Sentiment Analysis and Opinion Mining

Synthesis Lectures on Human Language Technologies

Editor

Graeme Hirst, University of Toronto

Synthesis Lectures on Human Language Technologies publishes monographs on topics relating to natural language processing, computational linguistics, information retrieval, and spoken language understanding. Emphasis is placed on important new techniques, on new applications, and on topics that combine two or more HLT subfields.

http://www.morganclaypool.com/toc/hlt/1/1

Sentiment Analysis and Opinion Mining
Bing Liu
2012

Discourse Processing
Manfred Stede
2011

Bitext Alignment
Jörg Tiedemann
2011

Linguistic Structure Prediction
Noah A. Smith
2011

Learning to Rank for Information Retrieval and Natural Language Processing
Hang Li
2011

Computational Modeling of Human Language Acquisition
Afra Alishahi
2010

Introduction to Arabic Natural Language Processing
Nizar Y. Habash
2010

Cross-Language Information Retrieval
Jian-Yun Nie
2010

Automated Grammatical Error Detection for Language Learners
Claudia Leacock, Martin Chodorow, Michael Gamon, Joel Tetreault
2010

Data-Intensive Text Processing with MapReduce
Jimmy Lin, Chris Dyer
2010

Semantic Role Labeling
Martha Palmer, Daniel Gildea, Nianwen Xue
2010

Spoken Dialogue Systems
Kristiina Jokinen, Michael McTear
2009

Introduction to Chinese Natural Language Processing
Kam-Fai Wong, Wenjie Li, Ruifeng Xu, Zheng-sheng Zhang
2009

Introduction to Linguistic Annotation and Text Analytics
Graham Wilcock
2009

Dependency Parsing
Sandra Kübler, Ryan McDonald, Joakim Nivre
2009

Statistical Language Models for Information Retrieval
ChengXiang Zhai
2008

Sentiment Analysis and Opinion Mining
Bing Liu

ISBN: 978-3-031-01017-0   paperback
ISBN: 978-3-031-02145-9   ebook

DOI 10.1007/978-3-031-021451-9

A Publication in the Springer series

SYNTHESIS LECTURES ON HUMAN LANGUAGE TECHNOLOGIES

Lecture #16

Series Editor: Graeme Hirst, University of Toronto

Series ISSN

ISSN   1947-4040   print
ISSN   1947-4059   electronic

Sentiment Analysis and Opinion Mining

Bing Liu
University of Illinois at Chicago

SYNTHESIS LECTURES ON HUMAN LANGUAGE TECHNOLOGIES #16

ABSTRACT

Sentiment analysis and opinion mining is the field of study that analyzes people's opinions, sentiments, evaluations, attitudes, and emotions from written language. It is one of the most active research areas in natural language processing and is also widely studied in data mining, Web mining, and text mining. In fact, this research has spread outside of computer science to the management sciences and social sciences due to its importance to business and society as a whole. The growing importance of sentiment analysis coincides with the growth of social media such as reviews, forum discussions, blogs, micro-blogs, Twitter, and social networks. For the first time in human history, we now have a huge volume of opinionated data recorded in digital form for analysis.

Sentiment analysis systems are being applied in almost every business and social domain because opinions are central to almost all human activities and are key influencers of our behaviors. Our beliefs and perceptions of reality, and the choices we make, are largely conditioned on how others see and evaluate the world. For this reason, when we need to make a decision we often seek out the opinions of others. This is true not only for individuals but also for organizations.

This book is a comprehensive introductory and survey text. It covers all important topics and the latest developments in the field with over 400 references. It is suitable for students, researchers and practitioners who are interested in social media analysis in general and sentiment analysis in particular. Lecturers can readily use it in class for courses on natural language processing, social media analysis, text mining, and data mining. Lecture slides are also available online.

KEYWORDS

sentiment analysis, opinion mining, emotion, affect, evaluation, attitude, mood, social media, natural language progressing, text mining.

Acknowledgments

I would like to thank my former and current students—Zhiyuan Chen, Xiaowen Ding, Geli Fei, Murthy Ganapathibhotla, Minqing Hu, Nitin Jindal, Huayi Li, Arjun Mukherjee, Quang Qiu (visiting student from Zhejiang University), William Underwood, Andrea Vaccari, Zhongwu Zhai (visiting student from Tsinghua University), and Lei Zhang—for contributing numerous research ideas over the years. Discussions with many researchers also helped shape the book: Malu G. Castellanos, Dennis Chong, Umesh Dayal, Eduard Dragut, Riddhiman Ghosh, Natalie Glance, Meichun Hsu, Jing Jiang, Birgit König, Xiaoli Li, Tieyun Qian, Gang Xu, Philip S. Yu, Clement Yu, and ChengXiang Zhai. I am also very grateful to two anonymous reviewers. Despite their busy schedules, they read the book very carefully and gave me many excellent suggestions. I have taken each and every one of them into consideration while improving the book. On the publication side, I thank the Editor, Dr. Graeme Hirst, and the President and CEO of Morgan & Claypool Publishers, Mr. Michael Morgan, who have managed to get everything done on time and provided me with many pieces of valuable advice. Finally, my greatest gratitude goes to my own family: Yue, Shelley, and Kate, who have helped in so many ways.

Contents

Preface...xiii

1. **Sentiment Analysis: A Fascinating Problem**...1
   1.1   Sentiment Analysis Applications...2
   1.2   Sentiment Analysis Research..3
         1.2.1   Different Levels of Analysis 4
         1.2.2   Sentiment Lexicon and Its Issues 5
         1.2.3   Natural Language Processing Issues 6
   1.3   Opinion Spam Detection 7
   1.4   What's Ahead..7

2. **The Problem of Sentiment Analysis** 9
   2.1   Problem Definitions 10
         2.1.1   Opinion Defintion..10
         2.1.2   Sentiment Analysis Tasks 14
   2.2   Opinion Summarization..17
   2.3   Different Types of Opinions...18
         2.3.1   Regular and Comparative Opinions 18
         2.3.2   Explicit and Implicit Opinions 19
   2.4   Subjectivity and Emotion 19
   2.5   Author and Reader Standpoint 21
   2.6   Summary...21

3. **Document Sentiment Classification**...23
   3.1   Sentiment Classification Using Supervised Learning................24
   3.2   Sentiment Classification Using Unsupervised Learning 28
   3.3   Sentiment Rating Prediction 30
   3.4   Cross-Domain Sentiment Classification 31

3.5   Cross-Language Sentiment Classification.. 34

3.6   Summary 36

4.   Sentence Subjectivity and Sentiment Classification 37

4.1   Subjectivity Classification.. 38

4.2   Sentence Sentiment Classification... 41

4.3   Dealing with Conditional Sentences 43

4.4   Dealing with Sarcastic Sentences 44

4.5   Cross-Language Subjectivity and Sentiment Classification 45

4.6   Using Discourse Information for Sentiment Classification 47

4.7   Summary 47

5.   Aspect-Based Sentiment Analysis 49

5.1   Aspect Sentiment Classification.. 50

5.2   Basic Rules of Opinions and Compositional Semantics............................ 53

5.3   Aspect Extraction.. 58

        5.3.1   Finding Frequent Nouns and Noun Phrases 59

        5.3.2   Using Opinion and Target Relations 61

        5.3.3   Using Supervised Learning 62

        5.3.4   Using Topic Models 62

        5.3.5   Mapping Implicit Aspects 66

5.4   Identifying Resource Usage Aspect 67

5.5   Simutaneous Opinion Lexicon Expansion and Aspect Extraction.................... 68

5.6   Grouping Aspects into Categories... 71

5.7   Entity, Opinion Holder, and Time Extraction 73

5.8   Coreference Resolution and Word Sense Disambiguation 75

5.9   Summary 76

6.   Sentiment Lexicon Generation 79

6.1   Dictionary-Based Approach... 80

6.2   Corpus-Based Approach 83

6.3   Desirable and Undesirable Facts... 87

6.4   Summary 88

7.   Opinion Summarization.. 91

7.1   Aspect-Based Opinion Summarization... 91

7.2   Improvements to Aspect-Based Opinion Summarization......................... 94

7.3   Contrastive View Summarization.. 95

7.4   Traditional Summarization.. 96

7.5   Summary.. 97

8.   **Analysis of Comparative Opinions** 99

8.1   Problem Definitions 99

8.2   Identify Comparative Sentences... 102

8.3   Identifying Preferred Entities.. 103

8.4   Summary... 105

9.   **Opinion Search and Retrieval** 107

9.1   Web Search vs. Opinion Search 107

9.2   Existing Opinion Retrieval Techniques... 108

9.3   Summary... 111

10.   **Opinion Spam Detection**... 113

10.1   Types of Spam and Spamming... 114

10.1.1 Harmful Fake Reviews 115

10.1.2 Individual and Group Spamming.. 115

10.1.3 Types of Data, Features, and Detection.................................. 116

10.2   Supervised Spam Detection... 117

10.3   Unsupervised Spam Detection 120

10.3.1 Spam Detection Based on Atypical Behaviors 120

10.3.2 Spam Detection Using Review Graph 123

10.4   Group Spam Detection 124

10.5   Summary.. 125

11.   **Quality of Reviews** 127

11.1   Quality as Regression Problem.. 127

11.2   Other Methods.. 129

11.3   Summary.. 130

12.   **Concluding Remarks**.. 133

Bibliography... 135

Author Biography 167

Preface

Opinions are central to almost all human activities and are key influencers of our behaviors. Our beliefs and perceptions of reality, and the choices we make, are, to a considerable degree, conditioned upon how others see and evaluate the world. For this reason, when we need to make a decision we often seek out the opinions of others. This is not only true for individuals but also true for organizations.

Opinions and related concepts such as sentiments, evaluations, attitudes, and emotions are the subjects of study of *sentiment analysis and opinion mining*. The inception and rapid growth of the field coincide with those of the social media on the Web, e.g., reviews, forum discussions, blogs, micro-blogs, Twitter, and social networks, because for the first time in human history, we have a huge volume of opinionated data recorded in digital forms. Since early 2000, sentiment analysis has grown to be one of the most active research areas in natural language processing. It is also widely studied in data mining, Web mining, and text mining. In fact, it has spread from computer science to management sciences and social sciences due to its importance to business and society as a whole. In recent years, industrial activities surrounding sentiment analysis have also thrived. Numerous startups have emerged. Many large corporations have built their own in-house capabilities. Sentiment analysis systems have found their applications in almost every business and social domain.

The goal of this book is to give an in-depth introduction to this fascinating problem and to present a comprehensive survey of all important research topics and the latest developments in the field. As evidence of that, this book covers more than 400 references from all major conferences and journals. Although the field deals with the natural language text, which is often considered the unstructured data, this book takes a structured approach in introducing the problem with the aim of bridging the unstructured and structured worlds and facilitating qualitative and quantitative analysis of opinions. This is crucial for practical applications. In this book, I first define the problem in order to provide an abstraction or structure to the problem. From the abstraction, we will naturally see its key sub-problems. The subsequent chapters discuss the existing techniques for solving these sub-problems.

This book is suitable for students, researchers, and practitioners who are interested in social media analysis in general and sentiment analysis in particular. Lecturers can readily use it in class for courses on natural language processing, social media analysis, text mining, and data mining. Lecture slides are also available online.

CHAPTER 1

Sentiment Analysis: A Fascinating Problem

Sentiment analysis, also called *opinion mining*, is the field of study that analyzes people's opinions, sentiments, evaluations, appraisals, attitudes, and emotions towards entities such as products, services, organizations, individuals, issues, events, topics, and their attributes. It represents a large problem space. There are also many names and slightly different tasks, e.g., *sentiment analysis, opinion mining, opinion extraction, sentiment mining, subjectivity analysis, affect analysis, emotion analysis, review mining*, etc. However, they are now all under the umbrella of sentiment analysis or opinion mining. While in industry, the term *sentiment analysis* is more commonly used, in academia both *sentiment analysis* and *opinion mining* are frequently employed. Regardless, they basically represent the same field of study. The term *sentiment analysis* perhaps first appeared in Nasukawa and Yi (2003), and the term *opinion mining* first appeared in Dave et al. (2003). However, the research on *sentiments* and *opinions* appeared earlier (Das and Chen, 2001; Morinaga et al., 2002; Pang et al., 2002; Tong, 2001; Turney, 2002; Wiebe, 2000). In this book, we use the terms *sentiment analysis* and *opinion mining* interchangeably. To simplify the presentation, throughout this book we will use the term *opinion* to denote opinion, sentiment, evaluation, appraisal, attitude, and emotion. However, these concepts are not equivalent. We will distinguish them when needed. The meaning of opinion itself is still very broad. Sentiment analysis and opinion mining mainly focus on opinions which express or imply positive or negative sentiments.

Although linguistics and natural language processing (NLP) have a long history, little research had been done about people's opinions and sentiments before the year 2000. Since then, the field has become a very active research area. There are several reasons for this. First, it has a wide arrange of applications, almost in every domain. The industry surrounding sentiment analysis has also flourished due to the proliferation of commercial applications. This provides a strong motivation for research. Second, it offers many challenging research problems, which had never been studied before. This book will systematically define and discuss these problems, and describe the current state-of-the-art techniques for solving them. Third, for the first time in human history, we now have a huge volume of opinionated data in the social media on the Web. Without this data, a lot of research would not have been possible. Not surprisingly, the inception and rapid growth of sentiment analysis coincide with those of the social media. In fact, sentiment analysis is now right at the center of the social media research. Hence, research in sentiment analysis not only has an important impact on NLP, but may also have a profound impact on management sciences, political science, economics, and social sciences as they are all affected by people's opinions. Although the sentiment analysis research mainly started from early 2000, there was some earlier work on interpretation of metaphors, sentiment adjectives, subjectivity, view points, and affects (Hatzivassiloglou and McKeown, 1997; Hearst, 1992; Wiebe, 1990, 1994; Wiebe et al., 1999). This book serves as an up-to-date and comprehensive introductory text, as well as a survey on the subject.

1.1   SENTIMENT ANALYSIS APPLICATIONS

Opinions are central to almost all human activities because they are key influencers of our behaviors. Whenever we need to make a decision, we want to know others' opinions. In the real world, businesses and organizations always want to find consumer or public opinions about their products and services. Individual consumers also want to know the opinions of existing users of a product before purchasing it, and others' opinions about political candidates before making a voting decision in a political election. In the past, when an individual needed opinions, he/she asked friends and family. When an organization or a business needed public or consumer opinions, it conducted surveys, opinion polls, and focus groups. Acquiring public and consumer opinions has long been a huge business itself for marketing, public relations, and political campaign companies.

With the explosive growth of social media (e.g., reviews, forum discussions, blogs, microblogs, Twitter, comments, and postings in social network sites) on the Web, individuals and organizations are increasingly using the content in these media for decision making. Nowadays, if one wants to buy a consumer product, one is no longer limited to asking one's friends and family for opinions because there are many user reviews and discussions in public forums on the Web about the product. For an organization, it may no longer be necessary to conduct surveys, opinion polls, and focus groups in order to gather public opinions because there is an abundance of such information publicly available. However, finding and monitoring opinion sites on the Web and distilling the information contained in them remains a formidable task because of the proliferation of diverse sites. Each site typically contains a huge volume of opinion text that is not always easily deciphered in long blogs and forum postings. The average human reader will have difficulty identifying relevant sites and extracting and summarizing the opinions in them. Automated sentiment analysis systems are thus needed.

In recent years, we have witnessed that opinionated postings in social media have helped reshape businesses, and sway public sentiments and emotions, which have profoundly impacted on our social and political systems. Such postings have also mobilized masses for political changes such as those happened in some Arab countries in 2011. It has thus become a necessity to collect and study opinions on the Web. Of course, opinionated documents not only exist on the Web (called external data), many organizations also have their internal data, e.g., customer feedback collected from emails and call centers or results from surveys conducted by the organizations.

Due to these applications, industrial activities have flourished in recent years. Sentiment analysis applications have spread to almost every possible domain, from consumer products, services, healthcare, and financial services to social events and political elections. I myself have implemented a sentiment analysis system called *Opinion Parser*, and worked on projects in all these areas in a start-up company. There have been at least 40–60 start-up companies in the space in the U.S. alone. Many big corporations have also built their own in-house capabilities, e.g., Microsoft, Google, Hewlett-Packard, SAP, and SAS. These practical applications and industrial interests have provided strong motivations for research in sentiment analysis.

Apart from real-life applications, many application-oriented research papers have also been published. For example, in Liu et al. (2007), a sentiment model was proposed to predict sales performance. In McGlohon et al. (2010), reviews were used to rank products and merchants. In Hong and Skiena (2010), the relationships between the NFL betting line and public opinions in blogs and Twitter were studied. In O'Connor et al. (2010), Twitter sentiment was linked with public opinion polls. In Tumasjan et al. (2010), Twitter sentiment was also applied to predict election results. In Chen et al. (2010), the authors studied political standpoints. In Yano and Smith (2010), a method was reported for predicting comment volumes of political blogs. In Asur and Huberman (2010), Joshi et al. (2010) and Sadikov et al. (2009), Twitter data, movie reviews, and blogs were used to predict box-office revenues for movies. In Miller et al. (2011), sentiment flow in social networks was investigated. In Mohammad and Yang (2011), sentiments in mails were used to find how genders differed on emotional axes. In Mohammad (2011), emotions in novels and fairy tales were tracked. In Bollen et al. (2011), Twitter moods were used to predict the stock market. In Bar-Haim et al. (2011) and Feldman et al. (2011), expert investors in microblogs were identified and sentiment analysis of stocks was performed. In Zhang and Skiena (2010), blog and news sentiment was used to study trading strategies. In Sakunkoo and Sakunkoo (2009), social influences in online book reviews were studied. In Groh and Hauffa (2011), sentiment analysis was used to characterize social relations. A comprehensive sentiment analysis system and some case studies were also reported in Castellanos et al. (2011). My own group has tracked opinions about movies on Twitter and predicted box-office revenues with very accurate results. We simply used our *Opinion Parser* system to analyze positive and negative opinions about each movie with no additional algorithms.

1.2   SENTIMENT ANALYSIS RESEARCH

As discussed above, pervasive real-life applications are only part of the reason why sentiment analysis is a popular research problem. It is also highly challenging as a NLP research topic, and covers many novel sub-problems as we will see later. Additionally, there was little research before the year 2000 in either NLP or in linguistics. Part of the reason is that before then there was little opinion text available in digital forms. Since the year 2000, the field has grown rapidly to become one of the most active research areas in NLP. It is also widely researched in data mining, Web mining, and information retrieval. In fact, it has spread from computer science to management sciences (Archak et al., 2007; Chen and Xie, 2008; Das and Chen, 2007; Dellarocas et al., 2007; Ghose et al., 2007; Hu, et al, 2006; Park et al. (2007).

1.2.1   Different Levels of Analysis

I now give a brief introduction to the main research problems based on the level of granularities of the existing research. In general, sentiment analysis has been investigated mainly at three levels.

Document level: The task at this level is to classify whether a whole opinion document expresses a positive or negative sentiment (Pang et al., 2002; Turney, 2002). For example, given a product review, the system determines whether the review expresses an overall positive or negative opinion about the product. This task is commonly known as *document-level sentiment classification*. This level of analysis assumes that each document expresses opinions on a single entity (e.g., a single product). Thus, it is not applicable to documents which evaluate or compare multiple entities.

Sentence level: The task at this level goes to the sentences and determines whether each sentence expressed a positive, negative, or neutral opinion. Neutral usually means no opinion. This level of analysis is closely related to *subjectivity classification* (Wiebe et al. 1999), which distinguishes sentences (called *objective sentences*) that express factual information from sentences (called *subjective sentences*) that express subjective views and opinions. However, we should note that subjectivity is not equivalent to sentiment as many objective sentences can imply opinions, e.g., "*We bought the car last month and the windshield wiper has fallen off.*" Researchers have also analyzed clauses (Wilson et al., 2004), but the clause level is still not enough, e.g., "*Apple is doing very well in this lousy economy.*"

Entity and Aspect level: Both the document-level and sentence-level analyses do not discover what exactly people liked and did not like. Aspect level performs finer-grained analysis. Aspect level was earlier called *feature level* (*feature-based opinion mining and summarization*) (Hu and Liu, 2004). Instead of looking at language constructs (documents, paragraphs, sentences, clauses, or phrases), aspect level directly looks at the opinion itself. It is based on the idea that an opinion consists of a *sentiment* (positive or negative) and a *target* (of opinion). An opinion without its target being identified is of limited use. Realizing the importance of opinion targets also helps us understand the sentiment analysis problem better. For example, although the sentence "*Although the service is not that great, I still love* *this restaurant.*" clearly has a positive tone, we cannot say that this sentence is entirely positive. In fact, the sentence is positive about the *restaurant* (emphasized), but negative about its *service* (not emphasized). In many applications, opinion targets are described by entities and/or their different aspects. Thus, the goal of this level of analysis is to discover sentiments on entities and/or their aspects. For example, the sentence "*The iPhone's call quality is good, but its battery life is short.*" evaluates two aspects: *call quality* and *battery life*, of *iPhone* (entity). The sentiment on iPhone's *call quality* is positive, but the sentiment on its *battery life* is negative. The *call quality* and *battery life* of iPhone are the opinion targets. Based on this level of analysis, a structured summary of opinions about entities and their aspects can be produced, which turns unstructured text to structured data and can be used for all kinds of qualitative and quantitative analyses. Both the document-level and sentence-level classifications are already highly challenging. The aspect-level is even more difficult. It consists of several sub-problems, which we will discuss in Chapters 2 and 5.

To make things even more interesting and challenging, there are two types of opinions, i.e., *regular opinions* and *comparative opinions* (Jindal and Liu, 2006b). A regular opinion expresses a sentiment only on an particular entity or an aspect of the entity, e.g., "*Coke tastes very good,*" which expresses a positive sentiment on the aspect *taste* of Coke. A comparative opinion compares multiple entities based on some of their shared aspects, e.g., "*Coke tastes better than Pepsi.*" which compares Coke and Pepsi based on their tastes (an aspect) and expresses a preference for Coke (see Chapter 8).

1.2.2 Sentiment Lexicon and Its Issues

Not surprisingly, the most important indicators of sentiments are *sentiment words*, also called *opinion words*. These are words that are commonly used to express positive or negative sentiments. For example, *good, wonderful*, and *amazing* are positive sentiment words, and *bad, poor*, and *terrible* are negative sentiment words. Apart from individual words, there are also phrases and idioms, e.g., *cost someone an arm and a leg*. Sentiment words and phrases are instrumental to sentiment analysis for obvious reasons. A list of such words and phrases is called a *sentiment lexicon* (or opinion lexicon). Over the years, researchers have designed numerous algorithms to compile such lexicons. We will discuss these algorithms in Chapter 6.

Although sentiment words and phrases are important for sentiment analysis, only using them is far from sufficient. The problem is much more complex. In other words, we can say that sentiment lexicon is necessary but not sufficient for sentiment analysis. Below, we highlight several issues.

1. A positive or negative sentiment word may have opposite orientations in different application domains. For example, "suck" usually indicates negative sentiment, e.g., "*This camera sucks.*" but it can also imply positive sentiment, e.g., "*This vacuum cleaner really sucks.*"

2. A sentence containing sentiment words may not express any sentiment. This phenomenon happens frequently in several types of sentences. Question (interrogative) sentences and conditional sentences are two important types, e.g., "*Can you tell me which Sony camera is good?*" and "*If I can find a good camera in the shop, I will buy it.*" Both these sentences contain the sentiment word "*good,*" but neither expresses a positive or negative opinion on any specific camera. However, not all conditional sentences or interrogative sentences express no sentiments, e.g., "*Does anyone know how to repair this terrible printer?*" and "*If you are looking for a good car, get Toyota Camry.*" We will discuss such sentences in Chapter 4.

3. Sarcastic sentences with or without sentiment words are hard to deal with, e.g., "*What a great car! It stopped working in two days.*" Sarcasms are not so common in consumer reviews about products and services, but are very common in political discussions, which make political opinions hard to deal with. We will discuss such sentences in Chapter 4.

4. Many sentences without sentiment words can also imply opinions. Many of these sentences are actually objective sentences that are used to express some factual information. Again, there are many types of such sentences. Here we just give two examples. The sentence "*This washer uses a lot of water.*" implies a negative sentiment about the washer since it uses a lot of resource (water). The sentence "*After sleeping on the mattress for two days, a valley has formed in the middle.*" expresses a negative opinion about the mattress. This sentence is objective as it states a fact. All these sentences have no sentiment words.

These issues all present major challenges. In fact, these are just some of the difficult problems. More will be discussed in Chapter 5.

1.2.3 Natural Language Processing Issues

Finally, we must not forget sentiment analysis is a NLP problem. It touches every aspect of NLP, e.g., coreference resolution, negation handling, and word sense disambiguation, which add more difficulties since these are not solved problems in NLP. However, it is also useful to realize that sentiment analysis is a highly restricted NLP problem because the system does not need to fully understand the semantics of each sentence or document but only needs to understand some aspects of it, i.e., positive or negative sentiments and their target entities or topics. In this sense, sentiment analysis offers a great platform for NLP researchers to make tangible progresses on all fronts of NLP with the potential of making a huge practical impact. In this book, I will describe the core problems and the current state-of-the-art algorithms. I hope to use this book to attract researchers from other areas of NLP to join force to make a concerted effort to solve the problem.

Prior to this book, there were a multi-author volume "*Computing Attitude and Affect in Text: Theory and Applications*" edited by Shanahan, Qu, and Wiebe (2006), and also a survey article/book by Pang and Lee (2008). Both these books have excellent contents. However, they were published relatively early in the development of the field. Since then, there have been significant advancements due to much more active research in the past 5 years. Researchers now also have a much better understanding of the whole spectrum of the problem, its structure, and core issues. Numerous new (formal) models and methods have been proposed. The research has not only deepened but also broadened significantly. Earlier research in the field mainly focused on classifying the sentiment or subjectivity expressed in documents or sentences, which is insufficient for most real-life applications. Practical applications often demand more in-depth and fine-grained analysis. Due to the maturity of the field, the book is also written in a more structured form in the sense that the problem is now structurally defined and different research directions are unified around the definition.

1.3   OPINION SPAM DETECTION

A key feature of social media is that it enables anyone from anywhere in the world to freely express his/her views and opinions without disclosing his/her true identify and without the fear of undesirable consequences. These opinions are thus highly valuable. However, this anonymity also comes with a price. It allows people with hidden agendas or malicious intentions to easily game the system to give people the impression that they are independent members of the public and post fake opinions to promote or to discredit target products, services, organizations, or individuals without disclosing their true intentions, or the person or organization that they are secretly working for. Such individuals are called *opinion spammers* and their activities are called *opinion spamming* (Jindal and Liu, 2007, 2008).

Opinion spamming has become a major issue. Apart from individuals who give fake opinions in reviews and forum discussions, there are also commercial companies that are in the business of writing fake reviews and bogus blogs for their clients. Several high profile cases of fake reviews have been reported in the news. It is important to detect such spamming activities to ensure that the opinions on the Web are a trusted source of valuable information. Unlike extraction of positive and negative opinions, opinion spam detection is not just a NLP problem as it involves the analysis of people's posting behaviors. It is thus also a data mining problem. Chapter 10 will discuss the current state-of-the-art detection techniques.

1.4   WHAT'S AHEAD

In this book, we explore this fascinating topic. Although the book deals with the natural language text, often called *unstructured data*, I take a structured approach to writing this book. The next chapter will formally define the problem, which allows us to see a structure of the problem. From the definition, we will see the key tasks of sentiment analysis. In the subsequent chapters, existing techniques for performing the tasks are described. Due to my research, consulting, and start-up experiences, the book not only discusses key research concepts but also looks at the technology from an application point of view in order to help practitioners in the field. However, I must apologize that when I talk about industrial systems, I cannot reveal the names of companies or their systems, partially because of my consulting/business agreements and partially because of the fact that the sentiment analysis market moves rapidly and the companies that I know of may have changed or improved their algorithms when you read this book. I do not want to create problems for them and for me.

Although I try to cover all major ideas and techniques in this book, it has become an impossible task. In the past decade, a huge number of research papers (probably more than 1,000) have been published on the topic. Although most papers appeared in NLP conferences and journals, many papers have also been published in data mining, Web mining, machine learning, information retrieval, e-commerce, management sciences, and many other fields. It is thus almost impossible to write a book that covers the ideas in every published paper. I am sorry if your good ideas or techniques are overlooked. However, a major advantage of publishing this book in the synthesis lecture series of Morgan & Claypool is that the authors can always add new or updated materials to the book because the printing is on demand. So if you find that some important ideas are not discussed, please do not hesitate to let me know and I will be very happy to include.

Finally, background knowledge in the following areas will be very helpful in reading this book: natural language processing (Indurkhya and Damerau, 2010; Manning and Schutze, 1999), machine learning (Bishop, 2006; Mitchell, 1997), data mining (Liu, 2006, 2011), and information retrieval (Manning et al., 2008).

·   ·   ·   ·

C H A P T E R   2

The Problem of Sentiment Analysis

In this chapter, we define an abstraction of the sentiment analysis or opinion mining problem. From a research point of view, this abstraction gives us a statement of the problem and enables us to see a rich set of inter-related sub-problems which make up the sentiment analysis problem. It is often said that if we cannot structure a problem, we probably do not understand the problem. The objective of the definitions is thus to abstract a structure from the complex and intimidating unstructured natural language text. They also serve as a common framework to unify various existing research directions, and to enable researchers to design more robust and accurate solution techniques by exploiting the inter-relationships of the sub-problems. From a practical application point of view, the definitions let practitioners see what sub-problems need to be solved in a practical system, how they are related, and what output should be produced.

Unlike factual information, opinions and sentiments have an important characteristic, namely, they are subjective. It is thus important to examine a collection of opinions from many people rather than only a single opinion from one person because such an opinion represents only the subjective view of that single person, which is usually not sufficient for application. Due to a large collection of opinions on the Web, some form of summary of opinions is needed (Hu and Liu, 2004). The problem definitions will state what kind of summary may be desired. Along with the problem definitions, the chapter will also discuss several related concepts such as subjectivity and emotion.

Note that throughout this chapter and also the whole book, I mainly use reviews and sentences from reviews as examples to introduce ideas and to define key concepts, but the ideas and the resulting definitions are general and applicable to all forms of formal and informal opinion text such as news articles, tweets (Twitter postings), forum discussions, blogs, and Facebook postings. Since product reviews are highly focused and opinion rich, they allow us to see different issues more clearly than from other forms of opinion text. Conceptually, there is no difference between them. The differences are mainly superficial and in the degree of difficulty in dealing with them. For example, Twitter postings (tweets) are short (at most 140 characters) and informal and use many Internet slangs and emoticons. Twitter postings are, in fact, easier to analyze due to the length limit because the authors are usually straight to the point. Thus, it is often easier to achieve high sentiment analysis accuracy. Reviews are also easier because they are highly focused with little irrelevant information. Forum discussions are perhaps the hardest to deal with because the users there can discuss anything and also interact with one another. In terms of the degree of difficulty, there is also the dimension of different application domains. Opinions about products and services are usually easier to analyze. Social and political discussions are much harder due to complex topic and sentiment expressions, sarcasms and ironies.

2.1 PROBLEM DEFINITIONS

As mentioned at the beginning of Chapter 1, sentiment analysis mainly studies opinions which express or imply positive or negative sentiments. This section thus defines the problem in this context.

2.1.1 Opinion Defintion

We use the following review about a Canon camera to introduce the problem (an id number is associated with each sentence for easy reference):

Posted by: John Smith   Date: September 10, 2011

"(1) *I bought a Canon G12 camera six months ago.* (2) *I simply love it.* (3) *The picture quality is amazing.* (4) *The battery life is also long.* (5) *However, my wife thinks it is too heavy for her.*"

From this review, we notice a few important points.

1. The review has a number of opinions, both positive and negative, about Canon G12 camera. Sentence (2) expresses a positive opinion about the Canon camera as a whole. Sentence (3) expresses a positive opinion about its picture equality. Sentence (4) expresses a positive opinion about its battery life. Sentence (5) expresses a negative opinion about the weight of the camera. From these opinions, we can make the following important observation:

   Observation: An opinion consists of two key components: a target g and a sentiment s on the target, i.e., (g, s), where g can be any entity or aspect of the entity about which an opinion has been expressed, and s is a positive, negative, or neutral sentiment, or a numeric rating score expressing the strength/intensity of the sentiment (e.g., 1–5 stars). Positive, negative, and neutral are called *sentiment* (or *opinion*) *orientations* (or *polarities*).

   For example, the target of the opinion in sentence (2) is *Canon G12*, and the target of the opinion in sentence (3) is the *picture quality of Canon G12*. Target is also called *topic* in the literature.

2. This review has opinions from two persons, which are called *opinion sources* or *opinion hold-ers* (Kim and Hovy, 2004; Wiebe et al., 2005). The holder of the opinions in sentences (2), (3), and (4) is the author of the review ("John Smith"), but for sentence (5), it is the wife of the author.

3. The date of the review is September 10, 2011. This date is important in practice because one often wants to know how opinions change with time and opinion trends.

We are now ready to define opinion as a quadruple.

Definition (Opinion): An *opinion* is a quadruple, (g, s, h, t), where g is the opinion (or sentiment) target, s is the sentiment about the target, h is the opinion holder, and t is the time when the opinion was expressed.

This definition, although quite concise, may not be easy to use in practice especially in the domain of online reviews of products, services, and brands because the full description of the target can be complex and may not even appear in the same sentence. For example, in sentence (3), the opinion target is actually "picture quality of Canon G12," but the sentence mentioned only "picture quality." In this case, the opinion target is not just "picture quality" because without knowing that the sentence is evaluating the picture quality of the Canon G12 camera, the opinion in sentence (3) alone is of little use. In practice, the target can often be decomposed and described in a structured manner with multiple levels, which greatly facilitate both mining of opinions and later use of the mined opinion results. For example, "picture quality of Canon G12" can be decomposed into an entity and an attribute of the entity and represented as a pair: (Cannon-G12, picture-quality).

Let us use the term *entity* to denote the target object that has been evaluated. Entity can be defined as follows (Hu and Liu, 2004; Liu, 2006 and 2011).

Definition (**entity**): An *entity* e is a product, service, topic, issue, person, organization, or event. It is described with a pair, e: (T, W), where T is a hierarchy of *parts*, *sub-parts*, and so on, and W is a set of *attributes* of e. Each part or sub-part also has its own set of attributes.

Example 1: A particular model of camera is an entity, e.g., Canon G12. It has a set of attributes, e.g., *picture quality*, *size*, and *weight*, and a set of parts, e.g., *lens*, *viewfinder*, and *battery*. *Battery* also has its own set of attributes, e.g., *battery life* and *battery weight*. A topic can be an entity too, e.g., *tax increase*, with its parts "*tax increase for the poor*," "*tax increase for the middle class*," and "*tax increase for the rich*."

This definition essentially describes a hierarchical decomposition of entity based on the *part-of* relation. The root node is the name of the entity, e.g., Canon G12 in the above review. All the other nodes are parts and sub-parts, etc. An opinion can be expressed on any node and any attribute of the node.

Example 2: In our example review above, sentence (2) expresses a positive opinion about the entity Canon G12 camera as a whole. Sentence (3) expresses a positive opinion on the attribute of picture quality of the camera. Clearly, one can also express opinions about parts or components of the camera.

This entity as a hierarchy of any number of levels needs a nested relation to represent it, which is often too complex for applications. The main reason is that since NLP is a very difficult task, recognizing parts and attributes of an entity at different levels of details is extremely hard. Most applications also do not need such a complex analysis. Thus, we simplify the hierarchy to two levels and use the term *aspects* to denote both parts and attributes. In the simplified tree, the root node is still the entity itself, but the second level (also the leaf level) nodes are different aspects of the entity. This simplified framework is what is typically used in practical sentiment analysis systems.

Note that in the research literature, entities are also called *objects*, and aspects are also called *features* (as in product features). However, features here can confuse with features used in machine learning, where a feature means a data attribute. To avoid confusion, aspects have become more popular in recent years. Note that some researchers also use the terms *facets*, *attributes*, and *topics*, and in specific applications, entities and aspects may also be called other names based on the application domain conventions.

After decomposing the opinion target, we can redefine an opinion (Hu and Liu, 2004; Liu, 2010).

Definition (opinion): An *opinion* is a quintuple, $(e_i, a_{ij}, s_{ijkl}, h_k, t_l)$, where e_i is the name of an entity, a_{ij} is an aspect of e_i, s_{ijkl} is the sentiment on aspect a_{ij} of entity e_i, h_k is the opinion holder, and t_l is the time when the opinion is expressed by h_k. The sentiment s_{ijkl} is positive, negative, or neutral, or expressed with different strength/intensity levels, e.g., 1–5 stars as used by most review sits on the Web. When an opinion is on the entity itself as a whole, the special aspect GENERAL is used to denote it. Here, e_i and a_{ij} together represent the opinion target.

Some important remarks about this definition are in order.

1. In this definition, we purposely use subscripts to emphasize that the five pieces of information in the quintuple must correspond to one another. That is, the opinion s_{ijkl} must be given by opinion holder h_k about aspect a_{ij} of entity e_i at time t_l. Any mismatch is an error.

2. The five components are essential. Missing any of them is problematic in general. For example, if we do not have the time component, we will not be able to analyze opinions on an entity according to time, which is often very important in practice because an opinion two years ago and an opinion yesterday is not the same. Without opinion holder is also problematic. For example, in the sentence " *The mayor is loved by the people in the city, but he has been criticized by the state government,* " the two opinion holders, "*people in the city*" and "*state government,*" are clearly important for applications.

3. The definition covers most but not all possible facets of the semantic meaning of an opinion, which can be arbitrarily complex. For example, it does not cover the situation in "*The view finder and the lens are too close,*" which expresses an opinion on the distance of two parts. It also does not cover the context of the opinion, e g., "*This car is too small for a tall person,*" which does not say the car is too small for everyone. "Tall person" is the context here. Note also that in the original definition of entity, it is a hierarchy of parts, sub-parts, and so on. Every part can have its set of attributes. Due to the simplification, the quintuple representation can result in information loss. For example, "ink" is a part/component of a printer. In a printer review, one wrote "*The ink of this printer is expensive.*" This does not say that the printer is expensive (which indicates the aspect *price*). If one does not care about any attribute of the ink, this sentence just gives a negative opinion to the ink, which is an aspect of the printer entity. However, if one also wants to study opinions about different aspects of the ink, e.g., price and quality, the ink needs to be treated as a separate entity. Then, the quintuple representation still applies, but the part-of relationship needs to be saved. Of course, conceptually we can also expand the representation of opinion target using a nested relation. Despite the limitations, the definition does cover the essential information of an opinion which is sufficient for most applications. As we mentioned above, too complex a definition can make the problem extremely difficult to solve.

4. This definition provides a framework to transform unstructured text to structured data. The quintuple above is basically a database schema, based on which the extracted opinions can be put into a database table. Then a rich set of qualitative, quantitative, and trend analyses of opinions can be performed using the whole suite of database management systems (DBMS) and OLAP tools.

5. The opinion defined here is just one type of opinion, called *regular opinion*. Another type is *comparative opinion* (Jindal and Liu, 2006b; Liu, 2006, 2011), which needs a different definition. Section 2.3 will discuss different types of opinions. Chapter 8 defines and analyzes comparative opinions. For the rest of this section, we only focus on regular opinions. For simplicity, we just called them opinions.

2.1.2 Sentiment Analysis Tasks

With the definition, we can now present the objective and the key tasks of sentiment analysis (Liu, 2006, 2011).

> **Objective of sentiment analysis:** Given an opinion document d, discover all opinion quintuples $(e_i, a_{ij}, s_{ijkl}, h_k, t_l)$ in d.

The key tasks are derived from the five components of the quintuple. The first component is the entity. That is, we need to extract entities. The task is similar to named entity recognition (NER) in information extraction (Hobbs and Riloff, 2010; Mooney and Bunescu, 2005; Sarawagi, 2008). Thus, the extraction itself is a problem. After extraction, we also need to categorize the extracted entities. In natural language text, people often write the same entity in different ways. For example, Motorola may be written as Mot, Moto, and Motorola. We need to recognize that they all refer to the same entity.

Definition (entity category and entity expression): An *entity category* represents a unique entity, while an *entity expression* is an actual word or phrase that appears in the text indicating an entity category.

Each entity category (or simply entity) should have a unique name in a particular application. The process of grouping entity expressions into entity categories is called *entity categorization*.

Now we look at aspects of entities. The problem is basically the same as for entities. For example, *picture*, *image*, and *photo* are the same aspect for cameras. We thus need to extract aspect expressions and categorize them.

Definition (aspect category and aspect expression): An *aspect category* of an entity represents a unique aspect of the entity, while an *aspect expression* is an actual word or phrase that appears in the text indicating an aspect category.

Each aspect category (or simply aspect) should also have a unique name in a particular application. The process of grouping aspect expressions into aspect categories (aspects) is called *aspect categorization*.

Aspect expressions are usually nouns and noun phrases but can also be verbs, verb phrases, adjectives, and adverbs. The following definitions are useful (Hu and Liu, 2004).

Definition (explicit aspect expression): Aspect expressions that are nouns and noun phrases are called *explicit aspect expressions*.

For example, "picture quality" in "*The picture quality of this camera is great*" is an explicit aspect expression.

Definition (**implicit aspect expression**): Aspect expressions that are not nouns or noun phrases are called *implicit aspect expressions*.

For example, "expensive" is an implicit aspect expression in "*This camera is expensive.*" It implies the aspect *price*. Many implicit aspect expressions are adjectives and adverbs that are used to describe or qualify some specific aspects, e.g., *expensive* (price), and *reliably* (reliability). They can also be verb and verb phrases, e.g., "*I can install the software easily.*" "Install" indicates the aspect *installation*. Implicit aspect expressions are not just adjectives, adverbs, verbs and verb phrases; they can also be very complex, e.g., "*This camera will not easily fit in a coat pocket.*" Here, "fit in a coat pocket" indicates the aspect *size* (and/or *shape*).

The third component in the opinion definition is the sentiment. This task classifies whether the sentiment on the aspect is positive, negative, or neutral. The fourth and fifth components are opinion holder and time respectively. They also need to be extracted and categorized as for entities and aspects. Note that an opinion holder (Bethard et al., 2004; Choi et al., 2005; Kim and Hovy, 2004) (also called opinion source in Wiebe et al., 2005) can be a person or organization who expressed an opinion. For product reviews and blogs, opinion holders are usually the authors of the postings. Opinion holders are more important for news articles as they often explicitly state the person or organization that holds an opinion. However, in some cases, identifying opinion holders can also be important in social media, e.g., identifying opinions from advertisers or people who quote advertisements of companies.

Based on the above discussions, we can define a model of entity and a model of opinion document (Liu, 2006, 2011).

> **Model of entity**: An entity e_i is represented by itself as a whole and a finite set of aspects $A_i = \{a_{i1}, a_{i2}, \ldots, a_{in}\}$. e_i can be expressed with any one of a finite set of its entity expressions $\{ee_{i1}, ee_{i2}, \ldots, ee_{is}\}$. Each aspect $a_{ij} \in A_i$ of entity e_i can be expressed with any one of its finite set of aspect expressions $\{ae_{ij1}, ae_{ij2}, \ldots, ae_{ijm}\}$.

> **Model of opinion document**: An opinion document d contains opinions on a set of entities $\{e_1, e_2, \ldots, e_r\}$ and a subset of their aspects from a set of opinion holders $\{h_1, h_2, \ldots, h_p\}$ at some particular time point.

Finally, to summarize, given a set of opinion documents D, sentiment analysis consists of the following six main tasks.

> **Task 1** (entity extraction and categorization): Extract all entity expressions in D, and categorize or group synonymous entity expressions into entity clusters (or categories). Each entity expression cluster indicates a unique entity e_i.

Task 2 (aspect extraction and categorization): Extract all aspect expressions of the entities, and categorize these aspect expressions into clusters. Each aspect expression cluster of entity e_i represents a unique aspect a_{ij}.

Task 3 (opinion holder extraction and categorization): Extract opinion holders for opinions from text or structured data and categorize them. The task is analogous to the above two tasks.

Task 4 (time extraction and standardization): Extract the times when opinions are given and standardize different time formats. The task is also analogous to the above tasks.

Task 5 (aspect sentiment classification): Determine whether an opinion on an aspect a_{ij} is positive, negative or neutral, or assign a numeric sentiment rating to the aspect.

Task 6 (opinion quintuple generation): Produce all opinion quintuples $(e_i, a_{ij}, s_{ijkl}, h_k, t_l)$ expressed in document d based on the results of the above tasks. This task is seemingly very simple but it is in fact very difficult in many cases as Example 4 below shows.

Sentiment analysis (or opinion mining) based on this framework is often called *aspect-based sentiment analysis* (or *opinion mining*), or *feature-based sentiment analysis* (or *opinion mining*) as it was called in Hu and Liu (2004) and Liu et al. (2005).

We now use an example blog to illustrate the tasks (a sentence id is again associated with each sentence) and the analysis results.

Example 4: Posted by: big John   Date: Sept. 15, 2011

(1) *I bought a Samsung camera and my friends brought a Canon camera yesterday.* (2) *In the past week, we both used the cameras a lot.* (3) *The photos from my Samy are not that great, and the battery life is short too.* (4) *My friend was very happy with his camera and loves its picture quality.* (5) *I want a camera that can take good photos.* (6) *I am going to return it tomorrow.*

Task 1 should extract the entity expressions, "Samsung," "Samy," and "Canon," and group "Samsung" and "Samy" together as they represent the same entity. Task 2 should extract aspect expressions "picture," "photo," and "battery life," and group "picture" and "photo" together as for cameras they are synonyms. Task 3 should find the holder of the opinions in sentence (3) to be big John (the blog author) and the holder of the opinions in sentence (4) to be big John's friend. Task 4 should also find the time when the blog was posted is Sept-15-2011. Task 5 should find that sentence (3) gives a negative opinion to the picture quality of the Samsung camera and also a negative opinion to its battery life. Sentence (4) gives a positive opinion to the Canon camera as a whole and also to its picture quality. Sentence (5) seemingly expresses a positive opinion, but it does not. To generate opinion quintuples for sentence (4) we need to know what "his camera" and "its" refer to. Task 6 should finally generate the following four opinion quintuples:

(Samsung, picture_quality, negative, bigJohn, Sept-15-2011)
(Samsung, battery_life, negative, bigJohn, Sept-15-2011)
(Canon, GENERAL, positive, bigJohn's_friend, Sept-15-2011)
(Canon, picture_quality, positive, bigJohn's_friend, Sept-15-2011)

2.2   OPINION SUMMARIZATION

Unlike factual information, opinions are essentially subjective. One opinion from a single opinion holder is usually not sufficient for action. In most applications, one needs to analyze opinions from a large number of people. This indicates that some form of summary of opinions is desired. Although an opinion summary can be in one of many forms, e.g., structured summary (see below) or short text summary, the key components of a summary should include opinions about different entities and their aspects and should also have a quantitative perspective. The quantitative perspective is especially important because 20% of the people being positive about a product is very different from 80% of the people being positive about the product. We will discuss this further in Chapter 7.

The opinion quintuple defined above actually provides a good source of information and also a framework for generating both *qualitative* and *quantitative* summaries. A common form of summary is based on aspects and is called *aspect-based opinion summary* (or *feature-based opinion summary*) (Hu and Liu, 2004; Liu et al., 2005). In the past few years, a significant amount of research has been done on opinion summary. Most of them are related to this framework (see Chapter 7).

Let us use an example to illustrate this form of summary, which was proposed in Hu and Liu (2004) and Liu et al. (2005) . We summarize a set of reviews of a digital camera, called *digital camera* 1. The summary looks like that in Figure 2.1, which is called a *structured summary* in contrast to a traditional text summary of a short document generated from one or multiple long documents. In the figure, GENERAL represents the camera itself (the entity). One hundred and five reviews expressed positive opinions about the camera and 12 expressed negative opinions. *Picture quality* and *battery life* are two camera aspects. Ninety-five reviews expressed positive opinions about the picture quality, and 10 expressed negative opinions. <*Individual review sentences*> is a link pointing to the sentences and/or the whole reviews that give the opinions. With such a summary, one can easily see how existing customers feel about the camera. If one is interested in a particular aspect and additional details, he/she can drill down by following the <*Individual review sentences*> link to see the actual opinion sentences or reviews.

Digital Camera **1:**
    Aspect: GENERAL
        Positive: 105   <Individual review sentences>
        Negative: 12   <Individual review sentences>
    Aspect: Picture quality
        Positive: 95   <Individual review sentences>
        Negative: 10   <Individual review sentences>
    Aspect: Battery life
        Positive: 50   <Individual review sentences>
        Negative: 9   <Individual review sentences>
    ...

FIGURE 2.1. AN ASPECT-BASED OPINION SUMMARY.

2.3   DIFFERENT TYPES OF OPINIONS

The type of opinions that we have discussed so far is called *regular opinion* (Liu, 2006, 2011). Another type is called *comparative opinion* (Jindal and Liu, 2006b). In fact, we can also classify opinions based on how they are expressed in text, *explicit opinion* and *implicit* (or *implied*) *opinion*.

2.3.1   Regular and Comparative Opinions

Regular opinion: A *regular opinion* is often referred to simply as an *opinion* in the literature and it has two main sub-types (Liu, 2006, 2011):

Direct opinion: A *direct opinion* refers to an opinion expressed directly on an entity or an entity aspect, e.g., "*The picture quality is great.*"

Indirect opinion: An *indirect opinion* is an opinion that is expressed indirectly on an entity or aspect of an entity based on its effects on some other entities. This sub-type often occurs in the medical domain. For example, the sentence "*After injection of the drug, my joints felt worse*" describes an undesirable effect of the drug on "my joints", which indirectly gives a negative opinion or sentiment to the drug. In the case, the entity is the *drug* and the aspect is the *effect on joints*.

Much of the current research focuses on direct opinions. They are simpler to handle. Indirect opinions are often harder to deal with. For example, in the drug domain, one needs to know whether some desirable and undesirable state is before or after using the drug. For example, the sentence "*Since my joints were painful, my doctor put me on this drug*" does not express a sentiment or opinion on the drug because "painful joints" (which is negative) happened before using the drug.

Comparative opinion: A *comparative opinion* expresses a relation of similarities or differences between two or more entities and/or a preference of the opinion holder based on some shared aspects of the entities (Jindal and Liu, 2006a, 2006b). For example, the sentences, "*Coke tastes better than Pepsi*" and "*Coke tastes the best*" express two comparative opinions. A comparative opinion is usually expressed using the *comparative* or *superlative* form of an adjective or adverb, although not always (e.g., *prefer*). Comparative opinions also have many types. We will discuss and define them in Chapter 8.

2.3.2   Explicit and Implicit Opinions

Explicit opinion: An *explicit opinion* is a subjective statement that gives a regular or comparative opinion, e.g.,

"*Coke tastes great,*" and

"*Coke tastes better than Pepsi.*"

Implicit (or implied) opinion: An *implicit opinion* is an objective statement that implies a regular or comparative opinion. Such an objective statement usually expresses a desirable or undesirable fact, e.g.,

"*I bought the mattress a week ago, and a valley has formed,*" and

"*The battery life of Nokia phones is longer than Samsung phones.*"

Explicit opinions are easier to detect and to classify than implicit opinions. Much of the current research has focused on explicit opinions. Relatively less work has been done on implicit opinions (Zhang and Liu, 2011b). In a slightly different direction, Greene and Resnik (2009) studied the influence of syntactic choices on perceptions of implicit sentiment. For example, for the same story, different headlines can imply different sentiments.

2.4   SUBJECTIVITY AND EMOTION

There are two important concepts that are closely related to sentiment and opinion, i.e., *subjectivity* and *emotion*.

Definition (sentence subjectivity): An *objective sentence* presents some factual information about the world, while a *subjective sentence* expresses some personal feelings, views, or beliefs.

An example objective sentence is "*iPhone is an Apple product.*" An example subjective sentence is "*I like iPhone.*" Subjective expressions come in many forms, e.g., opinions, allegations, desires, beliefs, suspicions, and speculations (Riloff et al., 2006; Wiebe, 2000). There is some confusion among researchers to equate *subjectivity* with *opinionated*. By *opinionated*, we mean that a document or sentence expresses or implies a positive or negative sentiment. The two concepts are not equivalent, although they have a large intersection. The task of determining whether a sentence is subjective or objective is called *subjectivity classification* (Wiebe and Riloff, 2005) (see Chapter 4). Here, we should note the following.

- A subjective sentence may not express any sentiment. For example, "*I think that he went home*" is a subjective sentence, but does not express any sentiment. Sentence (5) in Example 4 is also subjective but it does not give a positive or negative sentiment about anything.
- Objective sentences can imply opinions or sentiments due to desirable and undesirable facts (Zhang and Liu, 2011b). For example, the following two sentences which state some facts clearly imply negative sentiments (which are *implicit opinions*) about their respective products because the facts are undesirable:
    "*The earphone broke in two days.*"
    "*I brought the mattress a week ago and a valley has formed*"

Apart from explicit opinion bearing subjective expressions, many other types of subjectivity have also been studied although not as extensive, e.g., affect, judgment, appreciation, speculation, hedge, perspective, arguing, agreement and disagreement, political stances (Alm, 2008; Ganter and Strube, 2009; Greene and Resnik, 2009; Hardisty et al., 2010; Lin et al., 2006; Medlock and Briscoe, 2007; Mukherjee and Liu, 2012; Murakami and Raymond, 2010; Neviarouskaya et al., 2010; Somasundaran and Wiebe, 2009). Many of them may also imply sentiments.

Definition (emotion): Emotions are our subjective feelings and thoughts.

Emotions have been studied in multiple fields, e.g., psychology, philosophy, and sociology. The studies are very broad, from emotional responses of physiological reactions (e.g., heart rate changes, blood pressure, sweating and so on), facial expressions, gestures and postures to different types of subjective experiences of an individual's state of mind. Scientists have categorized people's emotions into some categories. However, there is still not a set of agreed basic emotions among researchers. Based on (Parrott, 2001), people have six primary emotions, i.e., *love*, *joy*, *surprise*, *anger*, *sadness*, and *fear*, which can be sub-divided into many secondary and tertiary emotions. Each emotion can also have different intensities.

Emotions are closely related to sentiments. The strength of a sentiment or opinion is typically linked to the intensity of certain emotions, e.g., *joy* and *anger*. Opinions that we study in sentiment analysis are mostly *evaluations* (although not always). According to consumer behavior research, evaluations can be broadly categorized into two types: *rational evaluations* and *emotional evaluations* (Chaudhuri, 2006).

Rational evaluation: Such evaluations are from rational reasoning, tangible beliefs, and utilitarian attitudes. For example, the following sentences express rational evaluations: *"The voice of this phone is clear," "This car is worth the price,"* and *"I am happy with this car."*

Emotional evaluation: Such evaluations are from non-tangible and emotional responses to entities which go deep into people's state of mind. For example, the following sentences express emotional evaluations: *"I love iPhone," "I am so angry with their service people"* and *"This is the best car ever built."*

To make use of these two types of evaluations in practice, we can design 5 sentiment ratings, *emotional negative* (-2), *rational negative* (-1), *neutral* (0), *rational positive* (+1), and *emotional positive* (+2). In practice, neutral often means no opinion or sentiment expressed.

Finally, we need to note that the concepts of emotion and opinion are clearly not equivalent. Rational opinions express no emotions, e.g., *"The voice of this phone is clear,"* and many emotional sentences express no opinion/sentiment on anything, e.g., *"I am so surprised to see you here."* More importantly, emotions may not have targets, but just people's internal feelings, e.g., *"I am so sad today."*

2.5   AUTHOR AND READER STANDPOINT

We can look at an opinion from two perspectives, i.e., the author (opinion holder) who expresses the opinion, and the reader who reads the opinion. For example, one wrote *"The housing price has gone down, which is bad for the economy."* Clearly, this author talks about the negative impact of the dropping housing price on the economy. However, this sentence can be perceived in both ways by readers. For sellers, this is indeed negative, but for buyers, this could well be a piece of good news. As another example, one wrote *"I am so happy that Google share price shot up today."* If a reader sold his Google shares yesterday at a loss, he will not be very happy, but if the reader bought a lot of Google shares yesterday, he will almost certainly be as happy as the author of the sentence.

I am not aware of any reported studies about this issue. In current research or applications, researchers either ignore the issue or assume a standpoint in their analysis. Usually, the opinion holders are assumed to be the consumers or the general public unless otherwise stated (e.g., the President of the United States). Product manufacturers or service providers' opinions are considered advertisements if they are marked explicitly or fake opinions if they are not marked explicitly (e.g., mixed with opinions from consumers).

2.6   SUMMARY

This chapter defined the concept of opinion in the context of sentiment analysis, the main tasks of sentiment analysis, and the framework of opinion summarization. Along with them, two relevant and important concepts of subjectivity and emotion were also introduced, which are highly related to but not equivalent to opinion. Existing studies about them have mostly focused on their intersections with opinion (although not always). However, we should realize that all these concepts and their definitions are rather fuzzy and subjective. For example, there is still not a set of emotions that all researchers agree. Opinion itself is a broad concept too. Sentiment analysis mainly deals with the evaluation type of opinions or opinions which imply positive or negative sentiments. I will not be surprised if you do not completely agree with everything in this chapter. The goal of this chapter is to give a reasonably precise definition of sentiment analysis and its related issues. I hope I have succeeded to some extent.

·   ·   ·   ·

CHAPTER 3

Document Sentiment Classification

Starting from this chapter, we discuss the current major research directions or topics and their core techniques. Sentiment classification is perhaps the most extensively studied topic (also see the Pang and Lee, 2008). It aims to classify an opinion document as expressing a positive or negative opinion or sentiment. The task is also commonly known as the *document-level sentiment classification* because it considers the whole document as a basic information unit. A large majority of research papers on this topic classifies online reviews. We thus also define the problem in the review context, but the definition is also applicable to other similar contexts.

Problem definition: Given an opinion document d evaluating an entity, determine the overall sentiment s of the opinion holder about the entity, i.e., determine s expressed on aspect GENERAL in the quintuple

$$(\_, GENERAL, s, \_, \_),$$

where the entity e, opinion holder h, and time of opinion t are assumed known or irrelevant (do not care).

There are two formulations based on the type of value that s takes. If s takes categorical values, e.g., positive and negative, then it is a classification problem. If s takes numeric values or ordinal scores within a given range, e.g., 1–5, the problem becomes regression.

To ensure that the task is meaningful in practice, existing research makes the following implicit assumption (Liu, 2010).

Assumption: Sentiment classification or regression assumes that the opinion document d (e.g., a product review) expresses opinions on a single entity e and contains opinions from a single opinion holder h.

In practice, if an opinion document evaluates more than one entity, then the sentiments on the entities can be different. For example, the opinion holder may be positive about some entities and negative about others. Thus, it does not make practical sense to assign one sentiment orientation to the entire document in this case. It also does not make much sense if multiple opinion holders express opinions in a single document because their opinions can be different too.

This assumption holds for reviews of products and services because each review usually focuses on evaluating a single product or service and is written by a single reviewer. However, the assumption may not hold for a forum and blog post because in such a post the author may express opinions on multiple entities and compare them using comparative sentences.

Below, we first discuss the classification problem to predict categorical class labels and then the regression problem to predict rating scores. Most existing techniques for document-level classification use supervised learning, although there are also unsupervised methods. Sentiment regression has been done mainly using supervised learning. Recently, several extensions to this research have also appeared, most notably, *cross-domain sentiment classification* (or *domain adaptation*) and *cross-language sentiment classification*, which will also be discussed at length.

3.1 SENTIMENT CLASSIFICATION USING SUPERVISED LEARNING

Sentiment classification is usually formulated as a two-class classification problem, *positive* and *negative*. Training and testing data used are normally product reviews. Since online reviews have rating scores assigned by their reviewers, e.g., 1–5 stars, the positive and negative classes are determined using the ratings. For example, a review with 4 or 5 stars is considered a positive review, and a review with 1–2 stars is considered a negative review. Most research papers do not use the neutral class, which makes the classification problem considerably easier, but it is possible to use the neutral class, e.g., assigning all 3-star reviews the neutral class.

Sentiment classification is essentially a text classification problem. Traditional text classification mainly classifies documents of different topics, e.g., politics, sciences, and sports. In such classifications, topic-related words are the key features. However, in sentiment classification, sentiment or opinion words that indicate positive or negative opinions are more important, e.g., *great*, *excellent*, *amazing*, *horrible*, *bad*, *worst*, etc.

Since it is a text classification problem, any existing supervised learning method can be applied, e.g., naïve Bayes classification, and support vector machines (SVM) (Joachims, 1999; Shawe-Taylor and Cristianini, 2000). Pang et al. (2002) was the first paper to take this approach to classify movie reviews into two classes, positive and negative. It was shown that using unigrams (a bag of words) as features in classification performed quite well with either naïve Bayes or SVM, although the authors also tried a number of other feature options.

In subsequent research, many more features and learning algorithms were tried by a large number of researchers. Like other supervised machine learning applications, the key for sentiment classification is the engineering of a set of effective features. Some of the example features are the following.

Terms and their frequency. These features are individual words (unigram) and their n-grams with associated frequency counts. They are also the most common features used in traditional topic-based text classification. In some cases, word positions may also be considered. The TF-IDF weighting scheme from information retrieval may be applied too. As in traditional text classification, these features have been shown highly effective for sentiment classification as well.

Part of speech. The part-of-speech (POS) of each word can be important too. Words of different parts of speech (POS) may be treated differently. For example, it was shown that adjectives are important indicators of opinions. Thus, some researchers treated adjectives as special features. However, one can also use all POS tags and their n-grams as features. Note that in this book, we use the standard *Penn Treebank POS Tags* as shown in Table 3.1 (Santorini, 1990). The Penn Treebank site is at http://www.cis.upenn.edu/~treebank/home .html.

Sentiment words and phrases. *Sentiment words* are words in a language that are used to express positive or negative sentiments. For example, *good, wonderful,* and *amazing* are positive sentiment words, and *bad, poor,* and *terrible* are negative sentiment words. Most sentiment words are adjectives and adverbs, but nouns (e.g., *rubbish, junk,* and *crap*) and verbs (e.g., *hate* and *love*) can also be used to express sentiments. Apart from individual words, there are also *sentiment phrases* and *idioms,* e.g., *cost someone an arm and a leg.*

Rules of opinions. Apart from sentiment words and phrases, there are also many other expressions or language compositions that can be used to express or imply sentiments and opinions. We will list and discuss some of such expressions in Section 5.2.

Sentiment shifters. These are expressions that are used to change the sentiment orientations, e.g., from positive to negative or vice versa. Negation words are the most important class of sentiment shifters. For example, the sentence "*I don't like this camera*" is negative. There are also several other types of sentiment shifters. We will discuss them in Section 5.2 too. Such shifters also need to be handled with care because not all occurrences of such words mean sentiment changes. For example, "not" in "not only . . . but also" does not change sentiment orientation.

Syntactic dependency. Words dependency-based features generated from parsing or dependency trees are also tried by researchers.

Instead of using a standard machine learning method, researchers have also proposed several custom techniques specifically for sentiment classification, e.g., the score function in Dave et al.

TABLE 3.1: Penn Treebank Part-Of-Speech (POS) tags

TAG	DESCRIPTION	TAG	DESCRIPTION
CC	Coordinating conjunction	PRP$	Possessive pronoun
CD	Cardinal number	RB	Adverb
DT	Determiner	RBR	Adverb, comparative
EX	Existential *there*	RBS	Adverb, superlative
FW	Foreign word	RP	Particle
IN	Preposition or subordinating conjunction	SYM	Symbol
JJ	Adjective	TO	*to*
JJR	Adjective, comparative	UH	Interjection
JJS	Adjective, superlative	VB	Verb, base form
LS	List item marker	VBD	Verb, past tense
MD	Modal	VBG	Verb, gerund or present participle
NN	Noun, singular or mass	VBN	Verb, past participle
NNS	Noun, plural	VBP	Verb, non-3rd person singular present
NNP	Proper noun, singular	VBZ	Verb, 3rd person singular present
NNPS	Proper noun, plural	WDT	Wh-determiner
PDT	Predeterminer	WP	Wh-pronoun
POS	Possessive ending	WP$	Possessive wh-pronoun

(2003) based on words in positive and negative reviews, and the aggregation method in Tong (2001) using manually compiled domain-specific words and phrases.

A large number of papers have been published in the literature. Here, we introduce them briefly. In Gamon (2004), classification was performed on customer feedback data, which are usually short and noisy compared to reviews. In Pang and Lee (2004), the minimum cut algorithm working on a graph was employed to help sentiment classification. In Mullen and Collier (2004) and Xia and Zong (2010), syntactic relations were used together with traditional features. In Kennedy and Inkpen (2006) and Li et al. (2010), the contextual valence and sentiment shifters were employed for classification. In Cui et al. (2006), an evaluation was reported with several sentiment classification algorithms available at that time. In Ng et al. (2006), the classification was done by using some linguistic knowledge sources. In Abbasi et al. (2008), a genetic algorithm based feature selection was proposed for sentiment classification in different languages. In Li et al. (2009), a non-negative matrix factorization method was proposed. In Dasgupta and Ng (2009), Li et al. (2011), and Zhou et al. (2010), semi-supervised learning and/or active learning were experimented. In Kim et al. (2009) and Paltoglou and Thelwall (2010), different IR term weighting schemes were studied and compared for sentiment classification. In Martineau and Finin (2009), a new term weighting scheme called Delta TFIDF was proposed. In Qiu et al. (2009), a lexicon-based and self-supervision approach was used. In He (2010), labeled features (rather than labeled documents) were exploited for classification. In Mejova and Srinivasan (2011), the authors explored various feature definition and selection strategies. In Nakagawa et al. (2010), a dependency tree-based classification method was proposed, which used conditional random fields (CRF) (Lafferty et al., 2001) with hidden variables. In Bickerstaffe and Zukerman (2010), a hierarchical multi-classifier considering inter-class similarity was reported. In Li et al. (2010), personal (I, we) and impersonal (they, it, this product) sentences were exploited to help classification. In Yessenalina et al. (2010), automatically generated annotator rationales was used to help classification. In Yessenalina et al. (2010), multi-level structured models were proposed. In Wang et al. (2011), the authors proposed a graph-based hashtag approach to classifying Twitter post sentiments, and in Kouloumpis et al. (2011), linguistic features and features that capture information about the informal and creative language used in microblogs were also utilized. In Maas et al. (2011), the authors used word vectors which can capture some latent aspects of the words to help classification. In Bespalov et al. (2011), sentiment classification was performed based on supervised latent n-gram analysis. In Burfoot et al. (2011), congressional floor debates were classified. In Becker and Aharonson (2010), the authors showed that sentiment classification should focus on the final portion of the text based on their psycholinguistic and psychophysical experiments. In Liu et al. (2010), different linguistic features were compared for both blog and review sentiment classification. In Tokuhisa et al. (2008), emotion classification of dialog utterances was investigated.

It first performed sentiment classification of three classes (positive, negative, and neutral) and then classified positive and negative utterances into 10 emotion categories.

3.2 SENTIMENT CLASSIFICATION USING UNSUPERVISED LEARNING

Since sentiment words are often the dominating factor for sentiment classification, it is not hard to imagine that sentiment words and phrases may be used for sentiment classification in an unsupervised manner. The method in Turney (2002) is such a technique. It performs classification based on some fixed syntactic patterns that are likely to be used to express opinions. The syntactic patterns are composed based on part-of-speech (POS) tags. The algorithm given in Turney (2002) consists of three steps.

Step 1. Two consecutive words are extracted if their POS tags conform to any of the patterns in Table 3.2. For example, pattern 2 means that two consecutive words are extracted if the first word is an adverb, the second word is an adjective, and the third word (not extracted) is not a noun. As an example, in the sentence "*This piano produces beautiful sounds*", "*beautiful sounds*" is extracted as it satisfies the first pattern. The reason these patterns are used is that JJ, RB, RBR, and RBS words often express opinions. The nouns or verbs act as the contexts because in different contexts a JJ, RB, RBR and RBS word may express different sentiments. For example, the adjective (JJ) "unpredictable" may have a negative sentiment in a car review as in "unpredictable steering," but it could have a positive sentiment in a movie review as in "unpredictable plot."

Step 2. It estimates the sentiment orientation (SO) of the extracted phrases using the *pointwise mutual information* (PMI) measure:

$$PMI(term_1, term_2) = \log_2 \left(\frac{\Pr(term_1 \wedge term_2)}{\Pr(term_1)\Pr(term_2)} \right). \tag{1}$$

PMI measures the degree of statistical dependence between two terms. Here, $\Pr(term_1 \wedge term_2)$ is the actual co-occurrence probability of $term_1$ and $term_2$, and $\Pr(term_1)\Pr(term_2)$ is the co-occurrence probability of the two terms if they are statistically independent. The sentiment orientation (SO) of a phrase is computed based on its association with the positive reference word "excellent" and the negative reference word "poor":

$$SO(phrase) = PMI(phrase, \text{"excellent"}) - PMI(phrase, \text{"poor"}). \tag{2}$$

	FIRST WORD	SECOND WORD	THIRD WORD (NOT EXTRACTED)
	TABLE 3.2: Patterns of POS tags for extracting two-word phrases		
1	JJ	NN or NNS	anything
2	RB, RBR, or RBS	JJ	not NN nor NNS
3	JJ	JJ	not NN nor NNS
4	NN or NNS	JJ	not NN nor NNS
5	RB, RBR, or RBS	VB, VBD, VBN, or VBG	Anything

The probabilities are calculated by issuing queries to a search engine and collecting the number of *hits*. For each search query, a search engine usually gives the number of relevant documents to the query, which is the number of hits. Thus, by searching the two terms together and separately, the probabilities in Eq. (1) can be estimated. In Turney (2002), the AltaVista search engine was used because it has a NEAR operator to constrain the search to documents that contain the words within ten words of one another in either order. Let *hits*(*query*) be the number of hits returned. Eq. (2) can be rewritten as:

$$SO(phrase) = \log_2 \left(\frac{hits \, (\text{phrase } NEAR \, \text{"excellent"}) \, hits \, (\text{"poor"})}{hits \, (\text{phrase } NEAR \, \text{"poor"}) \, hits \, (\text{"excellent"})} \right). \qquad (3)$$

Step 3. Given a review, the algorithm computes the average *SO* of all phrases in the review and classifies the review as positive if the average *SO* is positive and negative otherwise.

Final classification accuracies on reviews from various domains range from 84% for automobile reviews to 66% for movie reviews.

Another unsupervised approach is the lexicon-based method, which uses a dictionary of sentiment words and phrases with their associated orientations and strength, and incorporates intensification and negation to compute a sentiment score for each document (Taboada et al., 2011). This method was originally used in sentence and aspect-level sentiment classification (Ding, Liu and Yu, 2008; Hu and Liu, 2004; Kim and Hovy, 2004).

3.3 SENTIMENT RATING PREDICTION

Apart from classification of positive and negative sentiments, researchers also studied the problem of predicting the rating scores (e.g., 1–5 stars) of reviews (Pang and Lee, 2005). In this case, the problem can be formulated as a regression problem since the rating scores are ordinal, although not all researchers solved the problem using regression techniques. Pang and Lee (2005) experimented with SVM regression, SVM multiclass classification using the one-vs.-all (OVA) strategy, and a meta-learning method called metric labeling. It was shown that OVA based classification is significantly poorer than the other two approaches, which performed similarly. This is understandable as the numerical ratings are not categorical values. Goldberg and Zhu (2006) improved this approach by modeling rating prediction as a graph-based semi-supervised learning problem, which used both labeled (with ratings) and unlabeled (without ratings) reviews. The unlabeled reviews were also the test reviews whose ratings need to be predicted. In the graph, each node is a document (review) and the link between two nodes is the similarity value between the two documents. A large similarity weight implies that the two documents tend to have the same sentiment rating. The paper experimented with several different similarity schemes. The algorithm also assumed that initially a separate learner has already predicted the numerical ratings of the unlabeled documents. The graph-based method only improves them by revising the ratings through solving an optimization problem to force ratings to be smooth throughout the graph with regard to both the ratings and the link weights.

Qu et al. (2010) introduced a bag-of-opinions representation of documents to capture the strength of n-grams with opinions, which is different from the traditional bag-of-words representation. Each of the opinions is a triple, a sentiment word, a modifier, and a negator. For example, in "not very good," "good" is the sentiment word, "very" is the modifier, and "not" is the negator. For sentiment classification of two classes (positive and negative), the opinion modifier is not crucial but for rating prediction, it is very important and so is the impact of negation. A constrained ridge regression method was developed to learn the sentiment score or strength of each opinion from domain-independent corpora (of multiple domains) of rated reviews. The key idea of learning was to exploit an available opinion lexicon and the review ratings. To transfer the regression model to a newly given domain-dependent application, the algorithm derives a set of statistics over the opinion scores and then uses them as additional features together with the standard unigrams for rating prediction. Prior to this work, Liu and Seneff (2009) proposed an approach to extracting adverb-adjective-noun phrases (e.g., "very nice car") based on the clause structure obtained by parsing sentences into a hierarchical representation. They assigned sentiment scores based on a heuristic method which computes the contribution of adjectives, adverbs and negations to the sentiment degree based on the ratings of reviews where these words occurred. Unlike the above work, there was no learning involved in this work.

Instead of predicting the rating of each review, Snyder and Barzilay (2007) studied the problem of predicting the rating for each aspect. A simple approach to this task would be to use a standard regression or classification technique. However, this approach does not exploit the dependencies between users' judgments across different aspects. Knowledge of these dependencies is useful for accurate prediction. Thus, this paper proposed two models, aspect model (which works on individual aspects) and agreement model (which models the rating agreement among aspects). Both models were combined in learning. The features used for training were lexical features such as unigram and bigrams from each review.

Long et al. (2010) used a similar approach as that in Pang and Lee (2005) but with a Baysian network classifier for rating prediction of each aspect in a review. For good accuracy, instead of predicting for every review, they focused on predicting only aspect ratings for a selected subset of reviews which comprehensively evaluates the aspects. Clearly, the estimations from these reviews should be more accurate than for those of other reviews because these other reviews do not have sufficient information. The review selection method used an information measure based on Kolmogorov complexity. The aspect rating prediction for the selected reviews used machine learning. The features for training were only from those aspect related sentences. The aspect extraction was done in a similar way to that in Hu and Liu (2004).

3.4   CROSS-DOMAIN SENTIMENT CLASSIFICATION

It has been shown that sentiment classification is highly sensitive to the domain from which the training data is extracted. A classifier trained using opinion documents from one domain often performs poorly on test data from another domain. The reason is that words and even language constructs used in different domains for expressing opinions can be quite different. To make matters worse, the same word in one domain may mean positive but in another domain may mean negative. Thus, domain adaptation or transfer learning is needed. Existing researches are mainly based on two settings. The first setting needs a small amount of labeled training data for the new domain (Aue and Gamon, 2005). The second needs no labeled data for the new domain (Blitzer et al., 2007; Tan et al., 2007). The original domain with labeled training data is often called the *source domain*, and the new domain which is used for testing is called the *target domain*.

In Aue and Gamon (2005), the authors proposed transferring sentiment classifiers to new domains in the absence of large amounts of labeled data in these domains. They experimented with four strategies: (1) training on a mixture of labeled reviews from other domains where such data are available and testing on the target domain; (2) training a classifier as above, but limiting the set of features to those only observed in the target domain; (3) using ensembles of classifiers from domains with available labeled data and testing on the target domain; and (4) combining small amounts of labeled data with large amounts of unlabeled data in the target domain (this is the traditional semi-supervised learning setting). SVM was used for the first three strategies, and EM for semi-supervised learning (Nigam et al., 2000) was used for the fourth strategy. Their experiments showed that the strategy (4) performed the best because it was able to make use of both the labeled and unlabeled data in the target domain.

In Yang et al. (2006), a simple strategy based on feature selection was proposed for transfer learning for sentence-level classification. Their method first used two fully labeled training set from two domains to select features that were highly ranked in both domains. These selected features were considered domain independent features. The classifier built using these features was then applied to any target/test domains. Another simple strategy was proposed in Tan et al. (2007), which first trains a base classifier using the labeled data from the source domain, and then uses the classifier to label some informative examples in the target domain. Based on the selected examples in the target domain, a new classifier is learned, which is finally applied to classify the test cases in the target domain.

In Blitzer et al. (2007), the authors used a method called structural correspondence learning (SCL) for domain adaptation, which was proposed earlier in Blitzer et al. (2006). Given labeled reviews from a source domain and unlabeled reviews from both the source and target domains, SCL first chooses a set of m features which occur frequently in both domains and are also good predictors of the source label (the paper chose those features with highest mutual information to the source label). These features are called the *pivot features* which represent the shared feature space of the two domains. It then computes the correlations of each pivot feature with other non-pivot features in both domains. This produces a correlation matrix W where row i is a vector of correlation values of non-pivot features with the ith pivot feature. Intuitively, positive values indicate that those non-pivot features are positively correlated with the ith pivot feature in the source domain or in the new domain. This establishes a feature correspondence between the two domains. After that, singular value decomposition (SVD) is employed to compute a low-dimensional linear approximation θ (the top k left singular vectors, transposed) of W. The final set of features for training and for testing is the original set of features $\mathbf{x}$ combined with $\theta\mathbf{x}$ which produces k real-valued features. The classifier built using the combined features and labeled data in the source domain should work in both the source and the target domains.

Pan et al. (2010) proposed a method similar to SCL at the high level. The algorithm works in the setting where there are only labeled examples in the source domain and unlabeled examples in the target domain. It bridges the gap between the domains by using a spectral feature alignment (SFA) algorithm to *align* domain-specific words from different domains into unified clusters, with the help of domain independent words as the bridge. Domain-independent words are like pivot words in Blitzer et al. (2007) and can be selected similarly. SFA works by first constructing a bipartite graph with the domain-independent words as one set of nodes and the domain-specific words as the other set of nodes. A domain specific word is linked to a domain-independent word if they co-occur. The co-occurrence can be defined as co-occurring in the same document or within a window. The link weight is the frequency of their co-occurrence. A spectral clustering algorithm is then applied on the bipartite graph to co-align domain-specific and domain-independent words into a set of feature clusters. The idea is that if two domain-specific words have connections to more common domain-independent words in the graph, they tend to be aligned or clustered together with a higher probability. Similarly, if two domain-independent words have connections to more common domain-specific words in the graph, they tend to be aligned together with a higher probability. For the final cross-domain training and testing, all data examples are represented with the combination of these clusters and the original set of features.

Along the same line, He et al. (2011) used joint topic modeling to identify opinion topics (which are similar to clusters in the above work) from both domains to bridge them. The resulting topics which cover both domains are used as additional features to augment the original set of features for classification. In Gao and Li (2011), topic modeling was used too to find a common semantic space based on domain term correspondences and term co-occurrences in the two domains. This common semantic space was then used to learn a classifier which was applied to the target domain. Bollegala et al. (2011) proposed a method to automatically create a sentiment sensitive thesaurus using both labeled and unlabeled data from multiple source domains to find the association between words that express similar sentiments in different domains. The created thesaurus is then used to expand the original feature vectors to train a binary sentiment classifier. In Yoshida et al. (2011), the authors proposed a method for transfer from multiple source domains to multiple target domains by identifying domain dependent and independent word sentiments. In Andreevskaia and Bergler (2008), a method using an ensemble of two classifiers was proposed. The first classifier was built using a dictionary and the second was built using a small amount of in-domain training data.

In Wu et al. (2009), a graph-based method was proposed, which uses the idea of label propagation on a similarity graph (Zhu and Ghahramani, 2002) to perform the transfer. In the graph, each document is a node and each link between two nodes is a weight computed using the cosine similarity of the two documents. Initially, every document in the old domain has a label score of +1 (positive) or -1 (negative) and each document in the new domain is assigned a label score based a normal sentiment classifier, which can be learned from the old domain. The algorithm then iteratively updates the label score of each new domain document i by finding k nearest neighbors in the old domain and k nearest neighbors in the new domain. A linear combination of the neighbor label scores and link weights are used to assign a new score to node i. The iterative process stops when the label scores converge. The sentiment orientations of the new domain documents are determined by their label scores.

Xia and Zong (2011) found that across different domains, features of some types of part-of-speech (POS) tags are usually domain-dependent, while of some others are domain-free. Based on this observation, they proposed a POS-based ensemble model to integrate features with different types of POS tags to improve the classification performance.

3.5   CROSS-LANGUAGE SENTIMENT CLASSIFICATION

Cross-language sentiment classification means to perform sentiment classification of opinion documents in multiple languages. There are two main motivations for cross-language classification. First, researchers from different countries want to build sentiment analysis systems in their own languages. However, much of the research has been done in English. There are not many resources or tools in other languages that can be used to build good sentiment classifiers quickly in these languages. The natural question is whether it is possible to leverage the automated machine translation capability and existing sentiment analysis resources and tools available in English to help build sentiment analysis systems in other languages. The second motivation is that in many applications, companies want to know and compare consumer opinions about their products and services in different countries. If they have a sentiment analysis system in English, they want to quickly build sentiment analysis systems in other languages through translation.

Several researchers have studied this problem. Much of the current work focuses on sentiment classification at the document level, and subjectivity and sentiment classification at the sentence level. Limited work has been done at the aspect level except that in Guo et al. (2010). In this section, we focus on cross-language document-level sentiment classification. Section 4.5 in the next chapter focuses on the sentence level.

In Wan (2008), the author exploited sentiment resources in English to perform classification of Chinese reviews. The first step of the algorithm translates each Chinese review into English using multiple translators, which produce different English versions. It then uses a lexicon-based approach to classify each translated English version. The lexicon consists of a set of positive terms, a set of negative terms, a set of negation terms, and a set of intensifiers. The algorithm then sums up the sentiment scores of the terms in the review considering negations and intensifiers. If the final score is less than 0, the review is negative, otherwise positive. For the final classification of each review, it combines the scores of different translated versions using various ensemble methods, e.g., average, max, weighted average, voting, etc. If a Chinese lexicon is also available, the same technique can be applied to the Chinese version. Its result may also be combined with the results of those English translations. The results show that the ensemble technique is effective. Brooke (2009) also experimented with translation (using only one translator) from the source language (English) to the target language (Spanish) and then used a lexicon-based approach or machine learning for target language document sentiment classification.

In Wan (2009), a co-training method was proposed which made use of an annotated English corpus for classification of Chinese reviews in a supervised manner. No Chinese resources were used. In training, the input consisted of a set of labeled English reviews and a set of unlabeled Chinese reviews. The labeled English reviews were translated into labeled Chinese reviews, and the unlabeled Chinese reviews were translated into unlabeled English reviews. Each review was thus associated with an English version and a Chinese version. English features and Chinese features for each review were considered as two independent and redundant views of the review. A co-training algorithm using SVM was then applied to learn two classifiers. Finally, the two classifiers were combined into a single classifier. In the classification phase, each unlabeled Chinese review for testing was first translated into an English review, and then the learned classifier was applied to classify the review into either positive or negative.

Wei and Pal (2010) proposed to use a transfer learning method for cross-language sentiment classification. Due to the fact that machine translation is still far from perfect, to minimize the noise introduced in translation, they proposed to use the structural correspondence learning (SCL) method (Blitzer et al., 2007) discussed in the previous section to find a small set of core features shared by both languages (English and Chinese). To alleviate the problem of data and feature sparseness, they issued queries to a search engine to find other highly correlated features to those in the core feature set, and then used the newly discovered features to create extra pseudo-examples for training.

Boyd-Graber and Resnik (2010) extended the topic modeling method *supervised latent Dirichlet allocation* (SLDA) (Blei and McAuliffe, 2007) to work on reviews from multi-languages for review rating prediction. SLDA is able to consider the user-rating of each review in topic modeling. The extended model MLSLDA creates topics using documents from multiple languages at the same time. The resulting multi-language topics are globally consistent across languages. To bridge topic terms in different languages in topic modeling, the model used the aligned WordNets of different languages or dictionaries.

In Guo et al. (2010), a topic model-based method was proposed to group a set of given aspect expressions in different languages into aspect clusters (categories) for aspect-based sentiment comparison of opinions from different countries (see also Section 5.3.4).

In Duh et al. (2011), the authors presented their opinions about the research of cross-language sentiment classification. Based on their analysis, they claimed that domain mismatch was not caused by machine translation (MT) errors, and accuracy degradation would occur even with perfect MT. It also argued that the cross-language adaptation problem was qualitatively different from other (monolingual) adaptation problems in NLP; thus new adaptation algorithms should to be considered.

3.6 SUMMARY

Sentiment classification at the document level provides an overall opinion on an entity, topic or event. It has been studied by a large number of researchers. However, this level of classification has some shortcomings for applications.

- In many applications, the user needs to know additional details, e.g., what aspects of entities are liked and disliked by consumers. In typical opinion documents, such details are provided, but document sentiment classification does not extract them for the user.
- Document sentiment classification is not easily applicable to non-reviews such as forum discussions, blogs, and news articles, because many such postings can evaluate multiple entities and compare them. In many cases, it is hard to determine whether a posting actually evaluates the entities that the user is interested in, and whether the posting expresses any opinion at all, let alone to determine the sentiment about them. Document-level sentiment classification does not perform such fine-grained tasks, which require in-depth natural language processing. In fact, online reviews do not need sentiment classification because almost all reviews already have user-assigned star ratings. In practice, it is the forum discussions and blogs that need sentiment classification to determine people's opinions about different entities (e.g., products and services) and topics.

CHAPTER 4

Sentence Subjectivity and Sentiment Classification

As discussed in the previous chapter, document-level sentiment classification may be too crude for most applications. We now move to the sentence level, i.e., to classify sentiment expressed in each sentence. However, there is no fundamental difference between document and sentence-level classifications because sentences are just short documents. One assumption that researchers often make about sentence-level analysis is that a sentence usually contains a single opinion (although not true in many cases). A document typically contains multiple opinions. Let us start our discussion with an example review:

> "*I bought a Motorola phone two weeks ago. Everything was good initially. The voice was clear and the battery life was long, although it is a bit bulky. Then, it stopped working yesterday.*"

The first sentence expresses no opinion as it simply states a fact. All other sentences express either explicit or implicit sentiments. Note no opinion is usually regarded as neutral.

Problem definition: Given a sentence x, determine whether x expresses a positive, negative, or neutral (or no) opinion.

The quintuple (e, a, s, h, t) definition is not used here because sentence-level classification is an intermediate step. In most applications, one needs to know the opinion targets. Knowing only that a sentence expresses a positive or negative opinion, but not what entities/aspects the opinion is about, is of limited use. However, sentence-level classification is still useful because in many cases, if we know what entities and entity aspects are talked about in a sentence, this step can help determine whether the opinions about the entities and their aspects are positive or negative.

Sentence sentiment classification can be solved either as a three-class classification problem or as two separate classification problems. In the latter case, the first problem (also called the first step) is to classify whether a sentence expresses an opinion or not. The second problem (also called the second step) then classifies those opinion sentences into positive and negative classes. The first problem is usually called *subjectivity classification*, which determines whether a sentence expresses a piece of subjective information or factual (objective) information (Hatzivassiloglou and Wiebe, 2000; Riloff et al., 2006; Riloff and Wiebe, 2003; Wiebe et al., 2004; Wilson et al., 2004, 2006; Yu and Hatzivassiloglou, 2003). Objective sentences are regarded as expressing no sentiment or opinion. This can be problematic as we discussed earlier because objective sentences can also imply opinions. For example, "*Then, it stopped working yesterday*" in the above review is an objective sentence, but it implies a negative sentiment about the phone because of the undesirable fact. Thus, it is more appropriate for the first step to classify each sentence as opinionated or not opinionated, regardless whether it is subjective or objective. However, due to the common practice, we still use the term *subjectivity classification* in this chapter. Below, we first discuss existing work on sentence-level subjectivity classification and then sentiment classification.

4.1   SUBECTIVITY CLASSIFICATION

Subjectivity classification classifies sentences into two classes: subjective and objective (Wiebe et al., 1999). An objective sentence expresses some factual information, while a subjective sentence usually gives personal views and opinions. In fact, subjective sentences can express many types of information, e.g., opinions, evaluations, emotions, beliefs, speculations, judgments, allegations, stances, etc. (Quirk et al., 1985; Wiebe et al., 1999). Some of them indicate positive or negative sentiments and some of them do not. Early research solved subjectivity classification as a standalone problem, i.e., not for the purpose of sentiment classification. In more recent research, some researchers treated it as the first step of sentiment classification by using it to remove objective sentences which are assumed to express or imply no opinion.

Most existing approaches to subjectivity classification are based on supervised learning. For example, the early work reported in Wiebe et al. (1999) performed subjectivity classification using the naïve Bayes classifier with a set of binary features, e.g., the presence in the sentence of a pronoun, an adjective, a cardinal number, a modal other than *will* and an adverb other than *not*. Subsequent researches also used other learning algorithms and more sophisticated features.

Wiebe (2000) proposed an unsupervised method for subjectivity classification, which simply used the presence of subjective expressions in a sentence to determine the subjectivity of a sentence. Since there was not a complete set of such expressions, it provided some seeds and then used distributional similarity (Lin, 1998) to find similar words, which were also likely to be subjectivity indicators. However, words found this way had low precision and high recall. Then, the method in Hatzivassiloglou and McKeown (1997) and gradability in Hatzivassiloglou and Wiebe (2000) were applied to filter the wrong subjective expressions. We will discuss the method in Hatzivassiloglou and McKeown (1997) in Section 6.2. *Gradability* is a semantic property that enables a word to appear in a comparative construct and to accept modifying expressions that act as intensifiers or diminishers. Gradable adjectives express properties in varying degrees of strength, relative to a norm either explicitly mentioned or implicitly supplied by the modified noun (for example, a *small planet* is usually much larger than a *large house*). Gradable adjectives were found using a seed list of manually compiled adverbs and noun phrases (such as *a little, exceedingly, somewhat,* and *very*) that are frequently used as grading modifiers. Such gradable adjectives are good indicators of subjectivity.

Yu and Hatzivassiloglou (2003) performed subjectivity classifications using sentence similarity and a naïve Bayes classifier. The sentence similarity method is based on the assumption that subjective or opinion sentences are more similar to other opinion sentences than to factual sentences. They used the SIMFINDER system in Hatzivassiloglou et al. (2001) to measure sentence similarity based on shared words, phrases, and WordNet synsets. For naïve Bayes classification, they used features such as, words (unigram), bigrams, trigrams, part of speech, the presence of sentiment words, the counts of the polarities (or orientations) of sequences of sentiment words (e.g., "++" for two consecutive positively oriented words), and the counts of parts of speech combined with sentiment information (e.g., "JJ+" for positive adjective), as well as features encoding the sentiment (if any) of the head verb, the main subject, and their immediate modifiers. This work also does sentiment classification to determine whether a subjective sentence is positive or negative, which we will discuss in the next section.

One of the bottlenecks in applying supervised learning is the manual effort involved in annotating a large number of training examples. To save the manual labeling effort, a bootstrapping approach to label training data automatically was proposed in Riloff and Wiebe (2003). The algorithm works by first using two high-precision classifiers (HP-Subj and HP-Obj) to automatically identify some subjective and objective sentences. The high-precision classifiers use lists of lexical items (single words or *n*-grams) that are good subjectivity clues. HP-Subj classifies a sentence as subjective if it contains two or more strong subjective clues. HP-Obj classifies a sentence as objective if there are no strong subjective clues. These classifiers will give very high precision but low recall. The extracted sentences are then added to the training data to learn patterns. The patterns (which form the subjectivity classifiers in the next iteration) are then used to automatically identify more subjective and objective sentences, which are then added to the training set, and the next iteration of the algorithm begins.

For pattern learning, a set of syntactic templates are provided to restrict the kinds of patterns to be learned. Some example syntactic templates and example patterns are shown below.

Syntactic template	Example pattern
<subj> passive-verb	<subj> was satisfied
<subj> active-verb	<subj> complained
active-verb <dobj>	endorsed <dobj>
noun aux <dobj>	fact is <dobj>
passive-verb prep <np>	was worried about <np>

Wiebe and Riloff (2005) used such discovered patterns to generate a rule-based method to produce training data for subjectivity classification. The rule-based subjective classifier classifies a sentence as subjective if it contains two or more strong subjective clues (otherwise, it does not label the sentence). In contrast, the rule-based objective classifier looks for the absence of clues: it classifies a sentence as objective if there are no strong subjective clues in the sentence, and several other conditions. The system also learns new patterns about objective sentences using the information extraction system AutoSlog-TS (Riloff, 1996), which finds patterns based on some fixed syntactic templates. The data produced by the rule-based classifiers was used to train a naïve Bayes classifier. A related study was also reported in Wiebe et al. (2004), which used a more comprehensive set of features or subjectivity clues for subjectivity classification.

Riloff et al. (2006) studied relationships among different features. They defined subsumption relationships among unigrams, n-grams, and lexico-syntactic patterns. If a feature is subsumed by another, the subsumed feature is not needed. This can remove many redundant features.

In Pang and Lee (2004), a mincut based algorithm was proposed to classify each sentence as being subjective or objective. The algorithm works on a sentence graph of an opinion document, e.g., a review. The graph is first built based on local labeling consistencies (which produces an association score of two sentences) and individual sentence subjectivity score computed based on the probability produced by a traditional classification method (which produces a score for each sentence). Local labeling consistency means that sentences close to each other are more likely to have the same class label (subjective or objective). The mincut approach is able to improve individual sentence based subjectivity classification because of the local labeling consistencies. The purpose of this work was actually to remove objective sentences from reviews to improve document-level sentiment classification.

Barbosa and Feng (2010) classified the subjectivity of tweets (postings on Twitter) based on traditional features with the inclusion of some Twitter specific clues such as retweets, hashtags, links, uppercase words, emoticons, and exclamation and question marks. For sentiment classification of subjective tweets, the same set of features was also used.

Interestingly, in Raaijmakers and Kraaij (2008), it was found that character n-grams of subwords rather than words n-grams can also perform sentiment and subjectivity classification well. For example, for the sentence *"This car rocks"*, subword character bigrams are th, hi, is, ca, ar, ro, oc, ck, ks. In Raaijmakers et al. (2008) and Wilson and Raaijmakers (2008), word n-grams, character n-gram and phoneme n-grams were all experimented and compared for subjectivity classification. BoosTexter (Schapire and Singer, 2000) was used as the learning algorithm. Surprisingly, their experiments showed that character n-grams performed the best, and phoneme n-grams performed similarly to word n-grams.

Wilson et al. (2004) pointed out that a single sentence may contain both subjective and objective clauses. It is useful to pinpoint such clauses. It is also useful to identify the strength of subjectivity. A study of automatic subjectivity classification was presented to classify clauses of a sentence by the strength of subjectivity expressed in individual clauses, down to four levels deep (*neutral, low, medium,* and *high*). *Neutral* indicates the absence of subjectivity. Strength classification thus subsumes the task of classifying a sentence as subjective or objective. The authors used supervised learning. Their features included subjectivity indicating words and phrases, and syntactic clues generated from the dependency parse tree.

Benamara et al. (2011) performed subjectivity classification with four classes, *S, OO, O,* and *SN*, where *S* means subjective and evaluative (the sentiment can be positive or negative), *OO* means positive or negative opinion implied in an objective sentence or sentence segment, *O* means objective with no opinion, and *SN* means subjective but non-evaluative (no positive or negative sentiment). This classification is more complete and conforms to our discussion earlier and also in Section 2.4, which showed that a subjective sentence may not be evaluative (with positive or negative sentiment) and an objective sentence can imply sentiment too.

Additional works on subjectivity classification of sentences has also been done in Arabic (Abdul-Mageed et al., 2011) and Urdu languages (Mukund and Srihari, 2010) based on different machine learning algorithms using general and language specific features.

4.2 SENTENCE SENTIMENT CLASSIFICATION

If a sentence is classified as being subjective, we determine whether it expresses a positive or negative opinion. Supervised learning again can be applied just like that for document-level sentiment classification, and so can lexicon-based methods. Before discussing existing algorithms (some algorithms do not use the subjectivity classification step), let us point out an implicit assumption made in much of the research on the subject.

Assumption of sentence-level sentiment classification: A sentence expresses a single sentiment from a single opinion holder.

This assumption is appropriate for simple sentences with one sentiment, e.g., "*The picture quality of this camera is amazing.*" However, for compound and complex sentences, a single sentence may express more than one sentiment. For example, the sentence, "*The picture quality of this camera is amazing and so is the battery life, but the viewfinder is too small for such a great camera,*" expresses both positive and negative sentiments (or it has mixed sentiments). For "picture quality" and "battery life," the sentence is positive, but for "viewfinder," it is negative. It is also positive about the camera as a whole (which is the GENERAL aspect in Section 2.1).

For sentiment classification of subjective sentences, Yu and Hatzivassiloglou (2003) used a method similar to that in Turney (2002), which has been discussed in Section 3.2. Instead of using one seed word for positive and one for negative as in Turney (2002), this work used a large set of seed adjectives. Furthermore, instead of using PMI, this work used a modified log-likelihood ratio to determine the positive or negative orientation for each adjective, adverb, noun, and verb. To assign an orientation to each sentence, it used the average log-likelihood scores of its words. Two thresholds were chosen using the training data and applied to determine whether the sentence has a positive, negative, or neutral orientation. The same problem was also studied in Hatzivassiloglou and Wiebe (2000) considering gradable adjectives.

Hu and Liu (2004) proposed a lexicon-based algorithm for aspect level sentiment classification, but the method can determine the sentiment orientation of a sentence as well. It was based on a sentiment lexicon generated using a bootstrapping strategy with some given positive and negative sentiment word seeds and the synonyms and antonyms relations in WordNet. We will discuss various methods for generating sentiment lexicons in Chapter 6. The sentiment orientation of a sentence was determined by summing up the orientation scores of all sentiment words in the sentence. A positive word was given the sentiment score of +1 and a negative word was given the sentiment score of −1. Negation words and contrary words (e.g., *but* and *however*) were also considered. In Kim and Hovy (2004), a similar approach was also used. Their method of compiling the sentiment lexicon was also similar. However, they determined the sentiment orientation of a sentence by multiplying the scores of the sentiment words in the sentence. Again, a positive word was given the sentiment score of +1 and a negative word was given the sentiment score of −1. The authors also experimented with two other methods of aggregating sentiment scores but they were inferior. In Kim and Hovy (2004, 2007) and Kim et al. (2006), supervised learning was used to identify several specific types of opinions. Nigam and Hurst (2004) applied a domain specific lexicon and a shallow NLP approach to assessing the sentence sentiment orientation.

In Gamon et al. (2005), a semi-supervised learning algorithm was used to learn from a small set of labeled sentences and a large set of unlabeled sentences. The learning algorithm was based on Expectation Maximization (EM) using the naive Bayes as the base classifier (Nigam et al., 2000). This work performed three-class classification, positive, negative, and "other" (no opinion or mixed opinion).

In McDonald et al. (2007), the authors presented a hierarchical sequence learning model similar to conditional random fields (CRF) (Lafferty et al., 2001) to jointly learn and infer sentiment at both the sentence-level and the document-level. In the training data, each sentence was labeled with a sentiment, and each whole review was also labeled with a sentiment. They showed that learning both levels jointly improved accuracy for both levels of classification. In Täckström and McDonald (2011), a method was reported that learns from the document-level labeling only but performs both sentence and document-level sentiment classification. The method is thus partially supervised. In Täckström and McDonald (2011), a fully supervised model and a partially supervised model were integrated to perform multi-level sentiment classification.

In Hassan et al. (2010), a method was proposed to identify attitudes about participants in online discussions. Since their paper was only interested in the discussion recipient, the algorithm only used sentence segments with second person pronouns. Its first step finds sentences with attitudes using supervised learning. The features were generated using Markov models. Its second step determines the orientation (positive or negative) of the attitudes, for which it used a lexicon-based method similar to that in Ding et al. (2008) except that the shortest path in the dependence tree was utilized to determine the orientation when there were conflicting sentiment words in a sentence, while Ding et al. (2008) used words distance (see Section 5.1).

In Davidov et al. (2010), sentiment classification of Twitter postings (or tweets) was studied. Each tweet is basically a single sentence. The authors took a supervised learning approach. Apart from the traditional features, the method also used hashtags, smileys, punctuations, and their frequent patterns. These features were shown to be quite effective.

4.3   DEALING WITH CONDITIONAL SENTENCES

Much of the existing research on sentence-level subjectivity classification or sentiment classification focused on solving the general problem without considering that different types of sentences may need very different treatments. Narayanan et al. (2009) argued that it is unlikely to have a one-technique-fit-all solution because different types of sentences express sentiments in very different ways. A divide-and-conquer approach may be needed, i.e., focused studies on different types of sentences. Their paper focused on conditional sentences, which have some unique characteristics that make it hard for a system to determine their sentiment orientations.

Conditional sentences are sentences that describe implications or hypothetical situations and their consequences. Such a sentence typically contains two clauses—the condition clause and the consequent clause—that are dependent on each other. Their relationship has significant impact on whether the sentence expresses a positive or negative sentiment. A simple observation is that sentiment words (e.g., *great, beautiful, bad*) alone cannot distinguish an opinion sentence from a non-opinion one, e.g., *"If someone makes a reliable car, I will buy it"* and *"If your Nokia phone is not good, buy this Samsung phone.".* The first sentence expresses no sentiment towards any particular car, although *"reliable"* is a positive sentiment word, but the second sentence is positive about the Samsung phone and it does not express an opinion about the Nokia phone (although the owner of the Nokia phone may be negative about it). Hence, a method for determining sentiments in non-conditional sentences will not work for conditional sentences. A supervised learning approach was proposed to deal with the problem using a set of linguistic features, e.g., sentiment words/phrases and their locations, POS tags of sentiment words, tense patterns, conditional connectives, etc.

Another type of difficult sentences is the question sentences. For example, *"Can anyone tell me where I can find a good Nokia phone?"* clearly has no opinion about any particular phone. However,

"*Can anyone tell me how to fix this lousy Nokia phone?*" has a negative opinion about the Nokia phone. To my knowledge, there is no study on this problem. For more accurate sentiment analysis, I believe we need to handle different types of sentences differently. Much further research is needed in this direction.

4.4 DEALING WITH SARCASTIC SENTENCES

Sarcasm is a sophisticated form of speech act in which the speakers or the writers say or write the opposite of what they mean. Sarcasm has been studied in linguistics, psychology, and cognitive science (Gibbs and Colston, 2007; Gibbs, 1986; Kreuz and Caucci, 2007; Kreuz and Glucksberg, 1989; Utsumi, 2000). In the context of sentiment analysis, it means that when one says something positive he/she actually means negative, and vice versa. Sarcasm is very difficult to deal with. Some initial work has been done in González-Ibáñez et al. (2011) and Tsur et al. (2010). Based on my own experiences, sarcastic sentences are not very common in reviews of products and services, but are very frequent in online discussions and commentaries about politics.

In Tsur et al. (2010), a semi-supervised learning approach was proposed to identify sarcasms. It used a small set of labeled sentences (seeds), but did not use unlabeled examples. Instead, it expanded the seed set automatically through Web search. The authors posited that sarcastic sentences frequently co-occur in text with other sarcastic sentences. An automated web search using each sentence in the seed training set as a query was performed. The system then collected up to 50 search engine snippets for each seed example and added the collected sentences to the training set. This enriched training set was then used for learning and classification. For learning, it used two types of features: pattern-based features and punctuation-based features. A pattern is simply an ordered sequence of high frequency words. Two criteria were also designed to remove too general and too specific patterns. These patterns are similar to sequential patterns in data mining (Liu, 2006, 2011). Punctuation-based features include the number of "!", "?" and quotes, and the number of capitalized/all capital words in the sentence. For classification, a kNN-based method was employed. This work, however, did not perform sentiment classification. It only separated sarcastic and non-sarcastic sentences.

The work of González-Ibáñez et al. (2011) studied the problem in the context of sentiment analysis using Twitter data, i.e., to distinguish sarcastic tweets and non-sarcastic tweets that directly convey positive or negative opinions (neutral utterances were not considered). Again, a supervised learning approach was taken using SVM and logistic regression. As features, they used unigrams and some dictionary-based information. The dictionary-based features include: (i) word categories (Pennebaker et al., 2007); (ii) WordNet Affect (WNA) (Strapparava and Valitutti, 2004); and (iii) a list of interjections (e.g., ah, oh, yeah), and punctuations (e.g., !, ?). Features like emoticons, and *ToUser* (which marks if a tweet is a reply to another tweet, signaled by <@user>) were also used.

Experimental results for three-way classification (sarcastic, positive and negative) showed that the problem is very challenging. The best accuracy was only 57%. Again, this work did not classify sarcastic sentences into positive and negative classes.

4.5   CROSS-LANGUAGE SUBJECTIVITY AND SENTIMENT CLASSIFICATION

As in document-level cross-language sentiment classification, researchers have also studied cross-language subjectivity classification and sentiment classification at the sentence level. Again, the research focused on using extensive resources and tools available in English and automated translations to help build sentiment analysis systems in other languages which have few resources or tools. Current research proposed three main strategies.

1. Translate test sentences in the target language into the source language and classify them using a source language classifier.
2. Translate a source language training corpus into the target language and build a corpus-based classifier in the target language.
3. Translate a sentiment or subjectivity lexicon in the source language to the target language and build a lexicon-based classifier in the target language.

Kim and Hovy (2006) experimented with (1) translating German emails to English and applied English sentiment words to determine sentiment orientation, and (2) translating English sentiment words to German, and analyzing German emails using German sentiment words. Mihalcea et al. (2007) also experimented with translating English subjectivity words and phrases into the target language. In fact, they tried two translation strategies for cross-language subjectivity classification. First, they derived a subjectivity lexicon for the new language (in their case, Romanian) using an English subjectivity lexicon through translation. A rule-based subjectivity classifier similar to that in Riloff and Wiebe (2003) was then applied to classify Romanian sentences into subjective and objective classes. The precision was not bad, but the recall was poor. Second, they derived a subjectivity-annotated corpus in the new language using a manually translated parallel corpus. They first automatically classified English sentences in the corpus into subjective and objective classes using some existing tools, and then projected the subjectivity class labels to the Romanian sentences in the parallel corpus using the available sentence-level alignment in the parallel corpus. A subjectivity classifier based on supervised learning was then built in Romanian to classify Romanian sentences. In this case, the result was better than the first approach. However, it should be noted that the translation of the parallel corpus was done manually.

In Banea et al. (2008), three sets of experiments were reported. First, a labeled corpus in the source language (English) was automatically translated into the target language (Romanian). The subjectivity labels in the source language were then mapped to the translated version in the target language. Second, the source language text was automatically labeled for subjectivity and then translated into the target language. In both cases, the translated version with subjectivity labels in the target language was used to train a subjectivity classifier in the target language. Third, the target language was translated into the source language, and then a subjectivity classification tool was used to classify the automatically translated source language text. After classification, the labels were mapped back into the target language. The resulting labeled corpus was then used to train a subjectivity classifier in the target language. The final classification results were quite similar for the three strategies.

In Banea et al. (2010), extensive experiments for cross-language sentence-level subjectivity classification were conducted by translating from a labeled English corpus to 5 other languages. First, it was shown that using the translated corpus for training worked reasonably well consistently for all 5 languages. Combining the translated versions in different languages with the original English version to form a single training corpus can also improve the original English subjectivity classification itself. Second, the paper demonstrated that by combining the predictions made by monolingual classifiers using majority vote, it was able to generate a high precision sentence-level subjectivity classifier.

The technique in Bautin et al. (2008) also translated documents in the target language to English and used a English lexicon-based method to determine the sentiment orientation for each sentence containing an entity. This paper actually worked at the aspect level. The sentiment classification method was similar to that in Hu and Liu (2004).

In Kim et al. (2010), a concept called the multi-lingual comparability was introduced to evaluate multi-lingual subjectivity analysis systems. By multilingual comparability, they meant the level of agreement in the classification results of a pair of multilingual texts with an identical subjective meaning. Using a parallel corpus, they studied the agreement among the classification results of the source language and the target language using Cohen's Kappa. For the target language classification, several existing translation based cross-language subjectivity classification methods were experimented. Their results showed that classifiers trained on corpora translated from English to the target languages performed well for both subjectivity classification and multi-lingual comparability.

In Lu et al. (2011), a slightly different problem was attempted. The paper assumed that there was a certain amount of sentiment labeled data available for both the source and target languages, and there was also an unlabeled parallel corpus. Their method can simultaneously improve sentiment classification for both languages. The method is a maximum entropy-based EM algorithm which jointly learns two monolingual sentiment classifiers by treating the sentiment labels in the unlabeled parallel text as unobserved latent variables, and maximizing the regularized joint likelihood of the language-specific labeled data together with the inferred sentiment labels of the parallel text. In learning, it exploits the intuition that two sentences or documents that are parallel (i.e., translations of one another) should exhibit the same sentiment.

4.6   USING DISCOURSE INFORMATION FOR SENTIMENT CLASSIFICATION

Most existing works on both the document-level and the sentence-level sentiment classification do not use the discourse information either among sentences or among clauses in the same sentence. Sentiment annotation at the discourse level was studied in Asher et al. (2008) and Somasundaran et al. (2008). Asher et al. (2008) used five types of rhetorical relations: *Contrast, Correction, Support, Result,* and *Continuation* with attached sentiment information for annotation. Somasundaran et al. (2008) proposed a concept called *opinion frame.* The components of opinion frames are opinions and the relationships between their targets.

Somasundaran et al. (2009) performed sentiment classification based on the opinion frame annotation. The classification algorithm used was *collective classification* (Bilgic et al., 2007), which performs classification on a graph. The nodes are sentences (or other expressions) that need to be classified, and the links are relations. In the discourse context, they are sentiments related discourse relations. These relations can be used to generate a set of relational features for learning. Each node itself also generates a set of local features. The relational features allow the classification of one node to affect the classification of other nodes in the collective classification scheme. In Zhou et al. (2011), the discourse information within a single compound sentence was used to perform sentiment classification of the sentence. For example, the sentence *"Although Fujimori was criticized by the international community, he was loved by the domestic population because people hated the corrupted ruling class"* is a positive sentence although it has more negative opinion words (see also Section 4.7). This paper used pattern mining to find discourse patterns for classification. Zirn et al. (2011) proposed a method to classify discourse segments. Each segment expresses a single (positive or negative) opinion. Markov logic networks were used for classification which not only can utilize a sentiment lexicon but also the local/neighboring discourse context.

4.7   SUMMARY

Sentence-level subjectivity classification and sentiment classification goes further than document-level sentiment classification as it moves closer to opinion targets and sentiments on the targets. It can be regarded as an intermediate step in the overall sentiment analysis task. However, it still has several shortcomings for many real-life applications.

- In most applications, the user needs to know additional details, i.e., what entities or aspects of entities are liked and disliked. As the document-level analysis, the sentence-level analysis still does not do that.

- Although one may say that if we know the opinion targets (e.g., entities and aspects, or topics), we can assign the sentiment orientation of a sentence to the targets in the sentence. However, this is insufficient:

  1. Many complex sentences have different sentiments on different targets, e.g., *"Trying out Chrome because Firefox keeps crashing"* and *"Apple is doing very well in this lousy economy."* In this latter sentence, even the clause level classification is insufficient. We need to go to the opinion target or the aspect level.

  2. Although a sentence may have an overall positive or negative tone, some of its components may express opposite opinions. For example, some researchers regard the follow sentence as positive (Neviarouskaya et al., 2010; Zhou et al., 2011):

     "Despite the high unemployment rate, the economy is doing well."

     It is true that the overall tone of this sentence is positive or the author is trying to emphasize the positive side, but it does contain a negative sentiment on the *unemployment rate*, which we must not ignore. If we go to the aspect-level sentiment analysis, the problem is solved. That is, the sentence is positive about the overall economy but negative about the unemployment rate.

  3. Sentence-level sentiment classification cannot deal with opinions in comparative sentences, e.g., *"Coke tastes better than Pepsi."* In this case, we need different methods to extract and to analyze comparative opinions as they have quite different meanings from regular opinions. Although this sentence clearly expresses an opinion, we cannot simply classify the sentence as being positive, negative, or neutral.

We discuss aspect-level sentiment analysis in the next chapter and comparative opinion analysis in Chapter 8.

CHAPTER 5

Aspect-based Sentiment Analysis

Following the natural progression of chapters, this chapter should focus on phrase- and word-level sentiment classification as the last two chapters were about document- and sentence-level classification. However, we leave that topic to the next chapter. In this chapter, we focus on aspect-based sentiment analysis as it is time to deal with the full problem defined in Chapter 2 and many phrase and word sentiments depend on aspect contexts.

As we discussed in the two previous chapters, classifying opinion texts at the document level or the sentence level is often insufficient for applications because they do not identify opinion targets or assign sentiments to such targets. Even if we assume that each document evaluates a single entity, a positive opinion document about the entity does not mean that the author has positive opinions about all aspects of the entity. Likewise, a negative opinion document does not mean that the author is negative about everything. For more complete analysis, we need to discover the aspects and determine whether the sentiment is positive or negative on each aspect.

To extract such details, we go to the aspect level, which means that we need the full model of Chapter 2, i.e., *aspect-based sentiment analysis* (or *opinion mining*), which was also called the *feature-based opinion mining* in Hu and Liu (2004). Note that as discussed in Chapter 2, the opinion target is decomposed into entity and its aspects. The aspect GENERAL is used to represent the entity itself in the result. Thus, aspect-based sentiment analysis covers both entities and aspects. It also introduces a suite of problems which require deeper NLP capabilities and produce a richer set of results.

Recall that, at the aspect level, the objective is to discover every quintuple $(e_i, a_{ij}, s_{ijkl}, h_k, t_l)$ in a given document d. To achieve this goal, six tasks have to be performed. This chapter mainly focuses on the two core tasks listed below. They have been studied extensively by researchers. The other tasks will also be covered but relatively briefly.

1. **Aspect extraction**: This task extracts aspects that have been evaluated. For example, in the sentence, "*The voice quality of this phone is amazing*," the aspect is "voice quality" of the

entity represented by "this phone." Note that "this phone" does not indicate the aspect GENERAL here because the evaluation is not about the phone as a whole, but only about its voice quality. However, the sentence "*I love this phone*" evaluates the phone as a whole, i.e., the GENERAL aspect of the entity represented by "this phone." Bear in mind whenever we talk about an aspect, we must know which entity it belongs to. In our discussion below, we often omit the entity just for simplicity of presentation.

2. **Aspect sentiment classification**: This task determines whether the opinions on different aspects are positive, negative, or neutral. In the first example above, the opinion on the "voice quality" aspect is positive. In the second, the opinion on the aspect GENERAL is also positive.

Note that it is possible that in an application the opinion targets are given because the user is only interested in these particular targets (e.g., the BMW and Ford brands). In that case, we do not need to perform entity or aspect extraction, but only to determine the sentiments on the targets.

5.1 ASPECT SENTIMENT CLASSIFICATION

We study the second task first, i.e., determining the orientation of sentiment expressed on each aspect in a sentence. There are two main approaches, i.e., the supervised learning approach and the lexicon-based approach.

For the supervised learning approach, the learning based methods used for sentence-level and clause-level sentiment classification discussed in Chapter 4 are applicable. In Wei and Gulla (2010), a hierarchical classification model was also proposed. However, the key issue is how to determine the scope of each sentiment expression, i.e., whether it covers the aspect of interest in the sentence. The current main approach is to use parsing to determine the dependency and the other relevant information. For example, in Jiang et al. (2011), a dependency parser was used to generate a set of aspect dependent features for classification. A related approach was also used in Boiy and Moens (2009), which weighs each feature based on the position of the feature relative to the target aspect in the parse tree. For comparative sentences, "than" or other related words can be used to segment a sentence (Ding et al., 2009; Ganapathibhotla and Liu, 2008).

Supervised learning is dependent on the training data. As discussed in Section 3.4, a model or classifier trained from labeled data in one domain often performs poorly in another domain. Although domain adaptation (or transfer learning) has been studied by researchers (Section 3.4), the technology is still far from mature, and the current methods are also mainly used for document-level sentiment classification as documents are long and contain more features for classification than individual sentences or clauses. Thus, supervised learning has difficulty to scale up to a large number of application domains.

The lexicon-based approach can avoid some of the issues (Ding et al., 2008; Hu and Liu, 2004), and has been shown to perform quite well in a large number of domains. Such methods are typically unsupervised. They use a sentiment lexicon (which contains a list of sentiment words, phrases, and idioms), composite expressions, rules of opinions (Section 5.2), and (possibly) the sentence parse tree to determine the sentiment orientation on each aspect in a sentence. They also consider *sentiment shifters*, *but-clauses* (see below) and many other constructs which may affect sentiments. Of course, the lexicon-based approach also has its own shortcomings, which we will discuss later. An extension of this method to handling comparative sentences will be discussed in Section 8.2. Below, we introduce one simple lexicon-based method to give a flavor of this approach. The method is from Ding et al. (2008) and it has four steps. Here, we assume that entities and aspects are known. Their extraction will be discussed in Section 5.3.

1. **Mark sentiment words and phrases**: For each sentence that contains one or more aspects, this step marks all sentiment words and phrases in the sentence. Each positive word is assigned the sentiment score of +1 and each negative word is assigned the sentiment score of −1. For example, we have the sentence, "*The voice quality of this phone is not good, but the battery life is long.*" After this step, the sentence becomes "The *voice quality* of this phone is not **good** [+1], but the *battery life* is long" because "good" is a positive sentiment word (the aspects in the sentence are italicized). Note that "long" here is not a sentiment word as it does not indicate a positive or negative sentiment by itself in general, but we can infer its sentiment in this context shortly. In fact, "long" can be regarded as a context-dependent sentiment word, which we will discuss in Chapter 6. In the next section, we will see some other expressions that can give or imply positive or negative sentiments.

2. **Apply sentiment shifters:** Sentiment shifters (also called *valence shifters* in Polanyi and Zaenen, 2004) are words and phrases that can change sentiment orientations. There are several types of such shifters. Negation words like *not, never, none, nobody, nowhere, neither,* and *cannot* are the most common type. This step turns our sentence into "The *voice quality* of this phone is not **good**[−1], but the *battery life* is long" due to the negation word "not." We will discuss several other types of sentiment shifters in the next section. Note that not every appearance of a sentiment shifter changes the sentiment orientation, e.g., "not only . . . but also." Such cases need to be dealt with care. That is, such special uses and patterns need to be identified beforehand.

3. **Handle but-clauses:** Words or phrases that indicate *contrary* need special handling because they often change sentiment orientations too. The most commonly used contrary word in English is "but." A sentence containing a contrary word or phrase is handled by applying the following rule: the sentiment orientations before the contrary word (e.g., but) and after

the contrary word are opposite to each other if the opinion on one side cannot be determined. The if-condition in the rule is used because contrary words and phrases do not always indicate an opinion change, e.g., "*Car-x is great, but Car-y is better.*" After this step, the above sentence is turned into "The *voice quality* of this phone is not **good**[−1], but the *battery life* is *long*[+1]" due to "but" ([+1] is added at the end of the but-clause). Notice here, we can infer that "long" is positive for "battery life". Apart from *but*, phrases such as "with the exception of," "except that," and "except for" also have the meaning of contrary and are handled in the same way. As in the case of negation, not every *but* means contrary, e.g., "not only . . . but also." Such non-but phrases containing "but" also need to be identified beforehand.

4. **Aggregate opinions**: This step applies an opinion aggregation function to the resulting sentiment scores to determine the final orientation of the sentiment on each aspect in the sentence. Let the sentence be s, which contains a set of aspects $\{a_1, \ldots, a_m\}$ and a set of sentiment words or phrases $\{sw_1, \ldots, sw_n\}$ with their sentiment scores obtained from steps 1–3. The sentiment orientation for each aspect a_i in s is determined by the following aggregation function:

$$score(a_i, s) = \sum_{sw_j \in s} \frac{sw_j.so}{dist(sw_j, a_i)}, \tag{5}$$

where sw_j is an sentiment word/phrase in s, $dist(sw_j, a_i)$ is the distance between aspect a_i and sentiment word sw_j in s. $sw_j.so$ is the sentiment score of sw_j. The multiplicative inverse is used to give lower weights to sentiment words that are far away from aspect a_i. If the final score is positive, then the opinion on aspect a_i in s is positive. If the final score is negative, then the sentiment on the aspect is negative. It is neutral otherwise.

This simple algorithm performs quite well in many cases. It is able to handle the sentence "*Apple is doing very well in this bad economy*" with no problem. Note that there are many other opinion aggregation methods. For example, Hu and Liu (2004) simply summed up the sentiment scores of all sentiment words in a sentence or sentence segment. Kim and Hovy (2004) used multiplication of sentiment scores of words. Similar methods were also employed by other researchers (Wan, 2008; Zhu et al., 2009).

To make this method even more effective, we can determine the scope of each individual sentiment word instead of using words distance as above. In this case, parsing is needed to find the dependency as in the supervised method discussed above. We can also automatically discover the sentiment orientation of context dependent words such as "long" above. More details will be given in Chapter 6. In fact, the above simple approach can be enhanced in many directions. For example,

Blair-Goldensohn et al. (2008) integrated the lexicon-based method with supervised learning. Kessler and Nicolov (2009) experimented with four different strategies of determining the sentiment on each aspect/target (including a ranking method). They also showed several interesting statistics on why it is so hard to link sentiment words to their targets based on a large amount of manually annotated data.

Along with aspect sentiment classification research, researchers also studied the aspect sentiment rating prediction problem which has mostly been done together with aspect extraction in the context of topic modeling, which we discuss in Section 5.3.4.

As indicated above, apart from sentiment words and phrases, there are many other types of expressions that can convey or imply sentiments. Most of them are also harder to handle. Below, we list some of them, which are called the *basic rules of opinions* (Liu, 2010).

5.2   BASIC RULES OF OPINIONS AND COMPOSITIONAL SEMANTICS

An opinion rule expresses a concept that implies a positive or negative sentiment. It can be as simple as individual sentiment words with their implied sentiments or compound expressions that may need commonsense or domain knowledge to determine their orientations. This section describes some of these rules. One way of representing these rules is to use the idea of compositional semantics (Dowty et al., 1981; Montague, 1974), which states that the meaning of a compound expression is a function of the meaning of its constituents and of the syntactic rules by which they are combined. Below, we first describe the rules at the conceptual level without considering how they may be expressed in actual sentences because many of these rules can be expressed in numerous ways and can also be domain and context dependent. After that, we go to the expression level to discuss the current research on compositional semantics in the context of sentiment analysis, which aims to combine more than one input constituent expressions to derive an overall sentiment orientation for the composite expression.

The rules are presented using a formalism similar to the BNF form. The rules are from Liu (2010)

1.	POSITIVE	::=	P
2.		|	PO
3.		|	sentiment_shifter N
4.		|	sentiment_shifter NE
5.	NEGATIVE	::=	N
6.		|	NE
7.		|	sentiment_shifter P
8.		|	sentiment_shifter PO

The non-terminals P and PO represent two types of *positive sentiment expressions*. P indicates an atomic positive expression, a word or a phrase, while PO represents a positive expression composed of multiple expressions. Similarly, the non-terminals N and NE also represent two types of *negative sentiment expressions*. "sentiment_shifter N" and "sentiment_shifter NE" represent the negation of N and NE, respectively, and "sentiment_shifter P" and "sentiment_shifter PO" represent the negation of P and PO, respectively. We need to note that these are not expressed in the actual BNF form but a pseudo language stating some abstract concepts. It is hard to specify them precisely because in an actual sentence, the sentiment shifter may be in many different forms and can appear before or after N, NE, P, or PO and there may be words between the sentiment shifter and positive (or negative) sentiment expressions. POSITIVE and NEGATIVE are the final sentiments used to determine the opinions on the targets/aspects in a sentence.

Sentiment_shifters (or valence shifters; Polanyi and Zaenen, 2004): *Negation words* like *not, never, none, nobody, nowhere, neither,* and *cannot* are the most common type of sentiment shifters. *Modal auxiliary verbs* (e.g., *would, should, could, might, must,* and *ought*) are another type, e.g., "*The brake could be improved*," which may change sentiment orientation, but not always. Some *presuppositional items* are yet another type. This case is typical for adverbs like *barely* and *hardly* as shown by comparing "*It works*" with "*It hardly works*." "Works" indicates positive, but "hardly works" does not: it presupposes that better was expected. Words like *fail, omit, neglect* behave similarly, e.g., "*This camera fails to impress me*." Furthermore, sarcasm often changes orientations too, e.g., "*What a great car, it failed to start the first day*." Although it may not be hard to recognize such shifters manually, spotting them and handling them correctly in actual sentences by an automated system is challenging (see Section 4.4). Also, rules 11–14 below can be seen as sentiment shifters as well. We present them separately because they also cover comparative opinions. Note that several researchers also studied the application scope of negations (Ikeda et al., 2008; Jia et al., 2009; Li et al., 2010; Morante et al., 2011). We will discuss more about sentiment shifters when we discuss sentiment composition.

We now define N, NE, P, and PO, which contain no sentiment shifters. We group these expressions into six conceptual categories based on their specific characteristics.

1. *Sentiment word or phrase*: This is the simplest and also the most commonly used category, in which sentiment words or phrases alone can imply positive or negative opinions on aspects, e.g., "good" in "*The voice quality is good.*" These words or phrases are reduced to P and N.

   9. P   ::=   a_positive_sentiment_word_or_phrase
   10. N   ::=   a_negative_sentiment_word_or_phrase

   Again, the details of the right-hand sides are not specified (which also apply to all the subsequent rules). Much of the current research only uses words and phrases in this category.

2. *Decreased and increased quantity of an opinionated item* (N and P): This set of rules is similar to the negation (or sentiment shifter) rules 3, 4, 7, and 8 above. They express that decreasing or increasing the quantity associated with an opinionated item (often nouns and noun phrases) can change the orientation of the sentiment. For example, in the sentence "*This drug reduced my pain significantly,*" "pain" is a negative sentiment word, and the reduction of "pain" indicates a desirable effect of the drug. Thus, decreased pain implies a positive opinion on the drug. The concept of *decreasing* also extends to *removal* and *disappearance*, e.g., "*My pain disappeared after taking the drug.*" We then have the following rules:

11.	PO	::=	less_or_decreased N
12.		|	more_or_increased P
13.	NE	::=	less_or_decreased P
14.		|	more_or_increased N

Note that rules 12 and 14 do not change of sentiment orientation, but they can change the intensity of an opinion. The actual words or phrases representing the concepts of less_or_decreased and more_or_increased in a sentence may appear before or after N or P, e.g., "*My pain has subsided after taking the drug,*" and "*This drug has reduced my pain.*"

3. *High, low, increased and decreased quantity of a positive or negative potential item*: For some items, a small value/quantity of them is negative, and a large value/quantity of them is positive, e.g., "*The battery life is short*" and "*The battery life is long.*" We call such items *positive potential items* (PPI). Here "battery life" is a positive potential item. For some other aspects, a small value/quantity of them is positive, and a large value/quantity of them is negative, e.g., "*This phone costs a lot*" and "*Sony reduced the price of the camera.*" Such items are called *negative potential items* (NPI). "Cost" and "price" are negative potential items. Both positive and negative potential items themselves imply no opinions, i.e., "battery life" and "cost", but when they are modified by quantity adjectives or quantity change words or phrases, positive or negative sentiments may be implied. The following rules cover these cases:

15.	PO	::=	no_low_less_or_decreased_quantity_of NPI
16.		|	large_larger_or_increased_quantity_of PPI
17.	NE	::=	no_low_less_or_decreased_quantity_of PPI
18.		|	large_larger_or_increased_quantity_of NPI
19.	NPI	::=	a_negative_potential_item
20.	PPI	::=	a_positive_potential_item

In Wen and Wu (2011), a bootstrapping and classification method was proposed to discover PPI and NPI in Chinese.

4. *Desirable or undesirable fact*: The rules above all contain some subjective expressions. But objective expressions can imply positive or negative sentiments too as they can describe desirable and undesirable facts. Such sentences often do not use any sentiment words. For example, the sentence "*After my wife and I slept on the mattress for two weeks, I saw a mountain in the middle*" clearly implies a negative opinion about the mattress. However, the word "mountain" itself does not carry any opinion. Thus, we have the following two rules:

21. P   ::=   desirable_fact
22. N   ::=   undesirable_fact

5. *Deviation from the norm or a desired value range*: In some application domains, the value of an item has a desired range or norm. If the value deviates from the normal range, it is negative, e.g., "*After taking the drug, my blood pressure went to 410.*" Such sentences are often objective sentences as well. We thus have the following rules:

23. P   ::=   within the_desired_value_range
24. N   ::=   deviate_from the_desired_value_range

6. *Produce and consume resource and waste*: If an entity produces a large quantity of resources, it is desirable (or positive). If it consumes a large quantity of resources, it is undesirable (or negative). For example, *electricity* is a resource. The sentence, "*This computer uses a lot of electricity*" gives a negative opinion about power consumption of the computer. Likewise, if an entity produces a large quantity of wastes, it is negative. If it consumes a large quantity of wastes, it is positive. These give us the following rules:

25. P   ::=   produce a_large_quantity_of_or_more resource
26. | produce no,_little_or_less waste
27. | consume no,_little_or_less resource
28. | consume a_large_quantity_of_or_more waste
29. N   ::=   produce no,_little_or_less resource
30. | produce some_or_more waste
31. | consume a_large_quantity_of_or_more resource
32. | consume no,_little_or_less waste

These conceptual rules can appear in many (seemly unlimited number of) forms using different words and phrases in actual sentences, and in different domains they may also manifest in different ways. Thus, they are very hard to recognize. Without recognizing them, the rules cannot be applied.

This set of conceptual rules is by no means the complete set that governs opinions or sentiments. In fact, there are others, and with further research, more rules may be discovered. It is also important to note that like individual sentiment words an occurrence of any of the rules in a sentence does not always imply opinions. For example, "*I want a car with high reliability*" does not express a positive or negative opinion on any specific car, although "high reliability" satisfies rule 16. More complex rules or discourse level analysis may be needed to deal with such sentences.

We now discuss the existing work applying the principle of compositionality to express some of the above rules at the expression level. The most studied composition rules are those related to *sentiment reversal*, which are combinations of sentiment shifters and positive or negative sentiment words, e.g., "*not*" & POS("*good*") => NEG("*not good*"). We have discussed them at length above. Another main type is represented by rules 11–14 above, e.g., "*reduced*" & NEG("*pain*") => POS("*reduced pain*").

Such composition rules can express some of the opinion rules and also certain other expression level sentiment compositions. Apart from the above two composition types, Moilanen and Pulman (2007) also introduced *sentiment conflict*, which is used when multiple sentiment words occur together, e.g., "*terribly good*". Conflict resolution is achieved by ranking the constituents on the basis of relative weights assigned to them dictating which constituent is more important with respect to sentiment.

In Neviarouskaya et al. (2010), six types of composition rules were introduced, i.e., *sentiment reversal, aggregation, propagation, domination, neutralization*, and *intensification*. Sentiment reversal is the same as what we have discussed above. *Aggregation* is similar to *sentiment conflict* above, but defined differently. If the sentiments of terms in adjective-noun, noun-noun, adverb-adjective, adverb-verb phrases have opposite directions, mixed polarity with dominant polarity of a pre-modifier is assigned to the phrase, e.g., POS('*beautiful*') & NEG('*fight*') => POSneg('*beautiful fight*'). The rule of *propagation* is applied when a verb of "propagation" or "transfer" type is used in a phrase/clause and the sentiment of an argument that has prior neutral polarity needs to be determined, e.g., PROP-POS("*to admire*") & "*his behavior*" => POS("*his behavior*"); "*Mr. X*" & TRANS("*supports*") & NEG("*crime business*") => NEG('*Mr. X*'). The rules of *domination* are: (1) if polarities of a verb and an object in a clause have opposite directions, the polarity of verb is prevailing (e.g., NEG("*to deceive*") & POS("*hopes*") => NEG("*to deceive hopes*")); (2) if a compound sentence joints clauses using the coordinate connector "*but*", the attitude features of the clause following after the connector are dominant (e.g., 'NEG("*It was hard to climb a mountain all night long*"), *but* POS("*a magnificent view rewarded the traveler at the morning*").' => POS(whole sentence)). The rule of *neutralization* is applied when a preposition-modifier or condition operator relates to a sentiment statement, e.g., "*despite*" & NEG('*worries*') => NEUT("*despite worries*"). The rule of *intensification* strengthens or weakens a sentiment score (intensity), e.g., Pos_score("*happy*") < Pos_score("*extremely happy*")). Additional related works can be found in Choi and Cardie (2008), Ganapathibhotla and Liu (2008), Min and Park (2011), Nakagawa et al. (2010), Nasukawa and Yi (2003), Neviarouskaya et al. (2009), Polanyi and Zaenen (2004), Socher et al. (2011), **and** Yessenalina and Cardie (2011).

As we can see, some of the opinion rules have not been expressed with compositions, e.g., those involved in resource usages (rules 25–32). However, it is possible to express them to some extent using triples in Zhang and Liu (2011a). The desirable and undesirable facts or value ranges have not been included either (rules 21–24). They are, in fact, not directly related to composition because they are essentially context or domain implicit sentiment terms, which need to be discovered in a domain corpus (Zhang and Liu, 2011b).

5.3   ASPECT EXTRACTION

We now turn to aspect extraction, which can also be seen as an information extraction task. However, in the context of sentiment analysis, some specific characteristics of the problem can facilitate the extraction. The key characteristic is that an opinion always has a target. The target is often the aspect or topic to be extracted from a sentence. Thus, it is important to recognize each opinion expression and its target from a sentence. However, we should also note that some opinion expressions can play two roles, i.e., indicating a positive or negative sentiment and implying an (implicit) aspect (target). For example, in "*this car is expensive*," "expensive" is a sentiment word and also indicates the aspect *price*. We will discuss implicit aspects in Section 5.3.5. Here, we will focus on explicit aspect extraction. There are four main approaches:

1. Extraction based on frequent nouns and noun phrases
2. Extraction by exploiting opinion and target relations
3. Extraction using supervised learning
4. Extraction using topic modeling

Since existing research on aspect extraction (more precisely, *aspect expression extraction*) is mainly carried out in online reviews, we also use the review context to describe these techniques, but there is nothing to prevent them being used on other forms of social media text.

There are two common review formats on the Web.

> Format 1 - **Pros, Cons, and the detailed review:** The reviewer first describes some brief pros and cons separately and then writes a detailed/full review. An example of such a review is given in Figure 5.1.
>
> Format 2 - **Free format:** The reviewer writes freely, i.e., no brief pros and cons. An example of such a review is given in Figure 5.2.

Extracting aspects from Pros and Cons in reviews of Format 1 (not the detailed review, which is the same as that in Format 2) is a special case of extracting aspects from the full review and also relatively easy. In Liu et al. (2005), a specific method based on a sequential learning method was

My SLR is on the shelf
by camerafun 4. Aug 09 '04
Pros: Great photos, easy to use, very small
Cons: Battery usage; included memory is stingy.
I had never used a digital camera prior to purchasing this Canon A70.
I have always used a SLR …**Read the full review**

FIGURE 5.1: An example of a review of format 1.

GREAT Camera. , Jun 3, 2004
Reviewer: **jprice174** from Atlanta, Ga.
I did a lot of research last year before I bought this camera… It kinda hurt to leave behind my beloved nikon 35mm SLR, but I was going to Italy, and I needed something smaller, and digital.

The pictures coming out of this camera are amazing. The 'auto' feature takes great pictures most of the time. And with digital, you're not wasting film if the picture doesn't come out. …

FIGURE 5.2: An example of a review of format 2.

proposed to extract aspects from Pros and Cons, which also exploited a key characteristic of Pros and Cons, i.e., they are usually very brief, consisting of short phrases or sentence segments. Each segment typically contains only one aspect. Sentence segments can be separated by commas, periods, semi-colons, hyphens, &, *and*, *but*, etc. This observation helps the extraction algorithm to perform more accurately.

Since the same set of basic techniques can be applied to both Pros and Cons and full text, from now on we will not distinguish them, but will focus on different approaches.

5.3.1   Finding Frequent Nouns and Noun Phrases

This method finds *explicit aspect expressions* that are nouns and noun phrases from a large number of reviews in a given domain. Hu and Liu (2004) used a data mining algorithm. Nouns and noun phrases (or groups) were identified by a part-of-speech (POS) tagger. Their occurrence frequencies are counted, and only the frequent ones are kept. A frequency threshold can be decided experimentally. The reason that this approach works is that when people comment on different aspects of an entity, the vocabulary that they use usually converges. Thus, those nouns that are frequently talked about are usually genuine and important aspects. Irrelevant contents in reviews are often diverse, i.e., they are quite different in different reviews. Hence, those infrequent nouns are likely to be non-aspects or less important aspects. Although this method is very simple, it is actually quite effective. Some commercial companies are using this method with several improvements.

The precision of this algorithm was improved in Popescu and Etzioni (2005). Their algorithm tried to remove those noun phrases that may not be aspects of entities. It evaluated each discovered noun phrase by computing a pointwise mutual information (PMI) score between the phrase and some *meronymy discriminators* associated with the entity class, e.g., a camera class. The meronymy discriminators for the camera class are, "of camera," "camera has," "camera comes with," etc., which were used to find components or parts of cameras by searching the Web. The PMI measure was a simplified version of that in Section 3.2:

$$PMI(a,d) = \frac{hits(a \wedge d)}{hits(a)hits(d)},$$

(4)

where a is a candidate aspect identified using the frequency approach and d is a discriminator. Web search was used to find the number of hits of individual terms and also their co-occurrences. The idea of this approach is clear. If the PMI value of a candidate aspect is too low, it may not be a component of the product because a and d do not co-occur frequently. The algorithm also distinguishes components/parts from attributes using WordNet's *is-a* hierarchy (which enumerates different kinds of properties) and morphological cues (e.g., "-iness," "-ity" suffixes).

Blair-Goldensohn et al. (2008) refined the frequent noun and noun phrase approach by considering mainly those noun phrases that are in sentiment-bearing sentences or in some syntactic patterns which indicate sentiments. Several filters were applied to remove unlikely aspects, e.g., dropping aspects which do not have sufficient mentions along-side known sentiment words. They also collapsed aspects at the word stem level, and ranked the discovered aspects by a manually tuned weighted sum of their frequency in sentiment-bearing sentences and the type of sentiment phrases/patterns, with appearances in phrases carrying a greater weight. Using sentiment sentences is related to the approach in Section 5.3.2.

A frequency-based approach was also taken in Ku et al. (2006). The authors called the so discovered terms the major topics. Their method also made use of the TF-IDF scheme considering terms at the document level and paragraph level. Moghaddam and Ester (2010) augmented the frequency-based approach with an additional pattern-based filter to remove some non-aspect terms. Their work also predicted aspect ratings. Scaffidi et al. (2007) compared the frequency of extracted frequent nouns and noun phrases in a review corpus with their occurrence rates in a generic English corpus to identify true aspects.

Zhu et al. (2009) proposed a method based on the Cvalue measure from (Frantzi et al. (2000) for extracting multi-word aspects. The Cvalue method is also based on frequency, but it considers the frequency of multi-word term t, the length of t, and also other terms that contain t. However, Cvalue only helped find a set of candidates, which is then refined using a bootstrapping technique with a set of given seed aspects. The idea of refinement is based on each candidate's co-occurrence with the seeds.

Long et al. (2010) extracted aspects (nouns) based on frequency and information distance. Their method first finds the core aspect words using the frequency-based method. It then uses the information distance in Cilibrasi and Vitanyi (2007) to find other related words to an aspect, e.g., for aspect *price*, it may find "$" and "dollars." All these words are then used to select reviews which discuss a particular aspect most.

5.3.2   Using Opinion and Target Relations

Since opinions have targets, they are obviously related. Their relationships can be exploited to extract aspects which are opinion targets because sentiment words are often known. This method was used in Hu and Liu (2004) for extracting infrequent aspects. The idea is as follows. The same sentiment word can be used to describe or modify different aspects. If a sentence does not have a frequent aspect but has some sentiment words, the nearest noun or noun phrase to each sentiment word is extracted. Since no parser was used in Hu and Liu (2004), the "nearest" function approximates the dependency relation between sentiment word and noun or noun phrase that it modifies, which usually works quite well. For example, in the following sentence,

"The software is amazing."

If we know that "amazing" is a sentiment word, then "software" is extracted as an aspect. This idea turns out to be quite useful in practice even when it is applied alone. The sentiment patterns method in Blair-Goldensohn et al. (2008) uses a similar idea. Additionally, this relation-based method is also a useful method for discovering important or key aspects (or topics) in opinion documents because an aspect or topic is unlikely to be important if nobody expresses any opinion or sentiment about it.

In Zhuang et al. (2006), a dependency parser was used to identify such dependency relations for aspect extraction. Somasundaran and Wiebe (2009) employed a similar approach, and so did Kobayashi et al. (2006). The dependency idea was further generalized into the double-propagation method for simultaneously extracting both sentiment words and aspects in Qiu et al. (2011) (to be discussed in Section 5.5). In Wu et al. (2009), a phrase dependency parser was used rather than a normal dependency parser for extracting noun phrases and verb phrases, which form candidate aspects. The system then employed a language model to filter out those unlikely aspects. Note that a normal dependency parser identifies dependency of individual words only, but a phrase dependency parser identifies dependency of phrases, which can be more suitable for aspect extraction. The idea of using dependency relations has been used by many researchers for different purposes (Kessler and Nicolov, 2009).

5.3.3 Using Supervised Learning

Aspect extraction can be seen as a special case of the general information extraction problem. Many algorithms based on supervised learning have been proposed in the past for information extraction (Hobbs and Riloff, 2010; Mooney and Bunescu, 2005; Sarawagi, 2008). The most dominant methods are based on *sequential learning* (or *sequential labeling*). Since these are supervised techniques, they need manually labeled data for training. That is, one needs to manually annotate aspects and non-aspects in a corpus. The current state-of-the-art sequential learning methods are *Hidden Markov Models* (HMM) (Rabiner, 1989) and *Conditional Random Fields* (CRF) (Lafferty et al., 2001). Jin and Ho (2009) applied a lexicalized HMM model to learn patterns to extract aspects and opinion expressions. Jakob and Gurevych (2010) used CRF. They trained CRF on review sentences from different domains for a more domain independent extraction. A set of domain independent features were also used, e.g. tokens, POS tags, syntactic dependency, word distance, and opinion sentences. Li et al (2010) integrated two CRF variations, i.e., Skip-CRF and Tree-CRF, to extract aspects and also opinions. Unlike the original CRF, which can only use word sequences in learning, Skip-CRF and Tree-CRF enable CRF to exploit structure features. CRF was also used in Choi and Cardie (2010). Liu et al. (2005) and Jindal and Liu (2006b) used sequential pattern rules. These rules are mined based on sequential pattern mining considering labels (or classes).

One can also use other supervised methods. For example, the method in Kobayashi et al. (2007) first finds candidate aspect and opinion word pairs using a dependency tree, and then employs a tree-structured classification method to learn and to classify the candidate pairs as being an aspect and evaluation relation or not. Aspects are extracted from the highest scored pairs. The features used in learning include contextual clues, statistical co-occurrence clues, among others. Yu et al. (2011) used a partially supervised learning method called one-class SVM (Manevitz and Yousef, 2002) to extract aspects. Using one-class SVM, one only needs to label some positive examples, which are aspects, but not non-aspects. In their case, they only extracted aspects from Pros and Cons of review format 2 as in Liu et al. (2005). They also clustered those synonym aspects and ranked aspects based on their frequency and their contributions to the overall review rating of reviews. Ghani et al. (2006) used both traditional supervised learning and semi-supervised learning for aspect extraction. Kovelamudi et al. (2011) used a supervised method but also exploited some relevant information from Wikipedia.

5.3.4 Using Topic Models

In recent years, statistical topic models have emerged as a principled method for discovering topics from a large collection of text documents. Topic modeling is an unsupervised learning method that assumes each document consists of a mixture of topics and each topic is a probability distribution over words. A topic model is basically a document generative model which specifies a probabilistic procedure by which documents can be generated. The output of topic modeling is a set of word clusters. Each cluster forms a topic and is a probability distribution over words in the document collection.

There were two main basic models: pLSA (Probabilistic Latent Semantic Analysis) (Hofmann, 1999) and LDA (Latent Dirichlet allocation) (Blei et al., 2003; Griffiths and Steyvers, 2003; Steyvers and Griffiths, 2007). Technically, topic models are a type of graphical models based on Bayesian networks. Although they are mainly used to model and extract topics from text collections, they can be extended to model many other types of information simultaneously. For example, in the sentiment analysis context, one can design a joint model to model both sentiment words and topics at the same time, due to the observation that every opinion has a target. For readers who are not familiar with topic models, graphical models or Bayesian networks, apart from reading the topic modeling literature, the "pattern recognition and machine learning" book by Christopher M. Bishop (Bishop, 2006) is an excellent source of background knowledge.

Intuitively, topics from topic models are aspects in the sentiment analysis context. Topic modeling can thus be applied to extract aspects. However, there is also a difference. That is, topics can cover both aspect words and sentiment words. For sentiment analysis, they need to be separated. Such separations can be achieved by extending the basic model (e.g., LDA) to jointly model both aspects and sentiments. Below, we give an overview of the current research in sentiment analysis that has used topic models to extract aspects and to perform other tasks. Note that topic models not only discover aspects but also group synonym aspects.

Mei et al. (2007) proposed a joint model for sentiment analysis. Specifically, they built an aspect-sentiment mixture model, which was based on an aspect (topic) model, a positive sentiment model, and a negative sentiment model learned with the help of some external training data. Their model was based on pLSA. Most other models proposed by researchers are based on LDA.

Titov and McDonald (2008) showed that global topic models such as LDA (Blei et al., 2003) might not be suitable for detecting aspects. The reason is that LDA depends on topic distribution differences and word co-occurrences among documents to identify topics and word probability distribution in each topic. However, opinion documents such as reviews about a particular type of products are quite homogenous, meaning that every document talks about the same aspects, which makes global topic models ineffective and are only effective for discovering entities (e.g., different brands or product names). The authors then proposed the multigrain topic models. The global model discovers entities while the local model discovers aspects using a few sentences (or a sliding text window) as a document. Here, each discovered aspect is a unigram language model, i.e., a multinomial distribution over words. Different words expressing the same or related facets are automatically grouped together under the same aspect. However, this technique does not separate aspects and sentiment words.

Branavan et al. (2008) proposed a method which made use of the aspect descriptions as keyphrases in Pros and Cons of review format 1 to help finding aspects in the detailed review text. Their model consists of two parts. The first part clusters the keyphrases in Pros and Cons into some aspect categories based on distributional similarity. The second part builds a topic model modeling the topics or aspects in the review text. Their final graphical model models these two parts simultaneously. The two parts are integrated based on the idea that the model biases the assignment of hidden topics in the review text to be similar to the topics represented by the keyphrases in Pros and Cons of the review, but it also permits some words in the document to be drawn from other topics not represented by the keyphrases. This flexibility in the coupling allows the model to learn effectively in the presence of incomplete keyphrases, while still encouraging the keyphrase clustering to cohere with the topics supported by the review text. However, this approach still does not separate aspects and sentiments.

Lin and He (2009) proposed a joint topic-sentiment model by extending LDA, where aspect words and sentiment words were still not explicitly separated. Brody and Elhadad (2010) proposed to first identify aspects using topic models and then identify aspect-specific sentiment words by considering adjectives only. Li et al. (2010) proposed two joint models, Sentiment-LDA and Dependency-sentiment-LDA, to find aspects with positive and negative sentiments. It does not find aspects independently and it does not separate aspect words and sentiment words. Zhao et al. (2010) proposed the MaxEnt-LDA (a Maximum Entropy and LDA combination) hybrid model to jointly discover both aspect words and aspect-specific opinion words, which can leverage syntactic features to help separate aspects and sentiment words. The joint modeling is achieved through an *indicator variable* (also called a *switch variable*) which is drawn from a multinomial distribution governed by a set of parameters. The indicator variable determines whether a word in sentence is an aspect word, an opinion word or a background word. Maximum Entropy was used to learn the parameters of the variable using labeled training data.

A joint model was also proposed in Sauper et al. (2011) which worked only on short snippets already extracted from reviews, e.g., "*battery life is the best I've found.*" It combined topic modeling with a hidden Markov model (HMM), where the HMM models the sequence of words with types (aspect word, sentiment word, or background word). Their model is related to HMM-LDA proposed in Griffiths et al. (2005), which also models the word sequence. Variations of the joint topic modeling approach were also taken in Liu et al. (2007), Lu and Zhai (2008), and Jo and Oh (2011).

In Mukherjee and Liu (2012), a semi-supervised joint model was proposed, which allows the user to provide some seed aspect terms for some topics/aspects in order to guide the inference to produce aspect distributions that conform to the user's need.

Another line of work using topic modeling aimed to associate aspects with opinion/sentiment ratings, i.e., to predict aspect ratings based on joint modeling of aspects and ratings. Titov and McDonald (2008) proposed a model to discover aspects from reviews and also to extract textual evidence from reviews supporting each aspect rating. Lu et al. (2009) defined the problem of rated aspect summarization of short comments from eBay.com. Their aspect extraction was based on a topic model called structured pLSA. This model can model the dependency structure of phrases in short comments. To predict the rating for each aspect in a comment, it combined the overall rating of the comment and the classification result of a learned classifier for the aspect based on all the comments. Wang et al. (2010) proposed a probabilistic rating regression model to assign ratings to aspects. Their method first uses some given seed aspects to find more aspect words using a heuristic bootstrapping method. It then predicts aspect ratings using the proposed probabilistic rating regression model, which is also a graphical model. The model makes use of review ratings and assumes that the overall rating of a review is a linear combination of its aspect ratings. The model parameters are estimated using the Maximum Likelihood (ML) estimator and an EM style algorithm.

A series of joint models were also proposed in Lakkaraju et al. (2011) based on the composite topic model of HMM-LDA in Griffiths et al. (2005), which considers both word sequence and word-bag. The models thus can capture both syntactic structures and semantic dependencies similar to that in Sauper et al. (2011). They are able to discover latent aspects and their corresponding sentiment ratings. Moghaddam and Ester (2011) also proposed a joint topic model to find and group aspects and to derive their ratings.

Although topic modeling is a principled approach based on probabilistic inferencing and can be extended to model many types of information, it does have some weaknesses which limit its practical use in real-life sentiment analysis applications. One main issue is that it needs a large volume of data and a significant amount of tuning in order to achieve reasonable results. To make matters worse, most topic modeling methods use Gibbs sampling, which produces slightly different results in different runs due to MCMC (Markov chain Monte Carlo) sampling, which makes parameter tuning time consuming. While it is not hard for topic modeling to find those very general and frequent topics or aspects from a large document collection, it is not easy to find those locally frequent but globally not so frequent aspects. Such locally frequent aspects are often the most useful ones for applications because they are likely to be most relevant to the specific entities that the user is interested in. Those very general and frequent aspects can also be easily found by the methods discussed earlier. These methods can find less frequent aspects as well without the need of a large amount of data. In short, the results from current topic modeling methods are usually not granular or specific enough for many practical sentiment analysis applications. It is more useful for the user to get some high-level ideas about what a document collection is about.

That being said, topic modeling is a powerful and flexible modeling tool. It is also very nice conceptually and mathematically. I expect that continued research will make it more practically useful. One promising research direction is to incorporate more existing natural language and domain knowledge in the models. There are already some initial works in this direction (Andrzejewski and Zhu, 2009; Andrzejewski et al., 2009; Mukherjee and Liu, 2012; Zhai et al., 2011). We will discuss them in Section 5.6. However, I think they are still too statistics centric and come with their own limitations. It could be fruitful if we can shift more toward natural language and knowledge centric for a more balanced approach. Another direction would be to integrate topic modeling with some other techniques to overcome its shortcomings.

Apart from the main methods discussed above and in the previous three sections, there are still other works on aspect extraction. For example, Yi et al. (2003) used a mixture language model and likelihood ratio to extract product aspects. Ma and Wan (2010) used the centering theory and supervised learning. Meng and Wang (2009) extracted aspects from product specifications, which are structured data. Kim and Hovy (2006) used semantic role labeling. Stoyanov and Cardie (2008) exploited coreference resolution. Toprak et al. (2010) designed a comprehensive annotation scheme for aspect-based opinion annotation. Earlier annotations were partial and mainly for the special needs of individual papers. Carvalho et al. (2011) annotated a collection of political debates with aspects and other information.

5.3.5   Mapping Implicit Aspects

In Hu and Liu (2004), two kinds of aspects were identified: explicit aspects and implicit aspects. However, it only dealt with explicit aspects. Recall in Section 2.1, we call aspects that are expressed as nouns and noun phrases the *explicit aspects*, e.g., "picture quality" in "*The picture quality of this camera is great.*" All other expressions that indicate aspects are called *implicit aspects*. There are many types of implicit aspect expressions. Adjectives and adverbs are perhaps the most common types because most adjectives describe some specific attributes or properties of entities, e.g., *expensive* describes "price," and *beautiful* describes "appearance." Implicit aspects can be verbs too. In general, implicit aspect expressions can be very complex, e.g., "*This camera will not easily fit in a pocket.*" "fit in a pocket" indicates the aspect *size*.

Although explicit aspect extraction has been studied extensively, limited research has been done on mapping implicit aspects to their explicit aspects. In Su et al. (2008), a clustering method was proposed to map implicit aspect expressions, which were assumed to be sentiment words, to their corresponding explicit aspects. The method exploits the mutual reinforcement relationship between an explicit aspect and a sentiment word forming a co-occurring pair in a sentence. Such a pair may indicate that the sentiment word describes the aspect, or the aspect is associated with the sentiment word. The algorithm finds the mapping by iteratively clustering the set of explicit aspects and the set of sentiment words separately. In each iteration, before clustering one set, the clustering results of the other set is used to update the pairwise similarity of the set. The pairwise similarity in a set is determined by a linear combination of intra-set similarity and inter-set similarity. The intra-set similarity of two items is the traditional similarity. The inter-set similarity of two items is computed based on the degree of association between aspects and sentiment words. The association (or mutual reinforcement relationship) is modeled using a bipartite graph. An aspect and an opinion word are linked if they have co-occurred in a sentence. The links are also weighted based on the co-occurrence frequency. After the iterative clustering, the strongest *n* links between aspects and sentiment word groups form the mapping.

In Hai et al. (2011), a two-phase co-occurrence association rule mining approach was proposed to match implicit aspects (which are also assumed to be sentiment words) with explicit aspects. In the first phase, the approach generates association rules involving each sentiment word as the condition and an explicit aspect as the consequence, which co-occur frequently in sentences of a corpus. In the second phase, it clusters the rule consequents (explicit aspects) to generate more robust rules for each sentiment word mentioned above. For application or testing, given a sentiment word with no explicit aspect, it finds the best rule cluster and then assigns the representative word of the cluster as the final identified aspect.

5.4   IDENTIFYING RESOURCE USAGE ASPECT

As discussed in Section 4.3, researchers often try to solve a problem in a general fashion and in many cases based on a simplistic view. In the context of aspect extraction and aspect sentiment classification, it is not always the sentiment word and aspect word pairs that are important. As indicated in Section 5.2, the real world is much more complex and diverse than that. Here, we use resource usage as an example to show that a divide and conquer approach may be needed for aspect-based sentiment analysis.

In many applications, resource usage is an important aspect, e.g., *"This washer uses a lot of water."* Here, the water usage is an aspect of the washer, and this sentence indicates a negative opinion as consuming too much resource is undesirable. There is no opinion word in this sentence. Discovering resource words and phrases, which are called *resource terms*, are thus important for sentiment analysis. In Section 5.2, we presented some opinion rules involving resources. We reproduce two of them below:

1. P   ::=   consume no,_little_or_less resource
2. N   ::=   consume a_large_quantity_of_or_more resource

In Zhang and Liu (2011a), a method was proposed to extract resource terms. For example, in the above example, "water" should be extracted as a resource term. The paper formulated the problem based on a bipartite graph and proposed an iterative algorithm to solve the problem. The algorithm was based on the following observation:

Observation: The sentiment or opinion expressed in a sentence about resource usage is often determined by the following triple,

$$(verb, quantifier, noun\_term),$$

where *noun_term* is a noun or a noun phrase

For example, in "*This washer uses a lot of water*," "uses" is the main verb, "a lot of" is a quantifier phrase, and "water" is the noun representing a resource. The method used such triples to help identify resources in a domain corpus. The model used a circular definition to reflect a special reinforcement relationship between *resource usage verbs* (e.g., *consume*) and *resource terms* (e.g., *water*) based on the bipartite graph. The quantifier was not used in computation but was employed to identify candidate verbs and resource terms. The algorithm assumes that a list of quantifiers is given, which is not numerous and can be manually compiled. Based on the circular definition, the problem is solved using an iterative algorithm similar to the HITS algorithm in Kleinberg (1999). To start the iterative computation, some global *seed resources* are employed to find and to score some strong resource usage verbs. These scores are then applied as the initialization for the iterative computation for any application domain. When the algorithm converges, a ranked list of candidate resource terms is identified.

5.5 SIMUTANEOUS OPINION LEXICON EXPANSION AND ASPECT EXTRACTION

As mentioned in Chapter 2, an opinion always has a target. This property has been exploited in aspect extraction by several researchers (see Section 5.3.2). In Qiu et al. (2009) and Qiu et al. (2011), it was used to extract both sentiment words and aspects at the same time by exploiting certain syntactic relations between sentiments and targets, and a small set of seed sentiment words (no seed aspects are required) for extraction. The method is based on bootstrapping. Note that sentiment words generation is an important task itself (see Chapter 6).

Due to the relationships between sentiments/opinions and their targets (or aspects), sentiment words can be recognized by identified aspects, and aspects can be identified by known sentiment words. The extracted sentiment words and aspects are utilized to identify new sentiment words and new aspects, which are used again to extract more sentiment words and aspects. This propagation process ends when no more sentiment words or aspects can be found. As the process involves propagation through both sentiment words and aspects, the method is called *double propagation*. Extraction rules were based on certain special dependency relations among sentiment words and aspects. The *dependency grammar* (Tesniere, 1959) was adopted to describe the relations. The dependency parser used was minipar (Lin, 2007).

Some constraints were also imposed. Sentiment words were considered to be adjectives and aspects nouns or noun phrases. The dependency relations between sentiment words and aspects include *mod*, *pnmod*, *subj*, *s*, *obj*, *obj2*, and *desc*, while the relations for sentiment words and aspects themselves contain only the conjunction relation *conj*. OA-Rel denotes the relations between sentiment words and aspects, OO-Rel between sentiment words themselves, and AA-Rel between aspects. Each relation in OA-Rel, OO-Rel, or AA-Rel is a triple <POS(w_i), R, POS(w_j)>, where POS(w_i) is the POS tag of word w_i and R is one the dependency relations above.

The extraction process uses a rule-based approach. For example, in "*Canon G3 produces great pictures*," the adjective "great" is parsed as depending on the noun "pictures" through *mod*, formulated as an OA-Rel <*JJ, mod, NNS*>. If we know "great" is a sentiment word and are given the rule "a noun on which a sentiment word directly depends through *mod* is taken as an aspect," we can extract "pictures" as an aspect. Similarly, if we know "pictures" is an aspect, we can extract "great" as an opinion word using a similar rule. The propagation performs four subtasks:

1. extracting aspects using sentiment words;
2. extracting aspects using extracted aspects;
3. extracting sentiment words using extracted aspects; and
4. extracting sentiment words using both given and extracted opinion words.

OA-Rels are used for tasks (1) and (3), AA-Rels are used for task (2), and OO-Rels are used for task (4). Four types of rules are defined (shown in Table 5.1), respectively, for these four subtasks. In the table, *o* (or *a*) stands for the output (or extracted) sentiment word (or aspect). {O} (or {A}) is the set of known sentiment words (or aspects) either given or extracted. *H* means any word. *POS(O(or A))* and *O(or A)-Dep* stand for the POS tag and dependency relation of the word *O* (or *A*), respectively. {*JJ*} and {*NN*} are sets of POS tags of potential sentiment words and aspects respectively. {*JJ*} contains *JJ, JJR* and *JJS*; {*NN*} contains *NN* and *NNS*. {*MR*} consists of dependency relations, which is the set {*mod, pnmod, subj, s, obj, obj2*, and *desc*}. {*CONJ*} contains *conj* only. The arrows mean dependency. For example, $O \rightarrow O\text{-}Dep \rightarrow A$ means O depends on A through a relation O-Dep. Specifically, $R1_i$ is employed to extract aspects (*a*) using sentiment words (*O*), $R2_i$ to extract opinion words (*o*) using aspects (*A*), $R3_i$ to extract aspects (*a*) using extracted aspects (*A_i*), and $R4_i$ to extract sentiment words (*o*) using known sentiment words (*O_i*).

TABLE 5.1: Rules for aspect and opinion word extraction. Column 1 is the rule ID, column 2 is the observed relation (line 1) and the constraints that it must satisfy (lines 2 − 4), column 3 is the output, and column 4 is an example. In each example, the underlined word is the known word and the word with double quotes is the extracted word. The corresponding instantiated relation is given right below the example.

	OBSERVATIONS	OUTPUT	EXAMPLES
$R1_1$ (OA-Rel)	$O \rightarrow O\text{-}Dep \rightarrow A$ $s.t.\ O \in \{O\},\ O\text{-}Dep \in \{MR\},$ $POS(A) \in \{NN\}$	$a = A$	*The phone has a good "screen".* $good \rightarrow \textbf{mod} \rightarrow screen$
$R1_2$ (OA-Rel)	$O \rightarrow O\text{-}Dep \rightarrow H \leftarrow A\text{-}Dep \leftarrow A$ $s.t.\ O \in \{O\},\ O/A\text{-}Dep \in \{MR\},$ $POS(A) \in \{NN\}$	$a = A$	*"iPod" is the best mp3 player.* $best \rightarrow \textbf{mod} \rightarrow player \leftarrow \textbf{subj} \leftarrow iPod$
$R2_1$ (OA-Rel)	$O \rightarrow O\text{-}Dep \rightarrow A$ $s.t.\ A \in \{A\},\ O\text{-}Dep \in \{MR\},$ $POS(O) \in \{JJ\}$	$o = O$	same as $R1_1$ with *screen* as the known word and *good* as the extracted word
$R2_2$ (OA-Rel)	$O \rightarrow O\text{-}Dep \rightarrow H \leftarrow A\text{-}Dep \leftarrow A$ $s.t.\ A \in \{A\},\ O/A\text{-}Dep \in \{MR\},$ $POS(O) \in \{JJ\}$	$o = O$	same as $R1_2$ with *iPod* is the known word and *best* as the extract word.
$R3_1$ (AA-Rel)	$A_{i(j)} \rightarrow A_{i(j)}\text{-}Dep \rightarrow A_{j(i)}$ $s.t.\ A_{j(i)} \in \{A\},\ A_{i(j)}\text{-}Dep \in \{CONJ\},$ $POS(A_{i(j)}) \in \{NN\}$	$a = A_{i(j)}$	*Does the player play dvd with audio and "video"?* $video \rightarrow \textbf{conj} \rightarrow audio$
$R3_2$ (AA-Rel)	$A_i \rightarrow A_i\text{-}Dep \rightarrow H \leftarrow A_j\text{-}Dep \leftarrow A_j$ $s.t.\ A_i \in \{A\},\ A_i\text{-}Dep = A_j\text{-}Dep$ OR $(A_i\text{-}Dep = subj$ AND $A_j\text{-}Dep = obj),\ POS(A_j) \in \{NN\}$	$a = A_j$	*Canon "G3" has a great len.* $len \rightarrow \textbf{obj} \rightarrow has \leftarrow \textbf{subj} \leftarrow G3$
$R4_1$ (OO-Rel)	$O_{i(j)} \rightarrow O_{i(j)}\text{-}Dep \rightarrow O_{j(i)}$ $s.t.\ O_{j(i)} \in \{O\},\ O_{i(j)}\text{-}Dep \in \{CONJ\},$ $POS(O_{i(j)}) \in \{JJ\}$	$o = O_{i(j)}$	*The camera is amazing and "easy" to use.* $easy \rightarrow \textbf{conj} \rightarrow amazing$
$R4_2$ (OO-Rel)	$O_i \rightarrow O_i\text{-}Dep \rightarrow H \leftarrow O_j\text{-}Dep \leftarrow O_j$ $s.t.\ O_i \in \{O\},\ O_i\text{-}Dep = O_j\text{-}Dep$ OR $(O_i/O_j\text{-}Dep \in \{pnmod, mod\}),$ $POS(O_j) \in \{JJ\}$	$o = O_j$	*If you want to buy a sexy, "cool", accessory-available mp3 player, you can choose iPod.* $sexy \rightarrow \textbf{mod} \rightarrow player \leftarrow \textbf{mod} \leftarrow cool$

This method was originally designed for English, but it has also been used for Chinese online discussions (Zhai et al., 2011). This method can also be reduced for finding aspects only using a large sentiment lexicon. For practical use, the set of relations can be significantly expanded. Also, instead of using word-based dependency parsing, a phrase level dependency parsing may be better as many aspects are phrases (Wu et al., 2009). Zhang et al. (2010) improved this method by adding more relations and by ranking the extracted aspects using a graph method.

5.6 GROUPING ASPECTS INTO CATEGORIES

After aspect extraction, aspect expressions (actual words and phrases indicating aspects) need to be grouped into synonymous aspect categories. Each category represents a unique aspect. As in any writing, people often use different words and phrases to describe the same aspect. For example, "call quality" and "voice quality" refer to the same aspect for phones. Grouping such aspect expressions from the same aspect is critical for opinion analysis. Although WorldNet and other thesaurus dictionaries can help to some extent, they are far from sufficient because many synonyms are domain dependent (Liu et al., 2005). For example, "movie" and "picture" are synonyms in movie reviews, but they are not synonyms in camera reviews as "picture" is more likely to be synonymous to "photo" while "movie" to "video". Many aspect expressions are multi-word phrases, which cannot be easily handled with dictionaries. Furthermore, it is also important to note that many aspect expressions describing the same aspect are not general or domain specific synonyms. For example, "expensive" and "cheap" can both indicate the aspect *price* but they are not synonyms of each other (but antonyms) or synonyms of *price*.

Carenini et al. (2005) proposed the first method to deal with this problem. Their method was based on several similarity metrics defined using string similarity, synonyms, and lexical distances measured using WordNet. The method requires a taxonomy of aspects to be given for a particular domain. It merges each discovered aspect expression to an aspect node in the taxonomy based on the similarities. Experiments based on digital camera and DVD reviews showed promising results. In Yu et al. (2011), a more sophisticated method was presented to also use publicly available aspect hierarchies/taxonomies of products and the actual product reviews to produce the final aspect hierarchies. A set of distance measures was also used but was combined with an optimization strategy.

In Zhai et al. (2010), a semi-supervised learning method was proposed to group aspect expressions into some user-specified aspect categories. To reflect the user needs, he/she first labels a small number of seeds for each category. The system then assigns the rest of the aspect expressions to suitable categories using a semi-supervised learning method working with labeled and unlabeled examples. The method uses the Expectation-Maximization (EM) algorithm in Nigam et al. (2000).

The method also employed two pieces of prior knowledge to provide a better initialization for EM: (1) aspect expressions sharing some common words are likely to belong to the same group, e.g., "battery life" and "battery power;" and (2) aspect expressions that are synonyms in a dictionary are likely to belong to the same group, e.g., "movie" and "picture." These two pieces of knowledge help EM produce better classification results. In Zhai et al. (2011), soft constraints were used to help label some examples, i.e., sharing words and lexical similarity (Jiang and Conrath, 1997). The learning method also used EM, but it eliminated the need of asking the user to provide seeds. Note that the general NLP research on concept similarity and synonym discovery is also relevant here (Mohammad and Hirst, 2006; Wang and Hirst, 2011).

In Guo et al. (2009), a method called multilevel latent semantic association was presented. At the first level, all the words in aspect expressions (each aspect expression can have more than one word) are grouped into a set of concepts/topics using LDA. The results are used to build latent topic structures for aspect expressions. For example, we have four aspect expressions: "day photos," "day photo," "daytime photos," and "daytime photo." If LDA groups the individual words "day" and "daytime" into topic10, and "photo" and "photos" into topic12, the system will group all four aspect expressions into one group, call it "topic10-topic12", which is called a latent topic structure. At the second level, aspect expressions are grouped by LDA again but according to their latent topic structures produced at level 1 and their context snippets in reviews. Following the above example, "day photos," "day photo," "daytime photos," and "daytime photo" in "topic10-topic12" combined with their surrounding words form a document. LDA runs on such documents to produce the final result. In Guo et al. (2010), a similar idea was also used to group aspects from different languages into aspect categories, which can be used to compare opinions along different aspects from different languages (or countries).

Topic modeling methods discussed in Section 5.3.4 actually perform both aspect expression discovery and categorization at the same time in an unsupervised manner as topic modeling basically clusters terms in a document collection. Recently, some algorithms have also been proposed to use domain knowledge or constraints to guide topic modeling to produce better topic clusters (Andrzejewski et al., 2009). The constraints are in the form of *must-links* and *cannot-links*. A must-link constraint in clustering specifies that two data instances must be in the same cluster. A cannot-link constraint specifies that two data instances cannot be in the same cluster. However, the method can result in an exponential growth in the encoding of cannot-link constraints and thus have difficulty in processing a large number of constraints.

Constrained-LDA of Zhai et al. (2011) took a different but heuristic approach. Instead of treating constraints as priors, the constraints were used in Gibbs sampling to bias the conditional probability for topic assignment of a word. This method can handle a large number of must-link and cannot-link constraints. The constraints can also be relaxed, i.e., they are treated as soft (rather than hard) constraints and may not be satisfied. For aspect categorization, Constrained-LDA used the following constraints:

Must-link: If two aspect expressions a_i and a_j share one or more words, they form a must-link, i.e., they are likely to be in the same topic or category, e.g., "battery power" and "battery life."

Cannot-link: If two aspect expressions a_i and a_j in the same sentence, they form a cannot-link. The reason for this constraint is that people usually do not repeat the same aspect in the same sentence, e.g., "*I like the picture quality, battery life, and zoom of this camera.*"

In Mukherjee and Liu (2012), the domain knowledge came in the form of some user-provided seed aspect words to some topics (or aspects). The resulting model is thus semi-supervised. The model also separates aspect words and sentiment words. The model in Andrzejewski et al., (2009) or the Constrained-LDA method does not do that.

5.7   ENTITY, OPINION HOLDER, AND TIME EXTRACTION

Entity, opinion holder, and time extraction is the classic problem of named entity recognition (NER). NER has been studied extensively in several fields, e.g., information retrieval, text mining, data mining, machine learning, and natural language processing under the name of information extraction (Hobbs and Riloff, 2010; Mooney and Bunescu, 2005; Sarawagi, 2008). There are two main approaches to information extraction: rule-based and statistical. Early extraction systems were mainly based on rules (e.g., Riloff, 1993). Statistical methods were typically based on Hidden Markov Models (HMM) (Rabiner, 1989; Jin and Ho, 2009) and Conditional Random Fields (CRF) (Lafferty et al., 2001). Both HMM and CRF are supervised methods. Due to the prior work in the area, specific works in the context of sentiment analysis and opinion mining is not extensive. Thus, we will not discuss it further. See a comprehensive survey of information extraction tasks and algorithms in Sarawagi (2008). Here, we only discuss some specific issues in sentiment analysis applications.

In most applications that use social media, we do not need to extract opinion holders and the times of postings from the text as opinion holders are usually the authors of the reviews, blogs, or discussion postings, whose login ids are known although their true identities in the real world are unknown. The date and time when a posting was submitted are also known and displayed on the Web page. They can be scraped from the page using structured data extraction techniques (Liu, 2006, 2011). In some cases, opinion holders can be in the actual text and need to be extracted. We discuss it below.

Here we first discuss a specific problem of named entity extraction in the sentiment analysis context. In a typical sentiment analysis application, the user usually wants to find opinions about some competing entities, e.g., competing products or brands. However, he/she often can only provide a few names because there are so many different brands and models. Even for the same entity, Web users may write the entity in many different ways. For example, "Motorola" may be written as "Moto" or "Mot." It is thus important for a system to automatically discover them from the corpus (e.g., reviews, blogs, and forum discussions). The main requirement of this extraction is that the extracted entities must be of the same type as the entities provided by the user (e.g., phone brands and models).

Li et al. (2010) formulated the problem as a *set expansion problem* (Ghahramani and Heller, 2006; Pantel et al., 2009). The problem is stated as follows: Given a set Q of seed entities of a particular class C, and a set D of candidate entities, we wish to determine which of the entities in D belong to C. That is, we "grow" the class C based on the set of seed examples Q. Although this is a classification problem, in practice, the problem is often solved as a ranking problem, i.e., to rank the entities in D based on their likelihoods of belonging to C.

The classic methods for solving this problem in NLP are based on distributional similarity (Lee, 1999; Pantel et al., 2009). The approach works by comparing the similarity of the surround words of each candidate entity with those of the seed entities and then ranking the candidate entities based on the similarity values. In Li et al. (2010), it was shown that this approach was inaccurate. Learning from positive and unlabeled examples (PU learning) using the S-EM algorithm (Liu et al., 2002) was considerably better. To apply PU learning, the given seeds were used to automatically extract sentences that contain one or more of the seeds. The surrounding words of each seed in these sentences served as the context of the seed. The rest of the sentences were treated as unlabeled examples. Experimental results indicated that S-EM outperformed the machine learning technique *Bayesian Sets* (Ghahramani and Heller, 2006), which also outperformed the distributional similarity measure significantly.

About opinion holder extraction in the context of sentiment analysis, several researchers have investigated it. The extraction was mainly done in news articles. Kim and Hovy (2004) considered person and organization as the only possible opinion holders, and used a named entity tagger to identify them. Choi et al. (2006) used conditional random fields (CRF) for extraction. To train CRF, they used features such as surrounding words, part-of-speech of surrounding words, grammatical roles, sentiment words, etc. In Kim and Hovy (2006), the method first generates all possible holder candidates in a sentence, i.e., all noun phrases, including common noun phrases, named entities, and pronouns. It then parses the sentence and extracts a set of features from the parse tree. A learned Maximum Entropy (ME) model then ranks all holder candidates according to the scores obtained by the ME model. The system picks the candidate with the highest score as the holder of the opinion in the sentence. Johansson and Moschitti (2010) used SVM with a set of features. Wiegand and Klakow (2010) used convolution kernels, and Lu (2010) applied a dependency parser.

In Ruppenhofer et al. (2008), the authors discussed the issue of using automatic semantic role labeling (ASRL) to identify opinion holders. They argued that ASRL is insufficient and other linguistic phenomena such as the discourse structure may need to be considered. Earlier, Kim and Hovy (2006) also used semantic role labeling for that purpose.

5.8 COREFERENCE RESOLUTION AND WORD SENSE DISAMBIGUATION

Although we discuss only *coreference resolution* and *word sense disambiguation* in this section, we really want to highlight NLP issues and problems in the sentiment analysis context. Most of such issues have not been studied in sentiment analysis.

Coreference resolution has been studied extensively in the NLP community in general. It refers to the problem of determining multiple expressions in a sentence or document referring to the same thing, i.e., they have the same "referent." For example, in "*I bought an iPhone two days ago. It looks very nice. I made many calls in the past two days. They were great,*" "It" in the second sentence refers to iPhone, which is an entity, and "they" in the fourth sentence refers to "calls," which is an aspect. Recognizing these coreference relationships is clearly very important for aspect-based sentiment analysis. If we do not resolve them, but only consider opinion in each sentence in isolation, we lose recall. That is, although we know that the second and fourth sentences express opinions, we do not know about what. Then, from this piece of text we will get no useful opinion, but in fact, it has a positive opinion on iPhone itself and also a positive opinion on the call quality.

Ding and Liu (2010) proposed the problem of *entity and aspect coreference resolution.* The task aims to determine which mentions of entities and/or aspects that pronouns refer to. The paper took a supervised learning approach. The key interesting points were the design and testing of two opinion-related features, which showed that sentiment analysis was used for the purpose of coreference resolution. The first feature is based on sentiment analysis of regular sentences and comparative sentences, and the idea of *sentiment consistency.* Consider these sentences, "*The Nokia phone is better than this Motorola phone. It is cheap too.*" Our commonsense tells us that "It" means "Nokia phone" because in the first sentence, the sentiment about "Nokia phone" is positive (comparative positive), but it is negative (comparative negative) for "Motorola phone," and the second sentence is positive. Thus, we conclude that "It" refers to "Nokia phone" because people usually express sentiments in a consistent way. It is unlikely that "It" refers to "Motorola phone." However, if we change "*It is cheap too*" to "*It is also expensive,*" then "it" should now refer to "Motorola phone." To obtain this feature, the system needs to have the ability to determine positive and negative opinions expressed in both regular and comparative sentences.

The second feature considers what entities and aspects are modified by what opinion words. Consider these sentences, "*I bought a Nokia phone yesterday. The sound quality is good. It is cheap too.*" The question is what "It" refers to, "sound quality" or the "Nokia phone." Clearly, we know that "It" refers to "Nokia phone" because "sound quality" cannot be cheap. To obtain this feature, the system needs to identify what sentiment words are usually associated with what entities or aspects. Such relationships have to be mined from the corpus. These two features are semantic features that current general coreference resolution methods do not consider. These two features can help improve the coreference resolution accuracy.

Stoyanov and Cardie (2006) proposed the problem of *source coreference resolution*, which is the task of determining which mentions of opinion holders (sources) refer to the same entity. The authors used existing coreference resolution features in Ng and Cardie (2002). However, instead of employing supervised learning, they used partially supervised clustering.

Akkaya et al. (2009) studied *subjectivity word sense disambiguation* (SWSD). The task is to automatically determine which word instances in a corpus are being used with subjective senses, and which are being used with objective senses. Currently, most subjectivity or sentiment lexicons are compiled as lists of words, rather than word meanings (senses). However, many words have both subjective and objective senses. False hits—subjectivity clues used with objective senses—are a significant source of error in subjectivity and sentiment analysis. The authors built a supervised SWSD model to disambiguate members of a subjectivity lexicon as having a subjective sense or an objective sense in a corpus context. The algorithm relied on common machine learning features for word sense disambiguation (WSD). However, the performance was substantially better than the performance of full WSD on the same data, suggesting that the SWSD task was feasible, and that subjectivity provided a natural coarse grained grouping of senses. They also showed that SWSD can subsequently help subjectivity and sentiment analysis.

5.9 SUMMARY

Aspect-level sentiment analysis is usually the level of details required for practical applications. Most industrial systems are so based. Although a great deal of work has been done in the research community and many systems have also been built, the problem is still far from being solved. Every sub-problem remains to be highly challenging. As one CEO put it, "our sentiment analysis is as bad as everyone else's," which is a nice portrayal of the current situation and the difficulty of the problem.

Two most outstanding problems are aspect extraction and aspect sentiment classifications. The accuracies for both problems are not high because existing algorithms are still unable to deal with complex sentences that requires more than sentiment words and simple parsing, or to handle factual sentences that imply opinions. We discussed some of these problems in basic rules of opinions in Section 5.2.

On the whole, we seem to have met a long tail problem. While sentiment words can handle about 60% of the cases (more in some domains and less in others), the rest are highly diverse, numerous, and infrequent, which make it hard for statistical learning algorithms to learn patterns because there are simply not enough training data for them. In fact, there seem to be an unlimited number of ways that people can use to express positive or negative opinions. Every domain appears to have something special. In Wu et al. (2011), a more complex graph-based representation of opinions was proposed, which requires even more sophisticated solution methods.

So far, the research community has mainly focused on opinions about electronics products, hotels, and restaurants. These domains are easier (although not easy) and reasonably good accuracies can be achieved if one can focus on each domain and take care of its special cases. When one moves to other domains, e.g., mattress and paint, the situations get considerably harder because in these domains many factual statements imply opinions. Politics is another can of warms. Here, the current aspect extraction algorithms only had limited success because few political issues (aspects) can be described with one or two words. Political sentiments are also harder to determine due to complex mixture of factual reporting and subjective opinions, and heavy use of sarcastic sentences.

In term of the type of social media, researchers working on aspect-based sentiment analysis have focused mainly on product/service reviews and tweets from Twitter. These forms of data are also easier (again, not easy) to handle because reviews are opinion rich and have little irrelevant information while tweets are very short and often straight to the point. However, other forms of opinion text such as forum discussions and commentaries are much harder to deal with because they are mixed with all kinds of non-opinion contents and often talk about multiple entities and involve user interactions. This leads us to another major issue that we have not discussed so far as there is limited research on it. It is the data noise. Almost all forms of social media are very noisy (except reviews) and full of all kinds of spelling, grammatical, and punctuation errors. Most NLP tools such as POS taggers and parsers need clean data to perform accurately. Thus, a significant amount of pre-processing is needed before any analysis. See Dey and Haque (2008) for some pre-processing tasks and methods.

To make a significant progress, we still need novel ideas and to study a wide range of domains. Successful algorithms are likely to be a good integration of machine learning and domain and natural language knowledge.

CHAPTER 6

Sentiment Lexicon Generation

By now, it should be quite clear that words and phrases that convey positive or negative sentiments are instrumental for sentiment analysis. This chapter discusses how to compile such words lists. In the research literature, *sentiment words* are also called *opinion words*, *polar words*, or *opinion-bearing words*. Positive sentiment words are used to express some desired states or qualities while negative sentiment words are used to express some undesired states or qualities. Examples of positive sentiment words are *beautiful*, *wonderful*, and *amazing*. Examples of negative sentiment words are *bad*, *awful*, and *poor*. Apart from individual words, there are also sentiment phrases and idioms, e.g., *cost someone an arm and a leg*. Collectively, they are called *sentiment lexicon* (or *opinion lexicon*). For easy presentation, from now on when we say sentiment words, we mean both individual words and phrases.

Sentiment words can be divided into two types: *base type* and *comparative type*. All the example words above are of the base type. Sentiment words of the comparative type (which include the superlative type) are used to express comparative and superlative opinions. Examples of such words are *better*, *worse*, *best*, *worst*, etc., which are comparative and superlative forms of their base adjectives or adverbs, e.g., *good* and *bad*. Unlike sentiment words of the base type, sentiment words of the comparative type do not express a regular opinion on an entity but a comparative opinion on more than one entity, e.g., "*Pepsi tastes better than Coke.*" This sentence does not express an opinion saying that any of the two drinks is good or bad. It just says that compared to *Coke*, *Pepsi* tastes better. We will discuss comparative and superlative sentiment words further in Chapter 8. This chapter focuses only on sentiment words of the base type.

Researchers have proposed many approaches to compile sentiment words. Three main approaches are: *manual approach*, *dictionary-based approach*, and *corpus-based approach*. The manual approach is labor intensive and time consuming, and is thus not usually used alone but combined with automated approaches as the final check, because automated methods make mistakes. Below, we discuss the two automated approaches. Along with them, we will also discuss the issue of factual statements implying opinions, which has largely been overlooked by the research community.

6.1 DICTIONARY-BASED APPROACH

Using a dictionary to compile sentiment words is an obvious approach because most dictionaries (e.g., WordNet; Miller et al., 1990) list synonyms and antonyms for each word. Thus, a simple technique in this approach is to use a few seed sentiment words to bootstrap based on the synonym and antonym structure of a dictionary. Specifically, this method works as follows. A small set of sentiment words (seeds) with known positive or negative orientations is first collected manually, which is very easy. The algorithm then grows this set by searching in the WordNet or another online dictionary for their synonyms and antonyms. The newly found words are added to the seed list. The next iteration begins. The iterative process ends when no more new words can be found. This approach was used in Hu and Liu (2004). After the process completes, a manual inspection step was used to clean up the list. A similar method was also used by Valitutti et al. (2004). Kim and Hovy (2004) tried to clean up the resulting words (to remove errors) and to assign a sentiment strength to each word using a probabilistic method. Mohammad et al. (2009) additionally exploited many antonym-generating affix patterns like X and dis$X$ (e.g., honest-dishonest) to increase the coverage.

A more sophisticated approach was proposed in Kamps et al. (2004), which used a WordNet distance-based method to determine the sentiment orientation of a given adjective. The distance $d(t_1, t_2)$ between terms t_1 and t_2 is the length of the shortest path that connects t_1 and t_2 in WordNet. The orientation of an adjective term t is determined by its relative distance from two reference (or seed) terms *good* and *bad*, i.e., $SO(t) = (d(t, \text{bad}) - d(t, \text{good}))/d(\text{good}, \text{bad})$. t is positive iff $SO(t) > 0$, and is negative otherwise. The absolute value of $SO(t)$ gives the strength of the sentiment. Along a similar line, Williams and Anand (2009) studied the problem of assigning sentiment strength to each word.

In Blair-Goldensohn et al. (2008), a different bootstrapping method was proposed, which used a positive seed set, a negative seed set, and also a neutral seed set. The approach works based on a directed, weighted semantic graph where neighboring nodes are synonyms or antonyms of words in WordNet and are not part of the seed neutral set. The neutral set is used to stop the propagation of sentiments through neutral words. The edge weights are pre-assigned based on a scaling parameter for different types of edges, i.e., synonym or antonym edges. Each word is then scored (giving a sentiment value) using a modified version of the label propagation algorithm in Zhu and Ghahramani (2002). At the beginning, each positive seed word is given the score of +1, each negative seed is given the score of -1, and all other words are given the score of 0. The scores are revised during the propagation process. When the propagation stops after a number of iterations, the final scores after a logarithmic scaling are assigned to words as their degrees of being positive or negative.

In Rao and Ravichandran (2009), three graph-based semi-supervised learning methods were tried to separate positive and negative words given a positive seed set, a negative seed set, and a synonym graph extracted from the WordNet. The three algorithms were Mincut (Blum and Chawla, 2001), Randomized Mincut (Blum et al., 2004), and label propagation (Zhu and Ghahramani, 2002). It was shown that Mincut and Randomized Mincut produced better F scores, but label propagation gave significantly higher precisions with low recalls.

Hassan and Radev (2010) presented a Markov random walk model over a word relatedness graph to produce a sentiment estimate for a given word. It first uses WordNet synonyms and hypernyms to build a word relatedness graph. A measure, called the *mean hitting time* $h(i|S)$, was then defined and used to gauge the distance from a node i to a set of nodes (words) S, which is the average number of steps that a random walker, starting in state $i \notin S$, will take to enter a state $k \in S$ for the first time. Given a set of positive seed words S^+ and a set of negative seed words S^-, to estimate the sentiment orientation of a given word w, it computes the hitting times $h(w|S^+)$ and $h(w|S^-)$. If $h(w|S^+)$ is greater than $h(w|S^-)$, the word is classified as negative, otherwise positive. In Hassan et al. (2011), this method was applied to find sentiment orientations of foreign words. For this purpose, a multilingual word graph was created with both English words and foreign words. Words in different languages are connected based on their meanings in dictionaries. Other methods based on graphs include those in Takamura et al. (2005, 2006, 2007).

In Turney and Littman (2003), the same PMI based method as in Turney (2002) was used to compute the sentiment orientation of a given word. Specifically, it computes the orientation of the word from the strength of its association with a set of positive words (*good, nice, excellent, positive, fortunate, correct,* and *superior*), minus the strength of its association with a set of negative words (*bad, nasty, poor, negative, unfortunate, wrong,* and *inferior*). The association strength is measured using PMI.

Esuli and Sebastiani (2005) used supervised learning to classify words into positive and negative classes. Given a set P of positive seed words and a set N of negative seed words, the two seed sets are first expanded using synonym and antonym relations in an online dictionary (e.g., WordNet) to generate the expanded sets P' and N', which form the training set. The algorithm then uses all the glosses in the dictionary for each term in $P' \cup N'$ to generate a feature vector. A binary classifier is then built using different learning algorithms. The process can also be run iteratively. That is, the newly identified positive and negative terms and their synonyms and antonyms are added to the training set, an updated classifier can be constructed and so on. Esuli and Sebastiani (2006) also included the category *objective*. To expand the objective seed set, hyponyms were used in addition to synonyms and antonyms. They then tried different strategies to do the three-class classification. In Esuli and Sebastiani (2006), a committee of classifiers based on the above method was utilized to build the SentiWordNet, a lexical resource in which each synset of WordNet is associated with three numerical scores Obj(s), Pos(s), and Neg(s), describing how Objective, Positive, and Negative the terms contained in the synset are. The method of Kim and Hovy (2006) also started with three seed sets of positive, negative, and neutral words. It then finds their synonyms in WordNet. The expanded sets, however, have many errors. The method then uses a Bayesian formula to compute the closeness of each word to each category (positive, negative, and neutral) to determine the most probable class for the word.

Andreevskaia and Bergler (2006) proposed a more sophisticated bootstrapping method with several techniques to expand the initial positive and negative seed sets and to clean up the expanded sets (removing non-adjectives and words in both positive and negative sets). In addition, their algorithm also performs multiple runs of the bootstrapping process using non-overlapping seed subsets. Each run typically finds a slightly different set of sentiment words. A net overlapping score for each word is then computed based on how many times the word is discovered in the runs as a positive word and as a negative word. The score is then normalized to [0, 1] based on the fuzzy set theory.

In Kaji and Kitsuregawa (2006, 2007), many heuristics were used to build a sentiment lexicon from HTML documents based on Web page layout structures. For example, a table in a Web page may have a column clearly indicate positive or negative orientations (e.g., Pros and Cons) of the surround text. These clues can be exploited to extract a large number of candidate positive and negative opinion sentences from a large set of Web pages. Adjective phrases are then extracted from these sentences and assigned sentiment orientations based on different statistics of their occurrences in the positive and negative sentence sets, respectively.

Velikovich et al. (2010) also proposed a method to construct a sentient lexicon using Web pages. It was based on a graph propagation algorithm over a phrase similarity graph. It again assumed as input a set of positive seed phrases and a set of negative seed phrases. The nodes in the phrase graph were the candidate phrases selected from all n-grams up to length 10 extracted from 4 billion Web pages. Only 20 million candidate phrases were selected using several heuristics, e.g., frequency and mutual information of word boundaries. A context vector for each candidate phrase was then constructed based on a word window of size six aggregated over all mentions of the phrase in the 4 billion documents. The edge set was constructed through cosine similarity computation of the context vectors of the candidate phrases. All edges (v_i, v_j) were discarded if they were not one of the 25 highest weighted edges adjacent to either node v_i or v_j. The edge weight was set to the corresponding cosine similarity value. A graph-propagation method was used to calculate the sentiment of each phrase as the aggregate of all the best paths to the seed words.

In Dragut et al. (2010), yet another but very different bootstrapping method was proposed using WordNet. Given a set of seed words, instead of simply following the dictionary, the authors proposed a set of sophisticated inference rules to determine other words' sentiment orientations through a deductive process. That is, the algorithm takes words with known sentiment orientations (the seeds) as input and produces synsets (sets of synonyms) with orientations. The synsets with the deduced orientations can then be used to further deduce the polarities of other words.

Peng and Park (2011) presented a sentiment lexicon generation method using constrained symmetric nonnegative matrix factorization (CSNMF). The method first uses bootstrapping to find a set of candidate sentiment words in a dictionary and then uses a large corpus to assign polarity (or sentiment) scores to each word. This method thus uses both dictionary and corpus. Xu et al. (2010) presented several integrated methods as well using dictionaries and corpora to find emotion words. Their method is based on label propagation in a similarity graph (Zhu and Ghahramani, 2002).

In summary, we note that the advantage of using a dictionary-based approach is that one can easily and quickly find a large number of sentiment words with their orientations. Although the resulting list can have many errors, a manual checking can be performed to clean it up, which is time consuming (not as bad as people thought, only a few days for a native speaker) but it is only a one-time effort. The main disadvantage is that the sentiment orientations of words collected this way are general or domain and context independent. In other words, it is hard to use the dictionary-based approach to find domain or context dependent orientations of sentiment words. As discussed before, many sentiment words have context dependent orientations. For example, for a speaker phone, if it is quiet, it is usually negative. However, for a car, if it is quiet, it is positive. The sentiment orientation of *quiet* is domain or context dependent. The corpus-based approach below can help deal with this problem.

6.2 CORPUS-BASED APPROACH

The corpus-based approach has been applied to two main scenarios: (1) given a seed list of known (often general-purpose) sentiment words, discover other sentiment words and their orientations from a domain corpus; and (2) adapt a general-purpose sentiment lexicon to a new one using a domain corpus for sentiment analysis applications in the domain. However, the issue is more complicated than just building a domain specific sentiment lexicon because in the same domain the same word can be positive in one context but negative in another. Below, we discuss some of the existing works that tried to deal with these problems. Note that although the corpus-based approach may also be used to build a general-purpose sentiment lexicon if a very large and very diverse corpus is available, the dictionary-based approach is usually more effective for that because a dictionary has all words.

One of the key and also early ideas was proposed by Hazivassiloglou and McKeown (1997). The authors used a corpus and some seed adjective sentiment words to find additional sentiment adjectives in the corpus. Their technique exploited a set of linguistic rules or conventions on connectives to identify more adjective sentiment words and their orientations from the corpus. One of the rules is about the conjunction AND, which says that conjoined adjectives usually have the same orientation. For example, in the sentence, "*This car is beautiful and spacious*," if "beautiful" is known to be positive, it can be inferred that "spacious" is also positive. This is so because people usually express the same sentiment on both sides of a conjunction. The following sentence is not likely, "*This car is beautiful and difficult to drive.*" It is more acceptable if it is changed to "*This car is beautiful but difficult to drive.*" Rules were also designed for other connectives, i.e., OR, BUT, EITHER–OR, and NEITHER–NOR. This idea is called *sentiment consistency*. In practice, it is not always consistent. Thus, a learning step was also applied to determine if two conjoined adjectives have the same or different orientations. First, a graph was formed with same- and different-orientation links between adjectives. Clustering was then performed on the graph to produce two sets of words: positive and negative.

Kanayama and Nasukawa (2006) extended the approach by introducing the concepts of intra-sentential (within a sentence) and inter-sentential (between neighboring sentences) sentiment consistency, which they call *coherency*. The intra-sentential consistency is similar to the idea above. Inter-sentential consistency simply applies the idea to neighboring sentences. That is, the same sentiment orientation is usually expressed in consecutive sentences. Sentiment changes are indicated by adversative expressions such as *but* and *however*. Some criteria were also proposed to determine whether to add a word to the positive or negative lexicon. This study was based on Japanese text and was used to find domain dependent sentiment words and their orientations. Other related work includes those in Kaji and Kitsuregawa (2006, 2007).

Although finding domain-specific sentiment words and their orientations are useful, it is insufficient in practice. Ding et al. (2008) showed that many words in the same domain can have different orientations in different contexts. In fact, this phenomenon has been depicted by the basic rules of opinions in Section 5.2. For example, in the camera domain, the word "long" clearly expresses opposite opinions in the following two sentences: "*The battery life is long*" (positive) and "*It takes a long time to focus*" (negative). Such situations often occur with quantifiers, e.g., *long*, *short*, *large*, *small*, etc. However, it is not always. For example, in a car review, the sentence "*This car is very quiet*" is positive, but the sentence "*The audio system in the car is very quiet*" is negative. Thus, finding domain-dependent sentiment words and their orientations is insufficient. The authors found that both the aspect and the sentiment expressing words were both important. They then proposed to use the pair (*aspect, sentiment_word*) as an *opinion context*, e.g., ("battery life", "long"). Their method thus determines sentiment words and their orientations together with the aspects that they modify. In determining whether a pair is positive or negative, the above intra-sentential and inter-sentential sentiment consistency rules about connectives are still applied. The work in Ganapathibhotla and Liu (2008) adopted the same context definition but used it for analyzing comparative sentences. Wu and Wen (2010) dealt with a similar problem in Chinese. However, they only focused on pairs in which the adjectives are quantifiers such as *big*, *small*, *low* and *high*. Their method is based on syntactic patterns as in Turney (2002), and also use the Web search hit counts to solve the problem. Lu et al. (2011) used the same context definition as well. Like that in Ding et al. (2008), they assumed that the set of aspects was given. They formulated the problem of assigning each pair the positive or negative sentiment as an optimization problem with a number of constraints. The objective function and constraints were designed based on clues such as a general-purpose sentiment lexicon, the overall sentiment rating of each review, synonyms and antonyms, as well as conjunction "and" rules, "but" rules, and "negation" rules. To some extent, the methods in Takamura et al. (2007) and Turney (2002) can also be considered as an implicit method for finding context-specific opinions, but they did not use the sentiment consistency idea. Instead, they used the Web to find their orientations. However, we should note that all these context definitions are still not sufficient for all cases as the basic rules of opinions discussed in Section 5.2 showed, i.e., many contexts can be more complex, e.g., consuming a large amount of resources.

Along a similar line, Wilson et al. (2005) studied contextual subjectivities and sentiments at the phrase or expression level. Contextual sentiment means that although a word or phrase in a lexicon is marked positive or negative, but in the context of the sentence expression it may have no sentiment or have the opposite sentiment. In this work, the subjective expressions were first labeled in the corpus, i.e., those expressions that contain subjective words or phrases in a given subjectivity lexicon. Note that a subjectivity lexicon is slightly different from a sentiment lexicon as subjectivity lexicon may contains words that indicate only subjectivity but no sentiment, e.g., *feel*, and *think*. The goal of the work was to classify the contextual sentiment of the given expressions that contain instances of subjectivity clues in the subjectivity lexicon. The paper took a supervised learning approach with two steps. In the first step, it determines whether the expression is subjective or objective. In the second step, it determines whether the subjective expression is positive, negative, both, or neutral. *Both* means there are both positive and negative sentiments. Neutral is still included because the first step can make mistakes and left some neutral expressions unidentified. For subjectivity classification, a large and rich set of features was used, which included *word features*, *modification features* (dependency features), *structure features* (dependency tree based patterns), *sentence features*, and *document features*. For the second step of sentiment classification, it used features such as *word tokens*, *word prior sentiments*, *negations*, *modified by polarity*, *conj polarity*, etc. For both steps, the machine learning algorithm BoosTexter AdaBoost.HM (Schapire and Singer, 2000) was employed to build classifiers.

A related work on expression level sentiment classification was also done in Choi and Cardie (2008), where the authors classified the expressions annotated in Multi-Perspective Question Answering (MPQA) corpus (Wiebe et al., 2005). Both lexicon-based classification and supervised learning were experimented. In Breck et al. (2007), the authors studied the problem of extracting sentiment expressions with any number of words using Conditional Random Fields (CRF) (Lafferty et al., 2001).

The problem of adapting a general lexicon to a new one for domain specific expression level sentiment classification was studied in Choi and Cardie (2009). Their technique adapted the word-level polarities of a general-purpose sentiment lexicon for a particular domain by utilizing the expression-level polarities in the domain, and in return, the adapted word-level polarities were used to improve the expression-level polarities. The word-level and the expression-level polarity relationships were modeled as a set of constraints and the problem was solved using integer linear programming. This work assumed that there was a given general-purpose polarity lexicon L, and a polarity classification algorithm $f(e_l, L)$ that can determine the polarity of the opinion expression e_l based on the words in e_l and L. Jijkoun et al. (2010) proposed a related method to adapt a general sentiment lexicon to a topic specific one as well.

Du et al. (2010) studied the problem of adapting the sentiment lexicon from one domain (not a general-purpose lexicon) to another domain. As input, the algorithm assumes the availability of a set of in-domain sentiment-labeled documents, a set of sentiment words from these in-domain documents, and a set of out-of-domain documents. The task was to make the in-domain sentiment lexicon adapted for the out-of-domain documents. Two ideas were used in the study. First, a document should be positive (or negative) if it contains many positive (or negative) words, and a word should be positive (or negative) if it appears in many positive (or negative) documents. These are mutual reinforcement relationships. Second, even though the two domains may be under different distributions, it is possible to identify a common part between them (e.g. the same word has the same orientation). The sentiment lexicon adaption was solved using the information bottleneck framework. The same problem was also solved in Du and Tan (2009).

On a slightly different topic, Wiebe and Mihalcea (2006) investigated the possibility of assigning subjectivity labels to word senses based on a corpus. Two studies were conducted. The first study investigated the agreement between annotators who manually assigned labels *subjective*, *objective*, or *both* to WordNet senses. The second study evaluated a method for automatic assignment of subjectivity labels/scores to word senses. The method was based on distributional similarity (Lin, 1998). Their work showed that subjectivity is a property that can be associated with word senses, and word sense disambiguation can directly benefit from subjectivity annotations. A subsequent work was reported in Akkaya et al. (2009). Su and Markert (2008) also studied the problem and performed a case study for subjectivity recognition. In Su and Markert (2010), they further investigated this problem and applied it in a cross-lingual environment.

Brody and Diakopoulos (2011) studied the lengthening of words (e.g., *slooooow*) in microblogs. They showed that lengthening is strongly associated with subjectivity and sentiment, and presented an automatic way to leverage this association to detect domain sentiment and emotion words.

Finally, Feng et al. (2011) studied the problem of producing a connotation lexicon. A connotation lexicon differs from a sentiment lexicon in that the latter concerns words that express sentiment either explicitly or implicitly, while the former concerns words that are often associated with a specific polarity of sentiment, e.g., *award* and *promotion* have positive connotation and *cancer* and *war* have negative connotation. A graph-based method based on mutual reinforcement was proposed to solve the problem.

6.3   DESIRABLE AND UNDESIRABLE FACTS

Sentiment words and expressions that we have discussed so far are mainly subjective words and expressions that indicate positive or negative opinions. However, as mentioned earlier, many objective words and expressions can imply opinions too in certain domains or contexts because they can represent desirable or undesirable facts in these domains or contexts.

In Zhang and Liu (2011b), a method was proposed to identify nouns and noun phrases that are aspects and also imply sentiments in a particular domain. These nouns and noun phrases alone indicate no sentiments, but in the domain context they may represent desirable or undesirable facts. For example, "valley" and "mountain" do not have any sentiment connotation in general, i.e., they are objective. However, in the domain of mattress reviews, they often imply negative opinions as in "*Within a month, a valley has formed in the middle of the mattress.*" Here, "valley" implies a negative sentiment on the aspect of mattress quality. Identifying the sentiment orientations of such aspects is very challenging but critical for effective sentiment analysis in these domains.

The algorithm in Zhang and Liu (2011b) was based on the following idea. Although such sentences are usually objective with no explicit sentiments, in some cases the authors/reviewers may also give explicit sentiments, e.g., "*Within a month, a valley has formed in the middle of the mattress, which is terrible.*" The context of this sentence indicates that "valley" may not be desirable. Note that this work assumed that the set of aspects which are nouns and noun phrases are given. However, the problem with this approach is that those aspects (nouns and noun phrases) with no implied sentiment may also be in some positive or negative sentiment contexts, e.g., "voice quality" in "*The voice quality is poor.*" To distinguish these two cases, the following observation was used.

Observation: For normal aspects which themselves don't have positive or negative connotations, people can express different opinions, i.e., both positive and negative. For example, for aspect "voice quality," people can say "good voice quality" and "bad voice quality." However, for aspects which represent desirable or undesirable facts, they often have only a single sentiment, either positive or negative, but not both. For example, it is unlikely that both the following two sentences appear: "*A bad valley has formed*" and "*a good valley has formed.*"

With this observation in mind, the approach consists of two steps.

1. *Candidate identification*: This step determines the surrounding sentiment context of each noun aspect. If an aspect occurs in negative (respectively positive) sentiment contexts

significantly more frequently than in positive (or negative) sentiment contexts, it is inferred that its polarity is negative (or positive). This step thus produces a list of candidate aspects with positive opinions and a list of candidate aspects with negative opinions.

2. *Pruning*: This step prunes the two lists based on the observation above. The idea is that when a noun aspect is directly modified by both positive and negative sentiment words, it is unlikely to be an opinionated aspect. Two types of direct dependency relations were used.

Type 1: $O \rightarrow O\text{-}Dep \rightarrow F$

It means O depends on F through the relation $O\text{-}Dep$, e.g., "*This TV has a good picture quality.*"

Type 2: $O \rightarrow O\text{-}Dep \rightarrow H \leftarrow F\text{-}Dep \leftarrow F$

It means both O and F depend on H through relations $O\text{-}Dep$ and $F\text{-}Dep$ respectively, e.g., "*The springs of the mattress are bad.*"

where O is a sentiment word, $O\text{-}Dep / F\text{-}Dep$ is a dependency relation. F is the noun aspect. H means any word. For the first example, given aspect "picture quality," we can identify its modification sentiment word "good." For the second example, given aspect "springs," we can get its modification sentiment word "bad." Here H is the word "are."

This work is just the first attempt to tackle the problem. Its accuracy is still not high. Much further research is needed.

6.4   SUMMARY

Due to contributions of many researchers, several general-purpose subjectivity, sentiment, and emotion lexicons have been constructed, and some of them are also publically available, e.g.:

- General Inquirer lexicon (Stone, 1968): (http://www.wjh.harvard.edu/~inquirer/spread sheet_guide.htm)
- Sentiment lexicon (Hu and Liu, 2004): (http://www.cs.uic.edu/~liub/FBS/sentiment-analysis.html)
- MPQA subjectivity lexicon (Wilson et al., 2005): (http://www.cs.pitt.edu/mpqa/subj_lexicon.html)
- SentiWordNet (Esuli and Sebastiani, 2006): (http://sentiwordnet.isti.cnr.it/)
- Emotion lexicon (Mohammad and Turney, 2010): (http://www.purl.org/net/emolex)

However, domain and context-dependent sentiments remain to be highly challenging even with so much research. Recent work also used word vector and matrix to capture the contextual information of sentiment words (Maas et al., 2011; Yessenalina and Cardie, 2011). Factual words and expressions implying opinions have barely been studied (see Section 6.3), but they are very important for many domains.

Finally, we note that having a sentiment lexicon (even with domain specific orientations) does not mean that a word in the lexicon always expresses an opinion/sentiment in a specific sentence. For example, in *"I am looking for a good car to buy,"* "good" here does not express either a positive or negative opinion on any particular car.

CHAPTER 7

Opinion Summarization

As discussed in Chapter 2, in most sentiment analysis applications, one needs to study opinions from many people because due to the subjective nature of opinions, looking at only the opinion from a single person is usually insufficient. Some form of summary is needed. Chapter 2 indicated that the opinion quintuple provides the basic information for an opinion summary. Such a summary is called an *aspect-based summary* (or *feature-based summary*) and was proposed in Hu and Liu (2004) and Liu et al. (2005). Much of the opinion summarization research uses related ideas. This framework is also widely applied in industry. For example, the sentiment analysis systems of Microsoft Bing and Google Product Search use this form of summary. The output summary can be either in a structured form (see Section 7.1) or in an unstructured form as a short text document.

In general, opinion summarization can be seen as a form of *multi-document text summarization*. Text summarization has been studied extensively in NLP (Das, 2007). However, an opinion summary is quite different from a traditional single document or multi-document summary (of factual information) as an opinion summary is often centered on entities and aspects and sentiments about them, and also has a quantitative side, which are the essence of aspect-based opinion summary. Traditional single document summarization produces a short text from a long text by extracting some "important" sentences. Traditional multi-document summarization finds differences among documents and discards repeated information. Neither of them *explicitly* captures different topics/entities and their aspects discussed in the document, nor do they have a quantitative side. The "importance" of a sentence in traditional text summarization is often defined operationally based on the summarization algorithms and measures used in each system. Opinion summarization, on the other hand, can be conceptually defined. The summaries are thus structured. Even for output summaries that are short text documents, there are still some explicit structures in them.

7.1 ASPECT-BASED OPINION SUMMARIZATION

Aspect-based opinion summarization has two main characteristics. First, it captures the essence of opinions: opinion targets (entities and their aspects) and sentiments about them. Second, it is quantitative, which means that it gives the number or percent of people who hold positive or

Digital Camera 1:

Aspect: **GENERAL**

Positive:	105	<individual review sentences>
Negative:	12	<individual review sentences>

Aspect: **Picture quality**

Positive:	95	<individual review sentences>
Negative:	10	<individual review sentences>

Aspect: **Battery life**

Positive:	50	<individual review sentences>
Negative:	9	<individual review sentences>

...

FIGURE 7.1: An aspect-based opinion summary.

negative opinions about the entities and aspects. The quantitative side is crucial because of the subjective nature of opinions. The resulting opinion summary is a form of structured summary produced from the opinion quintuple in Section 2.1. We have described the summary in Section 2.2. It is reproduced here for completeness. Figure 7.1 shows an aspect-based summary of opinions about a digital camera (Hu and Liu, 2004). The aspect GENERAL represents opinions on the camera as a whole, i.e., the entity. For each aspect (e.g., picture quality), it shows how many people have positive and negative opinions respectively. <individual review sentences> links to the actual sentences (or full reviews or blogs). This structured summary can also be visualized (Liu et al., 2005).

Figure 7.2(A) uses a bar chart to visualize the summary in Figure 7.1. In the figure, each bar above the *X*-axis shows the number of positive opinions about the aspect given at the top. The corresponding bar below the *X*-axis shows the number of negative opinions on the same aspect. Clicking on each bar, we can see the individual sentences and full reviews. Obviously, other visualizations are also possible. For example, the bar charts of both Microsoft Bing search and Google Product Search use the percent of positive opinions on each aspect. Comparing opinion summaries of a few entities is even more interesting (Liu et al., 2005). Figure 7.2(B) shows the visual opinion comparison of two cameras. We can see how consumers view each of them along different aspect dimensions including the entities themselves.

The opinion quintuples in fact allows one to provide many more forms of structured summaries. For example, if time is extracted, one can show the trend of opinions on different aspects. Even without using sentiments, one can see the buzz (frequency) of each aspect mentions, which gives the user an idea what aspects people are most concerned about. In fact, with the quintuple, a full range of database and OLAP tools can be used to slice and dice the data for all kinds of qualitative and quantitative analysis. For example, in one practical sentiment analysis application in the automobile domain, opinion quintuples of individual cars were mined first. The user then compared

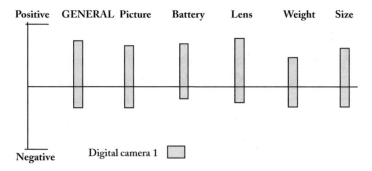

(A) Visualization of aspect-based summary of opinions on a digital camera

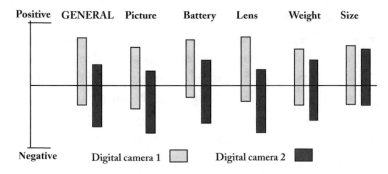

(B) Visual opinion comparison of two digital cameras

FIGURE 7.2: Visualization of aspect-based summaries of opinions.

sentiments about small cars, medium sized cars, German cars and Japanese cars, etc. In addition, the sentiment analysis results were also used as raw data for data mining. The user ran a clustering algorithm and found some interesting segments of the market. For example, it was found that one segment of the customers always talked about how beautiful and slick the car looked and how fun it was to drive, etc, while another segment of the customers talked a lot about back seats and trunk space, etc. Clearly, the first segment consisted of mainly young people, while the second segment consisted mainly of people with families and children. Such insights were extremely important. They enabled the user to see the opinions of different segments of customers.

This form of structured summary has also been adopted by other researchers to summarize movie reviews (Zhuang et al., 2006), to summarize Chinese opinion text (Ku et al., 2006), and to summarize service reviews (Blair-Goldensohn et al., 2008). However, we should note that aspect-based summary does not have to be in this structured form. It can also be in the form of a text document based on the same idea. In the next section, we discuss other related researches.

7.2 IMPROVEMENTS TO ASPECT-BASED OPINION SUMMARIZATION

Several improvements and refinements have been proposed by researchers for the basic aspect-based summary. Carenini et al. (2006) proposed integrating aspect-based summarization with two traditional text summarization approaches of factual documents, i.e., sentence selection (or extraction) and sentence generation. We discuss the integration with the sentence selection approach first. Their system first identifies aspect expressions from reviews of a particular entity (e.g., a product) using the method in Hu and Liu (2004). It then maps the aspect expressions to some given aspect categories organized as an ontology tree for the entity. These aspects in the tree are then scored based on their sentiment strength. Those sentences containing aspect expressions are also extracted. Each such sentence is then rated based on scores of aspects in the sentence. If multiple sentences have the same sentence rating, a traditional centroid based sentence selection method is used to break the tie (Radev et al., 2003). All relevant sentences are attached to their corresponding aspects in the ontology. The sentences for each aspect are then selected for the final summary based on sentence scores and aspect positions in the ontology tree. The integration with the sentence generation approach works similarly. First, a measure is used to score the aspects in the ontology based on their occurrence frequencies, sentiment strengths, and their positions in the ontology. An algorithm is also applied to select aspects in the ontology tree. Positive and negative sentiments are then computed for the aspects. Based on the selected aspects and their sentiments, a language generator generates the summary sentences which can be qualitative and quantitative. A user evaluation was carried out to assess the effectiveness of the two integration approaches. The results showed that they performed equally well, but for different reasons. The sentence selection method gave more varied languages and more details, while the sentence generation approach gives a better sentiment overview of the reviews.

Tata and Di Eugenio (2010) produced an opinion summary of song reviews similar to that in Hu and Liu (2004), but for each aspect and each sentiment (postive or ngative) they first selected a representative sentence for the group. The sentence should mention the fewest aspects (thus the representative sentence is focused). They then ordered the sentences using a given domain ontology by mapping sentences to the ontology nodes. The ontology basically encodes the key domain concepts and their relations. The sentences were ordered and organized into paragraphs following the tree such that they appear in a conceptually coherent fashion.

Lu et al. (2010) also used online ontologies of entities and aspects to organize and summarize opinions. Their method is related to the above two, but is also different. Their system first selects aspects that capture major opinions. The selection is done by frequency, opinion coverage (no redundancy), or conditional entropy. It then orders aspects and their corresponding sentences based on a coherence measure, which tries to optimize the ordering so that they best follow the sequences of aspect appearances in their original postings.

Ku et al. (2006) performed blog opinion summarization, and produced two types of summaries: brief and detailed summaries, based on extracted topics (aspects) and sentiments on the topics. For the brief summary, their method picks up the document/article with the largest number of positive or negative sentences and uses its headline to represent the overall summary of positive-topical or negative-topical sentences. For detailed summary, it lists positive-topical and negative-topical sentences with high sentiment degrees.

Lerman et al. (2009) defined opinion summarization in a slightly different way. Given a set of documents D (e.g., reviews) that contains opinions about some entity of interest, the goal of their opinion summarization system is to generate a summary S of that entity that is representative of the average opinion and speaks to its important aspects. This paper proposed three different models to perform summarization of reviews of a product. All these models choose some set of sentences from a review. The first model is called *sentiment match* (SM), which extracts sentences so that the average sentiment of the summary is as close as possible to the average sentiment rating of reviews of the entity. The second model, called *sentiment match + aspect coverage* (SMAC), builds a summary that trades-off between maximally covering important aspects and matching the overall sentiment of the entity. The third model, called *sentiment-aspect match* (SAM), not only attempts to cover important aspects, but cover them with appropriate sentiment. A comprehensive evaluation of human users was conducted to compare the three types of summaries. It was found that although the SAM model was the best, it is not significantly better than others.

In Nishikawa et al. (2010a), a more sophisticated summarization technique was proposed, which generates a traditional text summary by selecting and ordering sentences taken from multiple reviews, considering both informativeness and readability of the final summary. The informativeness was defined as the sum of frequency of each aspect-sentiment pair. Readability was defined as the natural sequence of sentences, which was measured as the sum of the connectivity of all adjacent sentences in the sequence. The problem was then solved through optimization. In Nishikawa et al. (2010b), the authors further studied this problem using an integer linear programming formulation. In Ganesan et al. (2010), a graphical model based method was used to generate an abstractive summary of opinions. In Yatani et al. (2011), adjective-noun pairs were extracted as a summary.

7.3   CONTRASTIVE VIEW SUMMARIZATION

Several researchers also studied the problem of summarizing opinions by finding contrastive viewpoints. For example, a reviewer may give a positive opinion about the voice quality of iPhone by saying "*The voice quality of iPhone is really good,*" but another reviewer may say the opposite, "*The voice quality of my iPhone is lousy."* Such pairs can give the reader a direct comparative view of different opinions.

Kim and Zhai (2009) proposed and studied this problem. Given a positive sentence set and a negative sentence set, this work performed contrastive opinion summarization by extracting a set of *k* contrastive sentence pairs from the sets. A pair of opinionated sentences (*x*, *y*) is called a *contrastive sentence pair* if sentence *x* and sentence *y* are about the same topic aspect, but have opposite sentiment orientations. The *k* chosen sentence pairs must also represent both the positive and negative sentence sets well. The authors formulated the summarization as an optimization problem and solved it based on several similarity functions.

Paul et al. (2010) worked on this problem as well. Their algorithm generates a macro multi-view summary and a micro multi-view summary. A macro multi-view summary contains multiple sets of sentences, each representing a different opinion. A micro multi-view summary contains a set of pairs of contrastive sentences (each pair consists of two sentences representing two different opinions). The algorithm works in two steps. In the first step, it uses a topic modeling approach to modeling and mining both topics (aspects) and sentiments. In the second step, a random walk formulation (similar to PageRank; Page et al., 1999) was proposed to score sentences and pairs of sentences from opposite viewpoints based on both their representativeness and their contrastiveness with each other. Along a similar line, Park et al. (2011) reported another method for generating contrasting opposing views in news articles.

Lerman and McDonald (2009) formulated a different contrastive summarization problem. They wanted to produce contrastive summaries of opinions about two different products to highlight the differences of opinions about them. Their approach is to jointly model the two summarization tasks and in optimization to explicitly consider the fact that it wants the two summaries to contrast.

7.4   TRADITIONAL SUMMARIZATION

Several researchers have also studied opinion summarization in the traditional fashion, e.g., producing a short text summary with limited or without consideration of aspects (or topics) and sentiments about them. A supervised learning method was proposed in Beineke et al. (2003) to select important sentences in reviews. A paragraph-clustering algorithm was proposed in Seki et al. (2006) to also select a set of important sentences.

Wang and Liu (2011) studied extractive summarizations (selection of important sentences) of opinions in conversations. They experimented with both the traditional sentence ranking and graph-based approaches, but also considered additional features such as topic relevance, sentiments, and the dialogue structure.

A weakness of such traditional summaries is that they only have limited or no consideration of target entities and aspects, and sentiments about them. Thus, they may select sentences which are not related to sentiments or any aspects. Another issue is that there is no quantitative perspective, which is often important in practice because one out of ten people hating something is very different from 5 out of ten people hating something.

7.5   SUMMARY

Opinion summarization is still an active research area. Most opinion summarization methods which produce a short text summary have not focused on the quantitative side (proportions of positive and negative opinions). Future research can deal with this problem while also producing human readable texts. We should note that the opinion summarization research cannot progress alone because it critically depends on results and techniques from other areas of research in sentiment analysis, e.g., aspect or topic extraction and sentiment classification. All these research directions will need to go hand-in-hand. Finally, we should also note that based on the structured summary in Section 7.1 one can generate natural language sentences as well based on what are shown in the bar charts using some predefined sentence templates. For instance, the first bar in Figure 7.2(B) can be summarized as "70% of the people are positive about digital camera 1 in general." However, this may not be the best sentence for people's reading pleasure.

· · · ·

CHAPTER 8

Analysis of Comparative Opinions

Apart from directly expressing positive or negative opinions about an entity and its aspects, one can also express opinions by comparing similar entities. Such opinions are called *comparative opinions* (Jindal and Liu, 2006a, 2006b). Comparative opinions are related to but are also different from regular opinions. They not only have different semantic meanings but also have different syntactic forms. For example, a typical regular opinion sentence is "*The voice quality of this phone is amazing*," and a typical comparative opinion sentence is "*The voice quality of Nokia phones is better than that of iPhones*." This comparative sentence does not say that any phone's voice quality is good or bad, but simply compares them. Due to this difference, comparative opinions require different analysis techniques. Like regular sentences, comparative sentences can be opinionated or not-opinionated. The comparative sentence above is opinionated because it explicitly expresses a comparative sentiment of its author, while the sentence "*iPhone is 1 inch wider than a normal Nokia phone*" expresses no sentiment. In this chapter, we first define the problem and then present some existing methods for solving it. We should also note that there are in fact two main types of opinions that are based on comparisons: *comparative opinions* and *superlative opinions*. In English, they are usually expressed using the *comparative* or *superlative* forms of adjectives or adverbs, but not always. However, in this chapter, we study them together and just call them comparative opinions in general because their semantic meanings and handling methods are similar.

8.1 PROBLEM DEFINITIONS

A comparative sentence expresses a relation based on similarities or differences of more than one entity. There are several types of comparisons. They can be grouped into two main categories: *gradable comparison* and *non-gradable comparison* (Jindal and Liu, 2006a; Kennedy, 2005).

> **Gradable comparison:** Such a comparison expresses an ordering relationship of entities being compared. It has three sub-types:

1. *Non-equal gradable comparison*: It expresses a relation of the type *greater* or *less than* that ranks a set of entities over another set of entities based on some of their shared aspects, e.g., "*Coke tastes better than Pepsi.*" This type also includes preference, e.g., "*I prefer Coke to Pepsi.*"

2. *Equative comparison*: It expresses a relation of the type *equal to* that states two or more entities are equal based on some of their shared aspects, e.g., "*Coke and Pepsi taste the same.*"

3. *Superlative comparison*: It expresses a relation of the type *greater* or *less than all others* that ranks one entity over *all* others, e.g., "*Coke tastes the best among all soft drinks.*"

Non-gradable comparison: Such a comparison expresses a relation of two or more entities but does not grade them. There are three main sub-types:

1. Entity A is similar to or different from entity B based on some of their shared aspects, e.g., "*Coke tastes differently from Pepsi.*"

2. Entity A has aspect a_1, and entity B has aspect a_2 (a_1 and a_2 are usually substitutable), e.g., "*Desktop PCs use external speakers but laptops use internal speakers.*"

3. Entity A has aspect a, but entity B does not have, e.g., "*Nokia phones come with earphones, but iPhones do not.*"

We only focus on gradable comparisons in this chapter. Non-gradable comparisons may also express opinions but they are often more subtle and difficult to recognize.

In English, comparisons are usually expressed using *comparative words* (also called *comparatives*) and *superlative words* (also called *superlatives*). Comparatives are formed by adding the suffix *-er* and superlatives are formed by adding the suffix *-est* to their *base adjectives* and *adverbs*. For example, in "*The battery life of Nokia phones is longer than Motorola phones,*" "longer" is the comparative form of the adjective "long." "longer" (and "than") here also indicates that this is a comparative sentence. In "*The battery life of Nokia phones is the longest,*" "longest" is the superlative form of the adjective "long", and it indicates that this is a superlative sentence. We call this type of comparatives and superlatives *Type 1 comparatives and superlatives*. Note that for simplicity, we often use *comparative* to mean both *comparative* and *superlative* if superlative is not explicitly stated.

However, adjectives and adverbs with two syllables or more and not ending in *y* do not form comparatives or superlatives by adding *-er* or *-est*. Instead, *more*, *most*, *less*, and *least* are used before such words, e.g., *more beautiful*. We call this type of comparatives and superlatives *Type 2 comparatives and superlatives*. Both Type 1 and Type 2 are called *regular comparatives and superlatives*.

English also has *irregular comparatives* and *superlatives*, i.e., *more, most, less, least, better, best, worse, worst, further/farther*, and *furthest/farthest*, which do not follow the above rules. However, they behave similarly to Type 1 comparatives and are thus grouped under Type 1.

These standard comparatives and superlatives are only some of the words that indicate comparisons. In fact, there are many other words and phrases that can be used to express comparisons, e.g., *prefer* and *superior*. For example, the sentence "*iPhone's voice quality is superior to that of Blackberry*" says that iPhone has a better voice quality and is preferred. In Jindal and Liu (2006a), a list of such words and phrases were compiled (which by no means is complete). Since these words and phrases usually behave similarly to Type 1 comparatives, they are also grouped under Type 1. All these words and phrases plus the above standard comparatives and superlatives are collectively called *comparative keywords*.

Comparative keywords used in non-equal gradable comparisons can be further grouped into two categories according to whether they express increased or decreased quantities, which are useful in sentiment analysis.

- *Increasing comparative:* Such a comparative expresses an increased quantity, e.g., *more* and *longer*.
- *Decreasing comparative:* Such a comparative expresses a decreased quantity, e.g., *less* and *fewer*.

Objective of mining comparative opinions (Jindal and Liu, 2006b; Liu, 2010): Given an opinion document d, discover in d all comparative opinion sextuples of the form:

$$(E_1, E_2, A, PE, h, t),$$

where E_1 and E_2 are the entity sets being compared based on their shared aspects A (entities in E_1 appear before entities in E_2 in the sentence), PE ($\in \{E_1, E_2\}$) is the preferred entity set of the opinion holder h, and t is the time when the comparative opinion is expressed. For a superlative comparison, if one entity set is implicit (not given in the text), we can use a special set U to denote it. For an equative comparison, we can use the special symbol EQUAL as the value for PE.

For example, consider the comparative sentence "*Canon's picture quality is better than those of LG and Sony,*" written by Jim on 9-25-2011. The extracted comparative opinion is:

$$(\{Canon\}, \{LG, Sony\}, \{picture\_quality\}, \{Canon\}, Jim, 9\text{-}25\text{-}2011)$$

The entity set E_1 is {Canon}, the entity set E_2 is {LG, Sony }, their shared aspect set A being compared is {picture_quality}, the preferred entity set is {Canon}, the opinion holder h is Jim, and the time t when this comparative opinion was written is 9-25-2011.

Note that the above representation may not be easily put in a database due to the use of sets, but it can be easily converted to multiple tuples with no sets, e.g., the above sets based sextuples can be expanded into two tuples:

(Canon, LG, picture_quality, Canon, Jim, Dec-25-2010)

(Canon, Sony, picture_quality, Canon, Jim, Dec-25-2010)

Like mining regular opinions, mining comparative opinions needs to extract entities, aspects, opinion holders, and times. The techniques used are similar too. In fact, these tasks are often easier for comparative sentences because entities are usually on the two sides of the comparative keyword, and aspects are also near. However, for sentiment analysis to identify the preferred entity set, a different method is needed which we will discuss in Section 8.3. We also need to identify comparative sentences themselves because not all sentences containing comparative keywords express comparisons and many comparative keywords and phrases are hard to identify (Jindal and Liu, 2006b). Below, we only focus on studying two comparative opinion sentiment analysis specific problems, i.e., identifying comparative sentences and determining the preferred entity set.

8.2   IDENTIFY COMPARATIVE SENTENCES

Although most comparative sentences contain comparative and superlative keywords, e.g., *better*, *superior*, and *best*, many sentences that contain such words are not comparative sentences, e.g., "*I cannot agree with you more.*"

Jindal and Liu (2006a) showed that almost every comparative sentence has a keyword (a word or phrase) indicating comparison. Using a set of keywords, 98% of comparative sentences (recall = 98%) were identified with a precision of 32% based on their data set. The keywords are:

1. Comparative adjectives (JJR) and comparative adverbs (RBR), e.g., *more*, *less*, *better*, and words ending with *-er*. These are counted as only two keywords.

2. Superlative adjectives (JJS) and superlative adverbs (RBS), e.g., *most*, *least*, *best*, and words ending with *-est*. These are also counted as only two keywords.

3. Other non-standard indicative words and phrases such as *favor*, *beat*, *win*, *exceed*, *outperform*, *prefer*, *ahead*, *than*, *superior*, *inferior*, *number one*, *up against*, etc. These are counted individually in the number of keywords.

Since keywords alone are able to achieve a high recall, they can be used to filter out those sentences that are unlikely to be comparative sentences. We just need to improve the precision on the remaining sentences.

It was also observed in Jindal and Liu (2006a) that comparative sentences have strong patterns involving comparative keywords, which is not surprising. These patterns can be used as features in learning. To discover these patterns, class sequential rule (CSR) mining was employed in Jindal and Liu (2006a). Class sequential rule mining is a special kind of sequential pattern mining

(Liu, 2006, 2011). Each training example is a pair (s_i, y_i), where s_i is a sequence and y_i is a class label, i.e., $y_i \in \{comparison, non\text{-}comparison\}$. The sequence is generated from a sentence. Using the training data, CSRs can be generated.

For classification model building, the left-hand side sequence patterns of the CSR rules with high conditional probabilities were used as features. Naïve Bayes was employed for model building. In Yang and Ko (2011), the same problem was studied but in the context of Korean language. The learning algorithm used was the transformation-based learning, which produces rules.

Classifying comparative sentences into four types: After comparative sentences are identified, the algorithm also classifies them into four types, *non-equal gradable*, *equative*, *superlative*, and *non-gradable*. For this task, (Jindal and Liu, 2006a) showed that keywords and keyphrases as features were already sufficient. SVM gave the best results.

Li et al. (2010) studied the problem of identifying comparative questions and the entities (which they call comparators) that are compared. Unlike the works above, this paper did not decide the types of comparison. For comparative sentences identification, they also used sequential patterns/rules. However, their patterns are different. They decided whether a question is a comparative question and the entities being compared at the same time. For example, the question sentence *"Which city is better, New York or Chicago?"* satisfies the sequential pattern <which NN is better, $C or $C ?>, where $C is an entity. A weakly supervised learning method based on the idea in Ravichandran and Hovy (2002) was used to learn such patterns. The algorithm is based on bootstrapping, which starts with a user-given pattern. From this pattern, the algorithm extracts a set of initial seed entity (comparators) pairs. For each entity pair, all questions containing the pair are retrieved from the question collection and regarded as comparative questions. From the comparative questions and entity pairs, all possible sequential patterns are learned and evaluated. The learning process is the traditional generalization and specialization process. Any words or phrases which match $C in a sentence are entities. Both Jindal and Liu (2006b) and Yang and Ko (2011) also extract compared entities. We will discuss them in Section 8.4. Other information extraction algorithms are applicable here as well.

8.3 IDENTIFYING PREFERRED ENTITIES

Unlike regular opinions, it does not make much sense to perform sentiment classification to a comparative opinion sentence as a whole because such a sentence does not express a direct positive or negative opinion. Instead, it compares multiple entities by ranking the entities based on their shared aspects to give a *comparative opinion*. That is, it expresses a preference order of the entities using comparison. Since most comparative sentences compare two sets of entities, the analysis of an opinionated comparative sentence means to identify the preferred entity set. However, for application purposes, one may assign positive opinions to the aspects of the entities in the preferred set, and negative opinions to the aspects of the entities in the not preferred set. Note that like regular sentences, it is still meaningful to classify whether a comparative sentence expresses an opinion or not, but little research has been done on such classification. Below we only describe a method for identifying the preferred entity set.

The method, proposed in Ding et al. (2009) and Ganapathibhotla and Liu (2008), basically extends the lexicon-based approach to aspect based sentiment classification of regular opinions to comparative opinions. It thus needs a sentiment lexicon for comparative opinions. Similar to opinion words of the base type, we can divide comparative opinion words into two categories.

1. *General-purpose comparative sentiment words*: For Type 1 comparatives, this category includes words like *better*, *worse*, etc., which often have domain independent positive or negative sentiments. In sentences involving such words, it is often easy to determine which entity set is preferred. In the case of Type 2 comparatives, formed by adding *more*, *less*, *most*, or *least* before adjectives/adverbs, the preferred entity sets are determined by both words. The following rules are applied:

$$
\begin{aligned}
\text{Comparative Negative} \quad ::= \quad & \text{increasing\_comparative N} \\
| \quad & \text{decreasing\_comparative P} \\
\text{Comparative Positive} \quad ::= \quad & \text{increasing\_comparative P} \\
| \quad & \text{decreasing\_comparative N}
\end{aligned}
$$

Here, P (respectively, N) denotes a positive (negative) sentiment word or phrase of the base type. The first rule above says that the combination of an increasing comparative (e.g., *more*) and a negative sentiment word (e.g., *awful*) implies a *negative comparative opinion* (on the left). The other rules have similar meanings. Note that the above four rules have already been discussed as basic rules of opinions in Section 5.2.

2. *Context-dependent comparative sentiment words*: In the case of Type 1 comparatives, such words include *higher*, *lower*, etc. For example, "*Nokia phones have longer battery life than Motorola phones*" carries a comparative positive sentiment about "Nokia phones" and a comparative negative sentiment about "Motorola phones," i.e., "Nokia phones" are preferred with respect to the *battery life* aspect. However, without domain knowledge it is hard to know whether "longer" is positive or negative for battery life. This issue is the same as for

regular opinions, and this case has also been included in the basic rules of opinions in Section 5.2. Here, "battery life" is a *positive potential item* (PPI).

In the case of Type 2 comparatives, the situation is similar. However, in this case the comparative word (*more, most, less,* or *least*), the adjective/adverb, and the aspect are all important in determining the preference. If we know whether the comparative word is an increasing or decreasing comparative (which is easy since there are only four of them), then the opinion can be determined by applying the four rules in (1).

As discussed in Section 6.2, the pair (*aspect, context_sentiment_word*) forms an opinion context. To determine whether a pair is positive or negative, the algorithm in Ganapathibhotla and Liu (2008) uses a large amount of external data. It employed a large corpus of Pros and Cons from product reviews. The idea is to determine whether the *aspect* and *context_sentiment_word* are more associated with each other in Pros or in Cons. If they are more associated in Pros, *context_sentiment_word* is most likely to be positive. Otherwise, it is likely to be negative. However, since Pros and Cons seldom use comparative opinions, the context opinion words in a comparative sentence have to be converted to its base form, which can be done using WordNet with the help of English comparative formation rules. This conversion is useful because of the following observation.

Observation: If an adjective or adverb of the base form is positive (or negative), then its comparative or superlative form is also positive (or negative), e.g., *good, better,* and *best.*

After the conversion, these words are manually categorized into increasing and decreasing comparatives. For context dependent opinion words, comparative words can also be converted to their base forms.

After the sentiment words and their orientations are identified, determining which entity set is preferred is fairly simple. Without negation, if the comparative is positive (or negative), then the entities before (or after) *than* is preferred. Otherwise, the entities after (or before) *than* are preferred. Additional details can be found in Ding et al. (2009) and Ganapathibhotla and Liu (2008).

8.4   SUMMARY

Although there have been some existing works, comparative sentences have not been studied as extensively as many other topics of sentiment analysis. Further research is still needed. One of the difficult problems is how to identify many types of non-standard or implicit comparative sentences, e.g., "*I am very happy that my iPhone is nothing like my old ugly Droid.*" Without identifying them, further sentiment analysis is hard to perform.

Apart from identifying comparative sentences and their types, several researchers have also studied the extraction of compared entities, compared aspects, and comparative words. Jindal and Liu (2006b) used label sequential rule mining, which is a supervised learning method based on sequential patterns. Yang and Ko (2011) applied the Maximum Entropy and SVM learning algorithms to extract compared entities and comparative predicates, which are aspects that are compared. As noted in Section 8.2, sequential patterns in Li et al. (2010) for identifying comparative questions can already identify compared entities. However, their work is limited in the sense that it only works with simple comparative questions. Fiszman et al. (2007) studied the problem of identifying which entity has more of certain aspects in comparative sentences in biomedical texts, but they did not analyze opinions in comparisons.

· · · ·

CHAPTER 9

Opinion Search and Retrieval

As Web search has proven to be a valuable service on the Web, it is not hard to imagine that opinion search will also be of great use. Two typical kinds of opinion search queries are:

1. Find public opinions about a particular entity or an aspect of the entity, e.g., find customer opinions about a digital camera or the picture quality of the camera, and find public opinions about a political issue or candidate.

2. Find opinions of a person or organization (i.e., opinion holder) about a particular entity or an aspect of the entity (or topic), e.g., find Barack Obama's opinion about abortion. This type of search is particularly relevant to news articles, where individuals or organizations who express opinions are explicitly stated.

For the first type of queries, the user may simply give the name of the entity or the name of the aspect together with the name of the entity. For the second type of queries, the user may give the name of the opinion holder and the name of the entity (or topic).

9.1 WEB SEARCH VS. OPINION SEARCH

Similar to traditional Web search, opinion search also has two major tasks: (1) retrieve relevant documents/sentences to the user query and (2) rank the retrieved documents or sentences. However, there are also major differences. On retrieval, opinion search needs to perform two sub-tasks:

1. Find documents or sentences that are relevant to the query. This is the only task performed in the traditional Web search or retrieval.

2. Determine whether the documents or sentences express opinions on the query topic (entity and/or aspect) and whether the opinions are positive or negative. This is the task of sentiment analysis. Traditional search does not perform this sub-task.

As for ranking, traditional Web search engines rank Web pages based on authority and relevance scores (Liu, 2006, 2011). The basic premise is that the top ranked pages (ideally the first page) contain sufficient information to satisfy the user's information need. This paradigm is adequate for factual information search because *one fact equals to any number of the same fact*. That is, if the first page contains the required information, there is no need to see the rest of the relevant pages. For opinion search, this paradigm is fine only for the second type of queries because the opinion holder usually has only one opinion about a particular entity or topic, and the opinion is contained in a single document or page. However, for the first type of opinion queries, this paradigm needs to be modified because ranking in opinion search has two objectives. First, it needs to rank those opinionated documents or sentences with high utilities or information contents at the top (see Chapter 11). Second, it needs to reflect the natural distribution of positive and negative opinions. This second objective is important because in most applications the actual proportions of positive and negative opinions are critical pieces of information. Only reading the top ranked result as in the traditional search is problematic because the top result only represents the opinion of a single opinion holder. Thus, ranking in opinion search needs to capture the natural distribution of positive and negative sentiments of the whole population. One simple solution for this is to produce two rankings, one for positive opinions and one for negative opinions, and also to display the numbers of positive and negative opinions.

Providing an aspect-based summary for each opinion search will be even better. However, it is an extremely challenging problem because aspect extraction, aspect categorization, and associating entities to its aspects are all very challenging problems. Without effective solutions for them, such a summary will not be possible.

9.2   EXISTING OPINION RETRIEVAL TECHNIQUES

Current research in opinion retrieval typically treats the task as a two-stage process. In the first stage, documents are ranked by topical relevance only. In the second stage, candidate relevant documents are re-ranked by their opinion scores. The opinion scores can be acquired by either a machine learning-based sentiment classifier, such as SVM, or a lexicon-based sentiment classifier using a sentiment lexicon and a combination of sentiment word scores and query term–sentiment word proximity scores. More advanced research models topic relevance and opinion at the same time, and produces rankings based on their integrated score.

To give a flavor of opinion search, we present an example system (Zhang and Yu, 2007), which was the winner of the blog track in the 2007 TREC evaluation (http://trec.nist.gov/). The task was exactly opinion search (or retrieval). This system has two components. The first component is for retrieving relevant documents for each query. The second component is for classifying the retrieved documents as being opinionated or not-opinionated. The opinionated documents are further classified into positive, negative, or mixed (containing both positive and negative opinions).

> **Retrieval component**: This component performs the traditional information retrieval (IR) task. It considers both keywords and concepts. Concepts are named entities (e.g., names of people or organizations) or various types of phrases from dictionaries and other sources (e.g., Wikipedia entries). The strategy for processing a user query is as follows (Zhang et al., 2008; Zhang and Yu, 2007): It first recognizes and disambiguates the concepts within the user query. It then broadens the search query with its synonyms. After that, it recognizes concepts in the retrieved documents and also performs pseudo-feedback to automatically extract relevant words from the top-ranked documents to expand the query. Finally, it computes a similarity (or relevance score) of each document with the expanded query using both concepts and keywords.
>
> **Opinion classification component**: This component performs two tasks: (1) classifying each document into one of the two categories, opinionated and not-opinionated and (2) classifying each opinionated document as expressing a positive, negative, or mixed opinion. For both tasks, the system uses supervised learning. For the first task, it obtains a large amount of opinionated (subjective) training data from review sites such as rate-itall.com and epinions.com. The data are also collected from different domains involving consumer goods and services as well as government policies and political viewpoints. The not-opinionated training data are obtained from sites that give objective information such as Wikipedia. From these training data, a SVM classifier is constructed.

This classifier is then applied to each retrieved document as follows. The document is first partitioned into sentences. The SVM classifier then classifies each sentence as opinionated or not-opinionated. If a sentence is classified to be opinionated, its strength, as determined by SVM, is also noted. A document is regarded opinionated if there is at least one sentence that is classified as opinionated. To ensure that the opinion of the sentence is directed at the query topic, the system requires that enough query concepts/words are found in its vicinity. The totality of the opinionated sentences and their strengths in a document together with the document's similarity with the query is used to rank the document.

To determine whether an opinionated document expresses a positive, negative or mixed opinion, a second classifier is constructed. The training data are reviews from review sites containing review ratings (e.g., rateitall.com). A low rating indicates a negative opinion while a high rating indicates a positive opinion. Using positive and negative reviews as training data, a sentiment classifier is built to classify each document as expressing a positive, negative, or mixed opinion.

There are also other approaches to opinion retrieval in TREC evaluations. The readers are encouraged to read the papers at the TREC Web site (http://trec.nist.gov/). For a summary of TREC evaluations, please refer to the overview paper of 2006 TREC blog track (Ounis et al., 2006), the overview paper of 2007 TREC blog track (Macdonald et al., 2007), and the overview paper of 2008 TREC blog track (Ounis et al., 2008). Below, we discuss research published in other forums.

Eguchi and Lavrenko (2006) proposed a sentiment retrieval technique based on generative language modeling. In their approach, the user needs to provide a set of query terms representing a particular topic of interest, and also sentiment polarity (orientation) interest, which is represented either as a set of seed sentiment words or a particular sentiment orientation (positive or negative). One main advance of their work is that they combined sentiment relevance models and topic relevance models with model parameters estimated from the training data, considering the topic dependence of the sentiment. They showed that the explicit modeling of dependency between topic and sentiment produced better retrieval results than treating them independently. A similar approach was also proposed by Huang and Croft (2009), which scored the relevance of a document using a topic reliance model and an opinion relevance model. Both these works took a linear combination of topic relevance and sentiment relevance for final ranking. In Zhang and Ye (2008), the authors used the product of the two relevance scores. The relevance formulation is also based on language modeling.

In Na et al. (2009), a lexicon-based approach was proposed for opinion retrieval. They also attempted to deal with the domain dependent lexicon construction issue. A relevant feedback style learning for generating query-specific sentiment lexicon was proposed, which made use of a set of top-ranked documents in response to a query.

Liu et al. (2009) explored various lexical and sentiment features and different learning algorithms for identifying opinionated blogs. They also presented results for the strategy that combines both the opinion analysis and the retrieval components for retrieving relevant and opinionated blogs.

Li et al. (2010) took a different approach. Their algorithm first finds topic and sentiment word pairs from each sentence of a document, and then builds a bipartite graph to link such pairs with the documents that contain the pairs. The graph based ranking algorithm HITS (Kleinberg, 1999) was applied to rank the documents, where documents were considered as authorities and pairs were considered as hubs. Each link connecting a pair and a document is weighted based on the contribution of the pair to the document.

In Pang and Lee (2008), a simple method was proposed for review search. It only re-ranks the top *k* topic-based search results by using an *idiosyncrasy* measure defined on the rarity of terms appeared in the initial search results. The rationale for the measure was explained in the paper.

The assumption was that the search engine has already found good results and only re-ranking is needed to put reviews at the top. The method is unsupervised and does not use any pre-existing lexicon.

9.3 SUMMARY

It will be really useful if a Web search engine such as Google or Microsoft Bing can provide a general opinion search service. Although both Google and Microsoft Bing already provide opinion summarization services for reviews of some products, their coverage is still very limited. For those not covered entities and topics, it is not easy to find opinions about them because their opinions are scattered all over the Internet. There are also some large and well-known review hosting sites such as amazon.com and Yelp.com. However, they do not cover all entities and topics either. For those not covered entities or topics, finding opinions about them remains to be a formidable task because of the proliferation of diverse sites and the difficulty of identifying relevant opinions. A lot of research is still needed before a breakthrough can be achieved.

· · · ·

CHAPTER 10

Opinion Spam Detection

Opinions from social media are increasingly used by individuals and organizations for making purchase decisions and making choices at elections and for marketing and product design. Positive opinions often mean profits and fames for businesses and individuals, which, unfortunately, give strong incentives for people to game the system by posting *fake opinions* or *reviews* to promote or to discredit some target products, services, organizations, individuals, and even ideas without disclosing their true intentions, or the person or organization that they are secretly working for. Such individuals are called *opinion spammers* and their activities are called *opinion spamming* (Jindal and Liu, 2007, 2008). Opinion spamming about social and political issues can even be frightening as they can warp opinions and mobilize masses into positions counter to legal or ethical mores. It is safe to say that as opinions in social media are increasingly used in practice, opinion spamming will become more and more rampant and also sophisticated, which presents a major challenge for their detection. However, they must be detected in order to ensure that the social media continues to be a trusted source of public opinions, rather than being full of fake opinions, lies, and deceptions.

Spam detection in general has been studied in many fields. Web spam and email spam are the two most widely studied types of spam. Opinion spam is, however, very different. There are two main types of Web spam, i.e., *link spam* and *content spam* (Castillo and Davison, 2010; Liu, 2006, 2011). Link spam is spam on hyperlinks, which hardly exist in reviews. Although advertising links are common in other forms of social media, they are relatively easy to detect. Content spam adds popular (but irrelevant) words in target Web pages in order to fool search engines to make them relevant to many search queries, but this hardly occurs in opinion postings. Email spam refers to unsolicited advertisements, which are also rare in online opinions.

> **Challenge**: The key challenge of opinion spam detection is that unlike other forms of spam, it is very hard, if not impossible, to recognize fake opinions by manually reading them, which makes it difficult to find opinion spam data to help design and evaluate detection algorithms. For other forms of spam, one can recognize them fairly easily.

In fact, in the extreme case, it is logically impossible to recognize spam by simply reading it. For example, one can write a truthful review for a good restaurant and post it as a fake review for a bad restaurant in order to promote it. There is no way to detect this fake review without considering information beyond the review text itself simply because the same review cannot be both truthful and fake at the same time.

This chapter uses consumer reviews as an example to study the problem. Little research has been done in the context of other forms of social media.

10.1   TYPES OF SPAM AND SPAMMING

Three types of spam reviews were identified in Jindal and Liu (2008):

> **Type 1 (fake reviews)**: These are untruthful reviews that are written not based on the reviewers' genuine experiences of using the products or services, but are written with hidden motives. They often contain undeserving positive opinions about some target entities (products or services) in order to promote the entities and/or unjust or false negative opinions about some other entities in order to damage their reputations.
>
> **Type 2 (reviews about brands only)**: These reviews do not comment on the specific products or services that they are supposed to review, but only comment on the brands or the manufacturers of the products. Although they may be genuine, they are considered as spam as they are not targeted at the specific products and are often biased. For example, a review for a specific HP printer says "*I hate HP. I never buy any of their products.*"
>
> **Type 3 (non-reviews)**: These are not reviews. There are two main sub-types: (1) advertisements and (2) other irrelevant texts containing no opinions (e.g., questions, answers, and random texts). Strictly speaking, they are not opinion spam as they do not give user opinions.

It has been shown in Jindal and Liu (2008) that types 2 and 3 spam reviews are rare and relatively easy to detect using supervised learning. Even if they are not detected, it is not a major problem because human readers can easily spot them during reading. This chapter thus focuses on type 1, fake reviews.

Fake reviews can be seen as a special form of deception (Hancock et al., 2007; Mihalcea and Strapparava, 2009; Newman et al., 2003; Pennebaker et al., 2007; Vrij, 2008; Zhou et al., 2008). However, traditional deceptions usually refer to lies about some facts or a person's true feeling. Researchers have identified many deception signals in text. For example, studies have shown that when people lie they tend to detach themselves and like to use words such as *you, she, he, they,* rather than *I, myself, mine,* etc. Liars also use words related to certainty more frequently to hide "fake" or to emphasize "truth". Fake reviews are different from lies in many aspects. First, fake reviewers actually like to use *I, myself, mine*, etc., to give readers the impression that their reviews express their true experiences. Second, fake reviews are not necessarily the traditional lies. For example, one wrote a book and pretended to be a reader and wrote a review to promote the book. The review might be the true feeling of the author. Furthermore, many fake reviewers might have never used the reviewed products/services, but simply tried to give positive or negative opinions about something that they do not know. They are not lying about any facts they know or their true feelings.

10.1.1 Harmful Fake Reviews

Not all fake reviews are equally harmful. Table 10.1 gives a conceptual view of different kinds of fake reviews. Here we assume we know the true quality of a product. The objective of fake reviews in regions 1, 3 and 5 is to promote the product. Although opinions expressed in region 1 may be true, the reviewers do not disclose their conflict of interests or hidden motives. The goal of fake reviews in regions 2, 4, and 6 is to damage the reputation of the product. Although opinions in the reviews of region 6 may be true, the reviewers have malicious intensions. Clearly, fake reviews in regions 1 and 6 are not very damaging, but fake reviews in regions 2, 3, 4, and 5 are very harmful. Thus, fake review detection algorithms should focus on identifying reviews in these regions. Some of the existing detection algorithms are already using this idea by employing different types of rating deviation features. Note that the good, bad, and average quality may be defined based on the average rating of the reviews given to the product. However, this can be invalid if there are many spammers or there are too few reviews.

10.1.2 Individual and Group Spamming

Fake reviews may be written by many types of people, e.g., friends and family, company employees, competitors, businesses that provide fake review writing services, and even genuine customers

TABLE 10.1: Fake reviews vs. product quality

	POSITIVE FAKE REVIEW	NEGATIVE FAKE REVIEW
Good quality product	1	*2*
Average quality product	*3*	*4*
Bad quality product	5	6

(some businesses give discounts and even full refunds to some of their customers on the condition that the customers write positive reviews for them). In other forms of social media, public or private agencies and political organizations may employ people to post messages to secretly influence social media conversations and to spread lies and disinformation.

In general, a spammer may work individually, or knowingly or unknowingly work as a member of a group (these activities are often highly secretive).

> *Individual spammers*: In this case, a spammer does not work with anyone. He/she just writes fake reviews him/herself using a single user-id, e.g., the author of a book.
>
> *Group spammers*: There are two main sub-cases (Mukherjee et al., 2011, 2012).

> • A group of spammers (persons) works in collusion to promote a target entity and/or to damage the reputation of another. The individual spammers in the group may or may not know each other.
> • A single person registers multiple user-ids and spam using these user-ids. These multiple user-ids behave just like a group in collusion. This case is often called *sock puppetting*.

> Group spamming is highly damaging because due to the sheer number of members in a group, it can take total control of the sentiment on a product and completely mislead potential customers, especially at the beginning of a product launch. Although group spammers can also be seen as many individual spammers, group spamming has some special characteristics which can give them away as we will see in Section 10.4.

We should also note that a spammer may work individually sometimes and as a member of a group some other times. A spammer may also be a genuine reviewer sometimes because he/she also purchases products as a consumer and may write reviews about them based on his/her true experiences. All these complicated situations make opinion spamming very difficult to detect.

10.1.3 Types of Data, Features, and Detection

Three main types of data have been used for review spam detection.

> *Review content*: The actual text content of each review. From the content, we can extract *linguistic features* such as word and POS n-grams and other syntactic and semantic clues for deceptions and lies. However, linguistic features may not be enough because one can fairly easily craft a fake review that is just like a genuine one. For example, one can write a fake positive review for a bad restaurant based on his true experience in a good restaurant.

Meta-data about the review: The data such as the star rating given to each review, user-id of the reviewer, the time when the review was posted, the time taken to write the review, the host IP address and MAC address of the reviewer's computer, the geo-location of the reviewer, and the sequence of clicks at the review site. From such data, we can mine many types of abnormal *behavioral patterns* of reviewers and their reviews. For example, from review ratings, we may find that a reviewer wrote only positive reviews for a brand and only negative reviews for a competing brand. Along a similar line, if multiple user-ids from the same computer posted a number of positive reviews about a product, these reviews are suspicious. Also, if the positive reviews for a hotel are all from the nearby area of the hotel, they are clearly not trustworthy.

Product information: Information about the entity being reviewed, e.g., the product description and sales volume/rank. For example, a product is not selling well but has many positive reviews, which is hard to believe.

These types of data have been used to produce many spam features. One can also classify the data into *public data* and *site private data*. By public data, we mean the data displayed on the review pages of the hosting site, e.g., the review content, the reviewer's user-id and the time when the review was posted. By private data, we mean the data that the site collects but is not displayed on their review pages for public viewing, e.g., the IP address and MAC address from the reviewer's computer, and the cookie information.

Opinion Spam Detection: The ultimate goal of opinion spam detection in the review context is to identify every fake review, fake reviewer, and fake reviewer group. The three concepts are clearly related as fake reviews are written by fake reviewers and fake reviewers can form fake reviewer groups. The detection of one type can help the detection of others. However, each of them also has its own special characteristics, which can be exploited for detection.

In the next two sections, we focus on detecting individual fake reviews and reviewers, and in Section 10.4 we discuss the detection of spammer groups.

10.2   SUPERVISED SPAM DETECTION

In general, opinion spam detection can be formulated as a classification problem with two classes, *fake* and *non-fake*. Supervised learning is naturally applicable. However, as we described above, a key difficulty is that it is very hard, if not impossible, to recognize fake reviews reliably by manually reading them because a spammer can carefully craft a fake review that is just like any innocent review (Jindal and Liu, 2008). Due to this difficulty, there is no reliable fake review and non-fake review data available to train a machine learning algorithm to recognize fake reviews. Despite these difficulties, several detection algorithms have been proposed and evaluated in various ways. This section discusses three supervised learning methods. The next section describes some unsupervised methods.

Due to the fact that there is no labeled training data for learning, Jindal and Liu (2008) exploited duplicate reviews. In their study of 5.8 million reviews and 2.14 million reviewers from amazon.com, a large number of duplicate and near-duplicate reviews were found, which indicated that review spam was widespread. Since writing new reviews can be taxing, many spammers use the same reviews or slightly revised reviews for different products. These duplicates and near-duplicates can be divided into four categories:

1. Duplicates from the same user-id on the same product;
2. Duplicates from different user-ids on the same product;
3. Duplicates from the same user-id on different products;
4. Duplicates from different user-ids on different products.

The first type of duplicates can be the results of reviewers mistakenly clicking the review submit button multiple times (which can be easily checked based on the submission dates). However, the last three types of duplicates are very likely to be fake. Thus, the last three types of duplicates were used as fake reviews and the rest of the reviews as non-fake reviews in the training data for machine learning. Three sets of features were employed.

Review centric features: These are features about each review. Example features include the actual words and n-grams of the review, the number of times that brand names are mentioned, the percent of opinion words, the review length, and the number of helpful feedbacks. In many review sites (e.g., amazon.com), the readers can provide feedback to each review by answering a question like "*Do you find this review helpful?*"

Reviewer centric features: These are features about each reviewer. Example features include the average rating given by the reviewer, the mean and the standard deviation in rating, the ratio of the number of reviews that this reviewer wrote which were the first reviews of products to the total number of reviews that he/she has written, and the ratio of the number of cases in which he/she was the only reviewer.

Product centric features: These features are about each product. Example features include the price of the product, the sales rank of the product (amazon.com assigns a sales rank to each product according to its sales volume), the mean and the standard deviation of review ratings of the product.

Logistic regression was used for model building. Experimental results showed some tentative but interesting results.

- Negative outlier reviews (ratings with significant negative deviations from the average rating of a product) tend to be heavily spammed. Positive outlier reviews are not badly spammed.
- Reviews that are the only reviews of some products are likely to be fake. This can be explained by the tendency of a seller promoting an unpopular product by writing a fake review.
- Top-ranked reviewers are more likely to be fake reviewers. amazon.com gives a rank to each reviewer based on its proprietary method. Analysis showed that top-ranked reviewers generally wrote a large number of reviews. People who wrote a large number of reviews are natural suspects. Some top reviewers wrote thousands or even tens of thousands of reviews, which is unlikely for an ordinary consumer.
- Fake reviews can get good feedbacks and genuine reviews can get bad feedbacks. This shows that if the quality of a review is defined based on helpfulness feedbacks, people can be fooled by fake reviews because spammers can easily craft a sophisticated review that can get many positive feedbacks.
- Products of lower sales ranks are more likely to be spammed. This indicates that spam activities seem to be limited to low selling products, which is intuitive as it is difficult to damage the reputation of a popular product, and an unpopular product needs some promotion.

It should be stressed again that these results are tentative because (1) it is not confirmed that the three types of duplicates are definitely fake reviews, and (2) many fake reviews are not duplicates and they are considered as non-fake reviews in model building in Jindal and Liu (2008).

In Li et al. (2011), another supervised learning approach was attempted to identify fake reviews. In their case, a manually labeled fake review corpus was built from Epinions reviews. In Epinions, after a review is posted, users can evaluate the review by giving it a helpfulness score. They can also write comments about the reviews. The authors manually labeled a set of fake and non-fake reviews by reading the reviews and the comments. For learning, several types of features were proposed, which are similar to those in Jindal and Liu (2008) with some additions, e.g., subjective and objectivity features, positive and negative features, reviewer's profile, authority score computed using PageRank (Page et al., 1999), etc. For learning, they used naïve Bayes classification which gave promising results. The authors also experimented with a semi-supervised learning method exploiting the idea that a spammer tends to write many fake reviews.

In Ott et al. (2011), supervised learning was also employed. In this case, the authors used Amazon Mechanical Turk to crowdsource fake hotel reviews of 20 hotels. Several provisions were made to ensure the quality of the fake reviews. For example, they only allowed each Turker to make a single submission, Turkers must be in the U.S., etc. The Turkers were also given the scenario that they worked in the hotels and their bosses asked them to write fake reviews to promote the hotels. Truthful reviews were obtained from the TripAdvisor Web site. The authors tried several classification approaches which have been used in related tasks such as genre identification, psycholinguistic deception detection, and text classification. All these tasks have some existing features proposed by researchers. Their experiments showed that text classification performed the best using only unigram and bigrams based on the 50/50 fake and non-fake class distribution. Traditional features for deceptions (Hancock et al., 2007; Mihalcea and Strapparava, 2009; Newman et al., 2003; Pennebaker et al., 2007; Vrij, 2008; Zhou et al., 2008) did not do well. However, like the previous studies, the evaluation data used here is also not perfect. The fake reviews from Amazon Mechanical Turk may not be true "fake reviews" as the Turkers do not know the hotels being reviewed although they were asked to pretend that they worked for the hotels. Furthermore, using 50/50 fake and non-fake data for testing may not reflect the true distribution of the real-life situation. The class distribution can have a significant impact on the precision of the detected fake reviews.

10.3   UNSUPERVISED SPAM DETECTION

Due to the difficulty of manually labeling of training data, using supervised learning alone for fake review detection is difficult. In this section, we discuss two unsupervised approaches. Techniques similar to these are already in use in many review hosting sites.

10.3.1 Spam Detection based on Atypical Behaviors

This sub-section describes some techniques that try to discover atypical behaviors of reviewers for spammer detection. For example, if a reviewer wrote all negative reviews for a brand but other reviewers were all positive about the brand, and wrote all positive reviews for a competing brand, then this reviewer is naturally suspicious.

The first technique is from Lim et al. (2010), which identified several unusual reviewer behavior models based on different review patterns that suggest spamming. Each model assigns a numeric spamming behavior score to a reviewer by measuring the extent to which the reviewer practices spamming behavior of the type. All the scores are then combined to produce the final spam score. Thus, this method focuses on finding spammers or fake reviewers rather than fake reviews. The spamming behavior models are:

a) **Targeting products**: To game a review system, it is hypothesized that a spammer will direct most of his efforts on promoting or victimizing a few target products. He is expected to monitor the products closely and mitigate the ratings by writing fake reviews when time is appropriate.

b) **Targeting groups**: This spam behavior model defines the pattern of spammers manipulating ratings of a set of products sharing some attribute(s) within a short span of time. For example, a spammer may target several products of a brand within a few hours. This pattern of ratings saves the spammers' time as they do not need to log on to the review system many times. To achieve maximum impact, the ratings given to these target groups of products are either very high or very low.

c) **General rating deviation**: A genuine reviewer is expected to give ratings similar to other raters of the same product. As spammers attempt to promote or demote some products, their ratings typically deviate a great deal from those of other reviewers.

d) **Early rating deviation**: Early deviation captures the behavior of a spammer contributing a fake review soon after product launch. Such reviews are likely to attract attention from other reviewers, allowing spammers to affect the views of subsequent reviewers.

The second technique also focused on finding fake reviewers or spammers (Jindal et al., 2010). Here, the problem was formulated as a data mining task of discovering unexpected class association rules. Unlike conventional spam detection approaches such as the above supervised and unsupervised methods, which first manually identify some heuristic spam features and then use them for spam detection. This technique is generic and can be applied to solve a class of problems due to its domain independence.

Class association rules are a special type of association rules (Liu et al., 1998) with a fixed class attribute. The data for mining class association rules (CARs) consists of a set of data records, which are described by a set of normal attributes $A = \{A_1, \cdots, A_n\}$, and a class attribute $C = \{c_1, \cdots, c_m\}$ of m discrete values, called *class labels*. A CAR rule is of the form: $X \rightarrow c_i$, where X is a set of conditions from the attributes in A and c_i is a class label in C. Such a rule computes the conditional probability of $\Pr(c_i \mid X)$ (called *confidence*) and the joint probability $\Pr(X, c_i)$ (called *support*).

For the spammer detection application, the data for CAR mining is produced as follows: Each review forms a data record with a set of attributes, e.g., *reviewer-id, brand-id, product-id,* and a class. The class represents the sentiment of the reviewer on the product, *positive*, *negative*, or *neutral* based on the review rating. In most review sites (e.g., amazon.com), each review has a rating between 1 (lowest) and 5 (highest) assigned by its reviewer. The rating of 4 or 5 is assigned positive, 3 neutral, and 1 or 2 negative. A discovered CAR rule could be that a reviewer gives all positive ratings to a particular brand of products. The method in Jindal et al. (2010) finds four types of unexpected rules based on four unexpectedness definitions. The unexpected rules represent atypical behaviors of reviewers. Below, an example behavior is given for each type of unexpectedness definition. The unexpectedness definitions are quite involved and can be found in Jindal et al. (2010).

- **Confidence unexpectedness**: Using this measure, one can find reviewers who give all high ratings to products of a brand, but most other reviewers are generally negative about the brand.
- **Support unexpectedness**: Using this measure, one can find reviewers who write multiple reviews for a single product, while other reviewers only write one review.
- **Attribute distribution unexpectedness**: Using this measure, one can find that most positive reviews for a brand of products are written by only one reviewer although there are a large number of reviewers who have reviewed the products of the brand.
- **Attribute unexpectedness**: Using this measure, one can find reviewers who write only positive reviews to one brand and only negative reviews to another brand.

The advantage of this approach is that all the unexpectedness measures are defined on CAR rules, and are thus domain independent. The technique can be used in other domains to find unexpected patterns. The weakness is that some atypical behaviors cannot be detected, e.g., time-related behaviors, because class association rules do not consider time.

It is important to note that the behaviors studied in published papers are all based on public data displayed on review pages of their respective review hosting sites. As mentioned earlier, review hosting sites also collect many other pieces of data about each reviewer and his/her activities at the sites. These data are not visible to the general public, but can be very useful, perhaps even more useful than the public data, for spam detection. For example, if multiple user-ids from the same IP address posted a number of positive reviews about a product, then these user-ids are suspicious. If the positive reviews for a hotel are all from the nearby area of the hotel, they are also doubtful. Some review hosting sites are already using these and other pieces of their internal data to detect fake reviewers and reviews.

Finally, Wu et al. (2010) also proposed an unsupervised method to detect fake reviews based on a distortion criterion (not on reviewers' behaviors as the above methods). The idea is that fake reviews will distort the overall popularity ranking for a collection of entities. That is, deleting a set of reviews chosen at random should not overly disrupt the ranked list of entities, while deleting fake reviews should significantly alter or distort the ranking of entities to reveal the "true" ranking. This distortion can be measured by comparing popularity rankings before and after deletion using rank correlation.

10.3.2 Spam Detection Using Review Graph

In Wang et al. (2011), a graph-based method was proposed for detecting spam in store or merchant reviews. Such reviews describe purchase experiences and evaluations of stores. This study was based on a snapshot of all reviews from resellerratings.com, which were crawled on October 6, 2010. After removing stores with no reviews, there were 343,603 reviewers who wrote 408,470 reviews about 14,561 stores.

Although one can borrow some ideas from product review spammer detection, their clues are insufficient for the store review context. For example, it is suspicious for a person to post multiple reviews to the same product, but it can be normal for a person to post more than one review to the same store due to multiple purchasing experiences. Also, it can be normal to have near-duplicate reviews from one reviewer for multiple stores because unlike different products, different stores basically provide the same type of services. Therefore, features or clues proposed in existing approaches to detecting fake product reviews and reviewers are not all appropriate for detecting spammers of store reviews. Thus, there is a need to look for a more sophisticated and complementary framework.

This paper used a heterogeneous review graph with three types of nodes, i.e., reviewers, reviews, and stores, to capture their relationships and to model spamming clues. A reviewer node has a link to each review that he/she wrote. A review node has an edge to a store node if the review is about that store. A store is connected to a reviewer via this reviewer's review about the store. Each node is also attached with a set of features. For example, a store node has features about its average rating, its number of reviews, etc. Based on the review graph, three concepts are defined and computed, i.e., the *trustiness* of reviewers, the *honesty* of reviews, and the *reliability* of stores. A reviewer is more trustworthy if he/she has written more honesty reviews; a store is more reliable if it has more positive reviews from trustworthy reviewers; and a review is more honest if it is supported by many other honest reviews. Furthermore, if the honesty of a review goes down, it affects the reviewer's trustiness, which has an impact on the store he/she reviewed. These intertwined relations are revealed in the review graph and defined mathematically. An iterative computation method was proposed to compute the three values, which are then used to rank reviewers, stores, and reviews. Those top ranked reviewers, stores and reviews are likely to be involved in review spamming. The evaluation was done using human judges by comparing with scores of stores from *Better Business Bureaus* (BBB), a well-known corporation in the U.S. that gathers reports on business reliability and alerts the public to business or consumer scams.

10.4   GROUP SPAM DETECTION

An initial group spam detection algorithm was proposed in Mukherjee et al. (2011), which was improved in Mukherjee et al. (2012). The algorithm finds groups of spammers who might have worked in collusion in promoting or demoting some target entities. It works in two steps.

1. **Frequent pattern mining**: First, it pre-processes the review data to produce a set of transactions. Each transaction represents a unique product and consists of all reviewers (their ids) who have reviewed that product. Using all the transactions, it performs frequent pattern mining to find a set of frequent patterns. Each pattern is basically a group of reviewers who have all reviewed a set of products. Such a group is regarded as a candidate spam group. The reason for using frequent pattern mining is as follows: If a group of reviewers who only worked together once to promote or to demote a single product, it can be hard to detect based on their collective behavior. However, these fake reviewers (especially those who get paid to write) cannot be just writing one review for a single product because they would not make enough money that way. Instead, they work on many products, i.e., write many reviews about many products, which also gives them away. Frequent pattern mining can find them working together on multiple products.

2. **Rank groups based on a set of group spam indicators**: The groups discovered in step 1 may not all be true spammer groups. Many of the reviewers are grouped together in pattern mining simply due to chance. Then, this step first uses a set of indicators to catch different types of unusual group and individual member behaviors. These indicators include writing reviews together in a short time window, writing reviews right after the product launch, group review content similarity, group rating deviation, etc. (Mukherjee et al. (2012). A relational model, called GSRank (Group Spam Rank), was then proposed to exploit the relationships of groups, individual group members, and products that they reviewed to rank candidate groups based on their likelihoods for being spammer groups. An iterative algorithm was then used to solve the problem. A set of spammer groups was also manually labeled and used to evaluate the proposed model, which showed promising results. One weakness of this method is that due to the frequency threshold used in pattern mining, if a group has not worked together many times (three or more times), it will not be detected by this method.

This method is unsupervised as it does not use any manually labeled data for training. Clearly, with the labeled data supervised learning can be applied as well. Indeed, Mukherjee et al. (2012) described experiments with several state-of-the-art supervised classification, regression and learning to rank algorithms but they were shown to be less effective.

10.5   SUMMARY

As social media is increasingly used for critical decision making by organizations and individuals, opinion spamming is also becoming more and more widespread. For many businesses, posting fake opinions themselves or employing others to do it for them has become a cheap way of marketing and brand promotion.

Although current research on opinion spam detection is still in its early stage, several effective algorithms have already been proposed and used in practice. Spammers, however, are also getting more sophisticated and careful in writing and posting fake opinions to avoid detection. In fact, we have already seen an arms race between detection algorithms and spammers. However, I am optimistic that more sophisticated detection algorithms will be designed to make it very difficult for spammers to post fake opinions. Such algorithms are likely to be holistic approaches that integrate all possible features or clues in the detection process.

Finally, we should note that opinion spamming occurs not only in reviews, but also in other forms of social media such as blogs, forum discussions, commentaries, and Twitter postings. However, so far little research has been done in these contexts.

· · · ·

CHAPTER 11

Quality of Reviews

In this chapter, we discuss the quality of reviews. The topic is related to opinion spam detection, but is also different because low-quality reviews may not be spam or fake reviews, and fake reviews may not be perceived as low-quality reviews by readers because as we discussed in the last chapter, by reading reviews it is very hard to spot fake reviews. For this reason, fake reviews may also be seen as helpful or high quality reviews if the imposters write their reviews early and craft them well.

The objective of this task is to determine the quality, helpfulness, usefulness, or utility of each review (Ghose and Ipeirotis, 2007; Kim et al., 2006; Liu et al., 2007; Zhang and Varadarajan, 2006). This is a meaningful task because it is desirable to rank reviews based on quality or helpfulness when showing reviews to the user, with the most helpful reviews first. In fact, many review aggregation or hosting sites have been practicing this for years. They obtain the helpfulness or quality score of each review by asking readers to provide helpfulness feedbacks to each review. For example, on amazon.com, the reader can indicate whether he/she finds a review helpful by responding to the question "*Was the review helpful to you?*" just below each review. The feedback results from all those responded are then aggregated and displayed right before each review, e.g., "*15 of 16 people found the following review helpful.*" Although most review hosting sites already provide the service, automatically determining the quality of each review is still useful because a good number of user feedbacks may take a long time to accumulate. That is why many reviews have few or no feedbacks. This is especially true for new reviews.

11.1 QUALITY AS REGRESSION PROBLEM

Determining the quality of reviews is usually formulated as a regression problem. The learned model assigns a quality score to each review, which can be used in review ranking or review recommendation. In this area of research, the ground truth data used for both training and testing are usually the user-helpfulness feedback given to each review, which as we discussed above is provided for each review at many review hosting sites. So, unlike fake review detection, the training and testing data here is not an issue. Researchers have used many types of features for model building.

In Kim et al. (2006), SVM regression was used to solve the problem. The feature sets included:

Structure features: review length, number of sentences, percentages of question sentences and exclamations, and the number of HTML bold tags <b> and line breaks <br>.;

Lexical features: unigrams and bigrams with tf-idf weights;

Syntactic features: percentage of parsed tokens that are of open-class (i.e., nouns, verbs, adjectives and adverbs), percentage of tokens that are nouns, percentage of tokens that are verbs, percentage of tokens that are verbs conjugated in the first person, and percentage of tokens that are adjectives or adverbs;

Semantic features: product aspects, and sentiment words; and

Meta-data features: review rating (number of stars).

Zhang and Varadarajan (2006) also treated the problem as a regressions problem. They used similar features, e.g., review length, review rating, counts of some specific POS tags, sentiment words, tf-idf weighting scores, wh-words, product aspect mentions, comparison with product specifications, comparison with editorial reviews, etc.

Unlike the above approaches, Liu et al. (2008) considered three main factors, i.e., reviewers' expertise, the timeliness of reviews, and review styles based on POS tags. A nonlinear regression model was proposed to integrate the factors. This work focused on movie reviews.

In Ghose and Ipeirotis (2007, 2010), three additional sets of features were used, namely, reviewer profile features which are available from the review site, reviewer history features which capture the helpfulness of his/her reviews in the past, and a set of readability features, i.e., spelling errors and readability indices from the readability research. For learning, the authors tried both regression and binary classification.

Lu et al. (2010) looked at the problem from an additional angle. They investigated how the social context of reviewers can help enhance the accuracy of a text-based review quality predictor. They argued that the social context can reveal a great deal of information about the quality of reviewers, which in turn affects the quality of their reviews. Specifically, their approach was based on the following hypotheses.

Author consistency hypothesis: reviews from the same author are of similar quality.

Trust consistency hypothesis: A link from a reviewer r_1 to a reviewer r_2 is an explicit or implicit statement of trust. Reviewer r_1 trusts reviewer r_2 only if the quality of reviewer r_2 is at least as high as that of reviewer r_1.

> *Co-citation consistency hypothesis*: People are consistent in how they trust other people. So if two reviewers, r_1 and r_2, are trusted by the same third reviewer r_3, then their quality should be similar.
>
> *Link consistency hypothesis*: If two people are connected in the social network (r_1 trusts r_2, or r_2 trusts r_1, or both), then their review quality should be similar.

These hypotheses were enforced as regularizing constraints and added into the text-based linear regression model to solve the review quality prediction problem. For experiments, the authors used the data from Ciao (www.ciao.co.uk), which is a community review Web site. In Ciao, people not only write reviews for products and services, but also rate the reviews written by others. Furthermore, people can add members to their network of trusted members or "Circle of Trust", if they find these members' reviews consistently interesting and helpful. Clearly, this technique will not be applicable to Web sites which do not have a trust social network in place.

11.2 OTHER METHODS

In O'Mahony and Smyth (2009), a classification approach was proposed to classify helpful and non-helpful reviews. Many features were used:

> *Reputation features*: the mean (R1) and standard deviation (R2) of review helpfulness over all reviews authored by the reviewer, the percentage of reviews authored by the reviewer which have received a minimum of T feedbacks (R3), etc.;
>
> *Content features*: review length (C1), the ratio of uppercase to lowercase characters in the review text (C3), etc.;
>
> *Social features*: the number of reviews authored by the reviewer (SL1), the mean (SL2), and standard deviation (SL3) of the number of reviews authored by all reviewers, etc.;
>
> *Sentiment features*: the rating score of the review (ST1), and the mean (ST5), and standard deviation (ST6) of the scores assigned by the reviewer over all reviews authored by the reviewer, etc.

In Liu et al. (2007), the problem was also formulated as a two-class classification problem. However, they argued that using the helpfulness votes as the ground truth may not be appropriate because of three biases: (1) vote imbalance (a very large percentage of votes are helpful votes); (2) early bird bias (early reviews tend to get more votes); (3) winner circle bias (when some reviews get many votes they are ranked high at the review sites which help them get even more votes). Those lowly ranked reviews get few votes, but they may not be of low quality. The authors then divided reviews into 4 categories—"best review," "good review," "fair review," and "bad review,"—based on whether reviews discuss many aspects of the product and provide convincing opinions. Manual labeling was carried out to produce the gold-standard training and testing data. In classification, they used SVM to perform binary classification. Only the "bad review" category was regarded as the low quality class and all the other three categories were regarded as belonging to the high quality class. The features for learning were informativeness, subjectiveness, and readability. Each of them contained a set of individual features.

Tsur and Rappoport (2009) studied the helpfulness of book reviews using an unsupervised approach which is quite different from the above supervised methods. The method works in three steps. Given a collection of reviews, it first identifies a set of important terms in the reviews. These terms together form a vector representing a virtual optimal or core review. Then, each actual review is mapped or converted to this vector representation based on occurrences of the discovered important terms in the review. After that, each review is assigned a rank score based on the distance of the review to the virtual review (both are represented as vectors).

In Moghaddam et al. (2012), a new problem of personalized review quality prediction for recommendation of helpful reviews was proposed. All of the above methods assume that the helpfulness of a review is the same for all users/readers, which the authors argued is not true. To solve the new problem, they proposed several factorization models. These models are based on the assumption that the observed review ratings depend on some latent features of the reviews, reviewers, raters/users, and products. In essence, the paper treated the problem as a personalized recommendation problem. The proposed technique to solve the problem is quite involved. Some background knowledge about this form of recommendation can be found in Chapter 12 of Liu (2006, 2011).

All the above approaches rank reviews based on the computed helpfulness or quality scores. However, Tsaparas et al. (2011) argued that these approaches do not consider an important fact that the top few high-quality reviews may be highly redundant and repeating the same information. In their work, they proposed the problem of selecting a *comprehensive* and yet a *small* set of high-quality reviews that cover many different aspects of the reviewed entity and also different viewpoints of the reviews. They formulated the problem as a maximum coverage problem, and presented an algorithm to solve the problem. An earlier work in Lappas and Gunopulos (2010) also studied the problem of finding a small set of reviews that cover *all* product aspects.

11.3 SUMMARY

In summary, determining review helpfulness is an important research topic. It is especially useful for products and services that have a large number of reviews. To help the reader get quality opinions quickly, review sites should provide good review rankings. However, I would also like to add some cautionary notes. First, as we discussed in the chapter about opinion search and retrieval, we argued that the review ranking (rankings) must reflect the natural distribution of positive and negative opinions. It is not a good idea to rank all positive (or all negative) reviews at the top simply because they have high-quality scores. The redundancy issue raised in Tsaparas et al. (2011) is also a valid concern. In my opinion, both quality and distribution (in terms of positive and negative viewpoints) are important. Second, readers tend to determine whether a review is helpful or not based on whether the review expresses opinions on many aspects of the product and appear to be genuine. A spammer can satisfy this requirement by carefully crafting a review that is just like a normal helpful review. Therefore, using the number of helpfulness feedbacks to define review quality or as the ground truth alone can be problematic. Furthermore, user feedbacks can be spammed too. Feedback spam is a sub-problem of click fraud in search advertising, where a person or robot clicks on some online advertisements to give the impression of real customer clicks. Here, a robot or a human spammer can click on the helpfulness feedback button to increase the helpfulness of a review.

. . . .

CHAPTER 12

Concluding Remarks

This book introduced the field of sentiment analysis and opinion mining and surveyed the current state-of-the-art. Due to many challenging research problems and a wide variety of practical applications, the research in the field has been very active in recent years. It has spread from computer science to management science (Archak et al., 2007; Chen and Xie, 2008; Das and Chen, 2007; Dellarocas et al., 2007; Ghose, et al., 2007; Hu et al., 2006; Park et al., 2007) as opinions about products are closely related to profits.

The book first defined the sentiment analysis problem, which provided a common framework to unify different research directions in the field. It then discussed the widely studied topic of document-level sentiment classification, which aims to determine whether an opinion document (e.g., a review) expresses a positive or negative sentiment. This was followed by the sentence-level subjectivity and sentiment classification, which determines whether a sentence is opinionated, and if so, whether it carries a positive or negative opinion. The book then described aspect-based sentiment analysis which explored the full power of the problem definition and showed that sentiment analysis is a multi-faceted problem with many challenging sub-problems. The existing techniques for dealing with them were discussed. After that, the book discussed the problem of sentiment lexicon generation. Two dominant approaches were covered. This was followed by the chapter on opinion summarization, which is a special form of multi-document summarization. However, it is also very different from the traditional multi-document summarization because opinion summarization can be done in a structured manner, which facilitates both qualitative and quantitative analysis, and visualization of opinions. Chapter 8 discussed the problem of analyzing comparative and superlative sentences. Such sentences represent a different type of evaluation from regular opinions which have been the focus of the current research. The topic of opinion search or retrieval was introduced in Chapter 9. Last but not least, we discussed opinion spam detection in Chapter 10 and assessing the quality of reviews in Chapter 11. Opinion spamming by writing fake reviews and posting bogus comments are increasingly becoming an important issue as more and more people are relying on the opinions on the Web for decision making. To ensure the trustworthiness of such opinions, combating opinion spamming is an urgent and critical task.

By reading this book thus far, it is not hard to see that sentiment analysis is very challenging technically. Although the research community has attempted so many sub-problems from many different angles and a large number of research papers have also been published, none of the sub-problems has been solved satisfactorily. Our understanding and knowledge about the whole problem and its solution are still very limited. The main reason is that this is a natural language processing task, and natural language processing has no easy problems. Another reason may be due to our popular ways of doing research. We probably relied too much on machine learning. Some of the most effective machine learning algorithms, e.g., support vector machines, naïve Bayes, and conditional random fields, produce no human understandable results such that although they may help us achieve improved accuracy, we know little about how and why apart from some superficial knowledge gained in the manual feature engineering process.

That being said, we have indeed made significant progresses over the past decade. This is evident from the large number of start-up and established companies that offer sentiment analysis services. There is a real and huge need in the industry for such services because every business wants to know how consumers perceive their products and services and those of their competitors. The same can also be said about consumers because whenever one wants to buy something, one wants to know the opinions of existing users. These practical needs and the technical challenges will keep the field vibrant and lively for years to come.

Building on what has been done so far, I believe that we just need to conduct more in-depth investigations and to build integrated systems that try to deal with all the sub-problems together because their interactions can help solve each individual sub-problem. I am optimistic that the whole problem will be solved satisfactorily in the near future for widespread applications.

For applications, a completely automated and accurate solution is nowhere in sight. However, it is possible to devise effective semi-automated solutions. The key is to fully understand the whole range of issues and pitfalls, cleverly manage them, and determine what portions can be done automatically and what portions need human assistance. In the continuum between the fully manual solution and the fully automated solution, as time goes by we can push more and more towards automation. I do not see a silver bullet solution soon. A good bet would be to work hard on a large number of diverse application domains, understand each of them, and design a general solution gradually.

· · · · ·

Bibliography

Abbasi, Ahmed, Hsinchun Chen, and Arab Salem. *Sentiment analysis in multiple languages: Feature selection for opinion classification in web forums. ACM Transactions on Information Systems (TOIS)*, 2008. **26**(3). doi:10.1145/1361684.1361685

Abdul-Mageed, Muhammad, Mona T. Diab, and Mohammed Korayem. *Subjectivity and sentiment analysis of modern standard Arabic* In *Proceedings of the 49th Annual Meeting of the Association for Computational Linguistics:shortpapers.* 2011.

Akkaya, Cem, Janyce Wiebe, and Rada Mihalcea. *Subjectivity word sense disambiguation.* In *Proceedings of the 2009 Conference on Empirical Methods in Natural Language Processing (EMNLP-2009).* 2009. doi:10.3115/1699510.1699535

Alm, Ebba Cecilia Ovesdotter. *Affect in text and speech,* 2008: ProQuest.

Andreevskaia, Alina and Sabine Bergler. *Mining WordNet for fuzzy sentiment: Sentiment tag extraction from WordNet glosses.* In *Proceedings of Conference of the European Chapter of the Association for Computational Linguistics (EACL-06).* 2006.

Andreevskaia, Alina and Sabine Bergler. *When specialists and generalists work together: Overcoming domain dependence in sentiment tagging.* In *Proceedings of the Annual Meeting of the Association for Computational Linguistics (ACL-2008).* 2008.

Andrzejewski, David and Xiaojin Zhu. *Latent Dirichlet Allocation with topic-in-set knowledge.* In *Proceedings of NAACL HLT.* 2009. doi:10.3115/1621829.1621835

Andrzejewski, David, Xiaojin Zhu, and Mark Craven. *Incorporating domain knowledge into topic modeling via Dirichlet forest priors.* In *Proceedings of ICML.* 2009. doi:10.1145/1553374.1553378

Archak, Nikolay, Anindya Ghose, and Panagiotis G. Ipeirotis. *Show me the money!: deriving the pricing power of product features by mining consumer reviews.* In *Proceedings of the ACM SIGKDD Conference on Knowledge Discovery and Data Mining (KDD-2007).* 2007.

Asher, Nicholas, Farah Benamara, and Yvette Yannick Mathieu. *Distilling opinion in discourse: A preliminary study.* In *Proceedings of the International Conference on Computational Linguistics (COLING-2008): Companion volume: Posters and Demonstrations.* 2008.

Asur, Sitaram and Bernardo A. Huberman. *Predicting the future with social media.* Arxiv preprint arXiv:1003.5699, 2010. doi:10.1109/WI-IAT.2010.63

Aue, Anthony and Michael Gamon. *Customizing sentiment classifiers to new domains: a case study*. In *Proceedings of Recent Advances in Natural Language Processing (RANLP-2005)*. 2005.

Banea, Carmen, Rada Mihalcea, and Janyce Wiebe. *Multilingual subjectivity: are more languages better?* In *Proceedings of the International Conference on Computational Linguistics (COLING-2010)*. 2010.

Banea, Carmen, Rada Mihalcea, Janyce Wiebe, and Samer Hassan. *Multilingual subjectivity analysis using machine translation*. In *Proceedings of the Conference on Empirical Methods in Natural Language Processing (EMNLP-2008)*. 2008. doi:10.3115/1613715.1613734

Barbosa, Luciano and Junlan Feng. *Robust sentiment detection on twitter from biased and noisy data*. In *Proceedings of the International Conference on Computational Linguistics (COLING-2010)*. 2010.

Bar-Haim, Roy, Elad Dinur, Ronen Feldman, Moshe Fresko, and Guy Goldstein. Identifying and Following Expert Investors in Stock Microblogs. In *Proceedings of the Conference on Empirical Methods in Natural Language Processing (EMNLP-2011)*, 2011.

Bautin, Mikhail, Lohit Vijayarenu, and Steven Skiena. *International sentiment analysis for news and blogs*. In *Proceedings of the International AAAI Conference on Weblogs and Social Media (ICWSM-2008)*. 2008.

Becker, Israela and Vered Aharonson. *Last but definitely not least: on the role of the last sentence in automatic polarity-classification*. In *Proceedings of the ACL 2010 Conference Short Papers*. 2010.

Beineke, Philip, Trevor Hastie, Christopher Manning, and Shivakumar Vaithyanathan. *An exploration of sentiment summarization*. In *Proceedings of AAAI Spring Symposium on Exploring Attitude and Affect in Text: Theories and Applications*. 2003.

Benamara, Farah, Baptiste Chardon, Yannick Mathieu, and Vladimir Popescu. *Towards Context-Based Subjectivity Analysis*. In *Proceedings of the 5th International Joint Conference on Natural Language Processing (IJCNLP-2011)*. 2011.

Bespalov, Dmitriy, Bing Bai, Yanjun Qi, and Ali Shokoufandeh. *Sentiment classification based on supervised latent n-gram analysis*. In *Proceeding of the ACM conference on Information and knowledge management (CIKM-2011)*. 2011. doi:10.1145/2063576.2063635

Bethard, Steven, Hong Yu, Ashley Thornton, Vasileios Hatzivassiloglou, and Dan Jurafsky. *Automatic extraction of opinion propositions and their holders*. In *Proceedings of the AAAI Spring Symposium on Exploring Attitude and Affect in Text*. 2004.

Bickerstaffe, A. and I. Zukerman. *A hierarchical classifier applied to multi-way sentiment detection*. In *Proceedings of the 23rd International Conference on Computational Linguistics (Coling 2010)*. 2010.

Bilgic, Mustafa, Galileo Mark Namata, and Lise Getoor. *Combining collective classification and link prediction*. In *Proceedings of Workshop on Mining Graphs and Complex Structures*. 2007. doi:10.1109/ICDMW.2007.35

Bishop, C. M. *Pattern recognition and machine learning*. Vol. 4. 2006: Springer, New York. doi:10.1117/1.2819119

Blair-Goldensohn, Sasha, Kerry Hannan, Ryan McDonald, Tyler Neylon, George A. Reis, and Jeff Reynar. *Building a sentiment summarizer for local service reviews*. In *Proceedings of WWW-2008 workshop on NLP in the Information Explosion Era*. 2008.

Blei, David M. and Jon D. McAuliffe. *Supervised topic models*. In *Proceedings of NIPS*. 2007.

Blei, David M., Andrew Y. Ng, and Michael I. Jordan. *Latent dirichlet allocation. The Journal of Machine Learning Research*, 2003. **3**: pp. 993–1022.

Blitzer, John, Mark Dredze, and Fernando Pereira. *Biographies, bollywood, boom-boxes and blenders: Domain adaptation for sentiment classification*. In *Proceedings of Annual Meeting of the Association for Computational Linguistics (ACL-2007)*. 2007.

Blitzer, John, Ryan McDonald, and Fernando Pereira. *Domain adaptation with structural correspondence learning*. In *Proceedings of the Conference on Empirical Methods in Natural Language Processing (EMNLP-2006)*. 2006. doi:10.3115/1610075.1610094

Blum, Avrim and Shuchi Chawla. *Learning from labeled and unlabeled data using graph mincuts*. In *Proceedings of International Conference on Machine Learning (ICML-2001)*. 2001.

Blum, Avrim, John Lafferty, Mugizi R. Rwebangira, and Rajashekar Reddy. *Semi-supervised learning using randomized mincuts*. In *Proceedings of International Conference on Machine Learning (ICML-2004)*. 2004. doi:10.1145/1015330.1015429

Boiy, Erik and Marie-Francine Moens. *A machine learning approach to sentiment analysis in multilingual Web texts. Information Retrieval*, 2009. **12**(5): pp. 526–558. doi:10.1007/s10791-008-9070-z

Bollegala, Danushka, David Weir, and John Carroll. *Using multiple sources to construct a sentiment sensitive thesaurus for cross-domain sentiment classification*. In *Proceedings of the 49th Annual Meeting of the Association for Computational Linguistics (ACL-2011)*. 2011.

Bollen, Johan, Huina Mao, and Xiao-Jun Zeng. *Twitter mood predicts the stock market. Journal of Computational Science*, 2011. doi:10.1016/j.jocs.2010.12.007

Boyd-Graber, Jordan and Philip Resnik. *Holistic sentiment analysis across languages: multilingual supervised latent Dirichlet allocation*. In *Proceedings of the Conference on Empirical Methods in Natural Language Processing (EMNLP-2010)*. 2010.

Branavan, S. R. K., Harr Chen, Jacob Eisenstein, and Regina Barzilay. *Learning document-level semantic properties from free-text annotations*. In *Proceedings of the Annual Meeting of the Association for Computational Linguistics (ACL-2008)*. 2008.

Breck, Eric, Yejin Choi, and Claire Cardie. *Identifying expressions of opinion in context*. In *Proceedings of the International Joint Conference on Artificial Intelligence (IJCAI-2007)*. 2007.

Brody, Samuel and Nicholas Diakopoulos. *Cooooooooooooooollllllllllllll!!!!!!!!!!!!!! Using Word Lengthening to Detect Sentiment in Microblogs*. In *Proceedings of the Conference on Empirical Methods in Natural Language Processing (EMNLP-2011)*. 2011.

Brody, Samuel and Noemie Elhadad. *An Unsupervised Aspect-Sentiment Model for Online Reviews.* In *Proceedings of The 2010 Annual Conference of the North American Chapter of the ACL.* 2010.

Brooke, Julian, Milan Tofiloski, and Maite Taboada. *Cross-linguistic sentiment analysis: From English to Spanish.* In *Proceedings of RANLP.* 2009.

Burfoot, Clinton, Steven Bird, and Timothy Baldwin. *Collective classification of congressional floor-debate transcripts.* In *Proceedings of the 49th Annual Meeting of the Association for Computational Linguistics (ACL-2011).* 2011.

Carenini, Giuseppe, Raymond Ng, and Adam Pauls. *Multi-document summarization of evaluative text.* In *Proceedings of the European Chapter of the Association for Computational Linguistics (EACL-2006).* 2006.

Carenini, Giuseppe, Raymond Ng, and Ed Zwart. *Extracting knowledge from evaluative text.* In *Proceedings of Third International Conference on Knowledge Capture (K-CAP-05).* 2005. doi: 10.1145/1088622.1088626

Carvalho, Paula, Luís Sarmento, Jorge Teixeira, and Mário J. Silva. *Liars and saviors in a sentiment annotated corpus of comments to political debates.* In *Proceedings of the 49th Annual Meeting of the Association for Computational Linguistics:shortpapers.* 2011.

Castellanos, Malu, Umeshwar Dayal, Meichun Hsu, Riddhiman Ghosh, Mohamed Dekhil, Yue Lu, Lei Zhang, and Mark Schreiman. *LCI: a social channel analysis platform for live customer intelligence.* In *Proceedings of the 2011 International Conference on Management of data (SIGMOD-2011).* 2011.

Castillo, Carlos and Brian D. Davison. *Adversarial web search. Foundations and Trends in Information Retrieval,* 2010. **4**(5): pp. 377–486. doi:10.1561/1500000021

Chaudhuri, Arjun. *Emotion and reason in consumer behavior.* 2006: Elsevier Butterworth-Heinemann. doi:10.1016/B978-0-7506-7976-3.50005-1

Chen, Bi, Leilei Zhu, Daniel Kifer, and Dongwon Lee. *What is an opinion about? exploring political standpoints using opinion scoring model.* In *Proceeedings of AAAI Conference on Artificial Intelligence (AAAI-2010).* 2010.

Chen, Yubo and Jinhong Xie. *Online consumer review: Word-of-mouth as a new element of marketing communication mix. Management Science,* 2008. **54**(3): pp. 477–491. doi:10.1287/mnsc.1070 .0810

Choi, Yejin, Eric Breck, and Claire Cardie. *Joint extraction of entities and relations for opinion recognition.* In *Proceedings of the Conference on Empirical Methods in Natural Language Processing (EMNLP-2006).* 2006. doi:10.3115/1610075.1610136

Choi, Yejin and Claire Cardie. *Adapting a polarity lexicon using integer linear programming for domain-specific sentiment classification.* In *Proceedings of the 2009 Conference on Empirical Methods in Natural Language Processing (EMNLP-2009).* 2009. doi:10.3115/1699571.1699590

Choi, Yejin and Claire Cardie. *Hierarchical sequential learning for extracting opinions and their attributes*. In *Proceedings of Annual Meeting of the Association for Computational Linguistics (ACL-2010)*. 2010.

Choi, Yejin and Claire Cardie. *Learning with compositional semantics as structural inference for subsentential sentiment analysis*. In *Proceedings of Conference on Empirical Methods in Natural Language Processing (EMNLP-2008)*. 2008. doi:10.3115/1613715.1613816

Choi, Yejin, Claire Cardie, Ellen Riloff, and Siddharth Patwardhan. *Identifying sources of opinions with conditional random fields and extraction patterns*. In *Proceedings of the Human Language Technology Conference and the Conference on Empirical Methods in Natural Language Processing (HLT/EMNLP-2005)*. 2005. doi:10.3115/1220575.1220620

Cilibrasi, Rudi L. and Paul M. B. Vitanyi. *The google similarity distance. IEEE Transactions on Knowledge and Data Engineering*, 2007. **19**(3): pp. 370–383. doi:10.1109/TKDE.2007.48

Cui, Hang, Vibhu Mittal, and Mayur Datar. *Comparative experiments on sentiment classification for online product reviews*. In *Proceedings of AAAI-2006*. 2006.

Das, Dipanjan. *A Survey on Automatic Text Summarization Single-Document Summarization*. Language, 2007. **4**: pp. 1–31.

Das, Sanjiv and Mike Chen. *Yahoo! for Amazon: Extracting market sentiment from stock message boards*. In *Proceedings of APFA-2001*. 2001.

Das, Sanjiv and Mike Chen. *Yahoo! for Amazon: Sentiment extraction from small talk on the web*. Management Science, 2007. **53**(9): pp. 1375–1388. doi:10.1287/mnsc.1070.0704

Dasgupta, Sajib and Vincent Ng. *Mine the easy, classify the hard: a semi-supervised approach to automatic sentiment classification*. In *Proceedings of the 47th Annual Meeting of the ACL and the 4th IJCNLP of the AFNLP (ACL-2009)*. 2009.

Dave, Kushal, Steve Lawrence, and David M. Pennock. *Mining the peanut gallery: Opinion extraction and semantic classification of product reviews*. In *Proceedings of International Conference on World Wide Web (WWW-2003)*. 2003.

Davidov, Dmitry, Oren Tsur, and Ari Rappoport. *Enhanced sentiment learning using twitter hashtags and smileys*. In *Proceedings of Coling-2010*. 2010.

Dellarocas, C., X. M. Zhang, and N. F. Awad. *Exploring the value of online product reviews in forecasting sales: The case of motion pictures. Journal of Interactive Marketing*, 2007. **21**(4): pp. 23–45. doi:10.1002/dir.20087

Dey, Lipika and S K Mirajul Haque. *Opinion mining from noisy text data*. In *Proceedings of the Second Workshop on Analytics for Noisy Unstructured Text Data (AND-2008)*. 2008. doi:10.1145/1390749.1390763

Ding, Xiaowen and Bing Liu. *Resolving Object and Attribute Coreference in Opinion Mining*. In *Proceedings of International Conference on Computational Linguistics (COLING-2010)*. 2010.

Ding, Xiaowen, Bing Liu, and Philip S. Yu. *A holistic lexicon-based approach to opinion mining*. In *Proceedings of the Conference on Web Search and Web Data Mining (WSDM-2008)*. 2008. doi: 10.1145/1341531.1341561

Ding, Xiaowen, Bing Liu, and Lei Zhang. *Entity discovery and assignment for opinion mining applications*. In *Proceedings of ACM SIGKDD International Conference on Knowledge Discovery and Data Mining (KDD-2009)*. 2009. doi:10.1145/1557019.1557141

Dowty, David R., Robert E. Wall, and Stanley Peters. *Introduction to Montague semantics*. Vol. 11. 1981: Springer. doi:10.1007/978-94-009-9065-4

Dragut, Eduard C., Clement Yu, Prasad Sistla, and Weiyi Meng. *Construction of a sentimental word dictionary*. In *Proceedings of ACM International Conference on Information and Knowledge Management (CIKM-2010)*. 2010. doi:10.1145/1871437.1871723

Du, Weifu and Songbo Tan. *Building domain-oriented sentiment lexicon by improved information bottleneck*. In *Proceedings of ACM Conference on Information and Knowledge Management (CIKM-2009)*. 2009. ACM. doi:10.1145/1645953.1646221

Du, Weifu, Songbo Tan, Xueqi Cheng, and Xiaochun Yun. *Adapting information bottleneck method for automatic construction of domain-oriented sentiment lexicon*. In *Proceedings of ACM International Confernece on Web search and data mining (WSDM-2010)*. 2010. doi:10.1145/1718487.1718502

Duh, Kevin, Akinori Fujino, and Masaaki Nagata. *Is machine translation ripe for cross-lingual sentiment classification?* in *Proceedings of the 49th Annual Meeting of the Association for Computational Linguistics:shortpapers (ACL-2011)*. 2011.

Eguchi, Koji and Victor Lavrenko. *Sentiment retrieval using generative models*. In *Proceedings of Conference on Empirical Methods in Natural Language Processing (EMNLP-2006)*. 2006. doi:10.3115/1610075.1610124

Esuli, Andrea and Fabrizio Sebastiani. *Determining term subjectivity and term orientation for opinion mining*. In *Proceedings of Conf. of the European Chapter of the Association for Computational Linguistics (EACL-2006)*. 2006.

Esuli, Andrea and Fabrizio Sebastiani. *Determining the semantic orientation of terms through gloss classification*. In *Proceedings of ACM International Conference on Information and Knowledge Management (CIKM-2005)*. 2005. doi:10.1145/1099554.1099713

Esuli, Andrea and Fabrizio Sebastiani. *SentiWordNet: A publicly available lexical resource for opinion mining*. In *Proceedings of Language Resources and Evaluation (LREC-2006)*. 2006.

Feldman, Ronen, Benjamin Rosenfeld, Roy Bar-Haim, and Moshe Fresko. The Stock Sonar - Sentiment Analysis of Stocks Based on a Hybrid Approach. In *Proceedings of 23rd IAAI Conference on Artificial Intelligence (IAAI-2011)*, 2011.

Feng, Song, Ritwik Bose, and Yejin Choi. *Learning general connotation of words using graph-based algorithms.* In *Proceedings of Confernece on Empirical Methods in Natural Language Processing (EMNLP-2011).* 2011.

Fiszman, Marcelo, Dina Demner-Fushman, Francois M. Lang, Philip Goetz, and Thomas C. Rindflesch. *Interpreting comparative constructions in biomedical text.* In *Proceedings of BioNLP.* 2007. doi:10.3115/1572392.1572417

Frantzi, Katerina, Sophia Ananiadou, and Hideki Mima. *Automatic recognition of multi-word terms:. the C-value/NC-value method. International Journal on Digital Libraries,* 2000. **3**(2): pp. 115–130. doi:10.1007/s007999900023

Gamon, Michael. *Sentiment classification on customer feedback data: noisy data, large feature vectors, and the role of linguistic analysis.* In *Proceedings of International Conference on Computational Linguistics (COLING-2004).* 2004.

Gamon, Michael, Anthony Aue, Simon Corston-Oliver, and Eric Ringger. *Pulse: Mining customer opinions from free text. Advances in Intelligent Data Analysis VI,* 2005: pp. 121–132. doi: 10.1007/11552253_12

Ganapathibhotla, Murthy and Bing Liu. *Mining opinions in comparative sentences.* In *Proceedings of International Conference on Computational Linguistics (COLING-2008).* 2008. doi:10.3115/1599081.1599112

Ganesan, Kavita, ChengXiang Zhai, and Jiawei Han. *Opinosis: a graph-based approach to abstractive summarization of highly redundant opinions.* In *Proceedings of the 23rd International Conference on Computational Linguistics (COLING-2010).* 2010.

Ganter, Viola and Michael Strube. *Finding hedges by chasing weasels: Hedge detection using Wikipedia tags and shallow linguistic features.* In *Proceedings of the ACL-IJCNLP 2009 Conference, Short Papers.* 2009.

Gao, Sheng and Haizhou Li. *A cross-domain adaptation method for sentiment classification using probabilistic latent analysis.* In *Proceeding of the ACM Conference on Information and knowledge management (CIKM-2011).* 2011. doi:10.1145/2063576.2063728

Ghahramani, Zoubin and Katherine A. Heller. *Bayesian sets. Advances in Neural Information Processing Systems,* 2006. **18**: pp. 435.

Ghani, Rayid, Katharina Probst, Yan Liu, Marko Krema, and Andrew Fano. *Text mining for product attribute extraction. ACM SIGKDD Explorations Newsletter,* 2006. **8**(1): pp. 41–48. doi:10.1145/1147234.1147241

Ghose, Anindya and Panagiotis G. Ipeirotis. *Designing novel review ranking systems: predicting the usefulness and impact of reviews.* In *Proceedings of the International Conference on Electronic Commerce.* 2007.

Ghose, Anindya and Panagiotis G. Ipeirotis. *Estimating the helpfulness and economic impact of product reviews: Mining text and reviewer characteristics. IEEE Transactions on Knowledge and Data Engineering*, 2010. doi:10.1109/TKDE.2010.188

Ghose, Anindya, Panagiotis G. Ipeirotis, and Arun Sundararajan. *Opinion mining using econometrics: A case study on reputation systems.* In *Proceedings of the Association for Computational Linguistics (ACL-2007).* 2007.

Gibbs, Raymond W and Herbert L. Colston. *Irony in language and thought: A cognitive science reader,* 2007: Lawrence Erlbaum.

Gibbs, Raymond W. *On the psycholinguistics of sarcasm. Journal of Experimental Psychology: General,* 1986. **115**(1): p. 3. doi:10.1037//0096-3445.115.1.3

Goldberg, Andrew B. and Xiaojin Zhu. *Seeing stars when there aren't many stars: graph-based semi-supervised learning for sentiment categorization.* In *Proceedings of HLT-NAACL 2006 Workshop on Textgraphs: Graph-based Algorithms for Natural Language Processing.* 2006.

González-Ibáñez, Roberto, Smaranda Muresan, and Nina Wacholder. *Identifying sarcasm in Twitter: a closer look.* In *Proceedings of the 49th Annual Meeting of the Association for Computational Linguistics:shortpapers (ACL-2011).* 2011.

Greene, Stephan and Philip Resnik. *More than words: Syntactic packaging and implicit sentiment.* In *Proceedings of Human Language Technologies: The 2009 Annual Conference of the North American Chapter of the ACL (NAACL-2009).* 2009.

Griffiths, Thomas L. and Mark Steyvers. *Prediction and semantic association.* In *Neural Information Processing Systems 15.* 2003.

Griffiths, Thomas L., Mark Steyvers, David M. Blei, and Joshua B. Tenenbaum. *Integrating topics and syntax.* Advances in Neural Information Processing Systems, 2005. **17**: pp. 537–544.

Groh, Georg and Jan Hauffa. *Characterizing Social Relations Via NLP-based Sentiment Analysis.* In *Proceedings of the Fifth International AAAI Conference on Weblogs and Social Media (ICWSM-2011).* 2011.

Guo, Honglei , Huijia Zhu, Zhili Guo, Xiaoxun Zhang, and Zhong Su. *OpinionIt: a text mining system for cross-lingual opinion analysis.* In *Proceeding of the ACM conference on Information and knowledge management (CIKM-2010).* 2010.

Guo, Honglei , Huijia Zhu, Zhili Guo, Xiaoxun Zhang, and Zhong Su. *Product feature categorization with multilevel latent semantic association.* In *Proceedings of ACM International Conference on Information and Knowledge Management (CIKM-2009).* 2009. doi:10.1145/1645953 .1646091

Hai, Zhen, Kuiyu Chang, and Jung-jae Kim. *Implicit feature identification via co-occurrence association rule mining. Computational Linguistics and Intelligent Text Processing,* 2011: pp. 393-404. doi:10.1007/978-3-642-19400-9_31

Hancock, Jeffrey T., Lauren E. Curry, Saurabh Goorha, and Michael Woodworth. *On lying and being lied to: A linguistic analysis of deception in computer-mediated communication. Discourse Processes*, 2007. **45**(1): pp. 1–23. doi:10.1080/01638530701739181

Hardisty, Eric A., Jordan Boyd-Graber, and Philip Resnik. *Modeling perspective using adaptor grammars.* In *Proceedings of the 2010 Conference on Empirical Methods in Natural Language Processing (EMNLP-2010).* 2010.

Hassan, Ahmed, Amjad Abu-Jbara, Rahul Jha, and Dragomir Radev. *Identifying the semantic orientation of foreign words.* In *Proceedings of the 49th Annual Meeting of the Association for Computational Linguistics:shortpapers (ACL-2011).* 2011.

Hassan, Ahmed, Vahed Qazvinian, and Dragomir Radev. *What's with the attitude?: identifying sentences with attitude in online discussions.* In *Proceedings of the 2010 Conference on Empirical Methods in Natural Language Processing (EMNLP-2010).* 2010.

Hassan, Ahmed and Dragomir Radev. *Identifying text polarity using random walks.* In *Proceedings of Annual Meeting of the Association for Computational Linguistics (ACL-2010).* 2010.

Hatzivassiloglou, Vasileios, Judith L. Klavans, Melissa L. Holcombe, Regina Barzilay, Min-Yen Kan, and Kathleen R. McKeown. *Simfinder: A flexible clustering tool for summarization.* In *Proceedings of the Workshop on Summarization in NAACL-01.* 2001.

Hatzivassiloglou, Vasileios and Kathleen R. McKeown. *Predicting the semantic orientation of adjectives.* In *Proceedings of Annual Meeting of the Association for Computational Linguistics (ACL-1997).* 1997. doi:10.3115/976909.979640

Hatzivassiloglou, Vasileios and Janyce Wiebe. *Effects of adjective orientation and gradability on sentence subjectivity.* In *Proceedings of Interntional Conference on Computational Linguistics (COLING-2000).* 2000. doi:10.3115/990820.990864

He, Yulan. *Learning sentiment classification model from labeled features.* In *Proceeding of the ACM conference on Information and knowledge management (CIKM-2011).* 2010. doi:10.1145/1871 437.1871704

He, Yulan, Chenghua Lin, and Harith Alani. *Automatically extracting polarity-bearing topics for cross-domain sentiment classification.* In *Proceedings of the 49th Annual Meeting of the Association for Computational Linguistics (ACL-2011).* 2011.

Hearst, Marti. *Direction-based text interpretation as an information access refinement*, in *Text-Based Intelligent Systems*, P. Jacobs, Editor 1992, Lawrence Erlbaum Associates. pp. 257–274.

Hobbs, Jerry R. and Ellen Riloff. *Information Extraction*, in *Handbook of Natural Language Processing, 2nd Edition*, N. Indurkhya and F. J. Damerau, Eds. 2010, Chapman & Hall/CRC Press.

Hofmann, Thomas. *Probabilistic latent semantic indexing.* In *Proceedings of Conference on Uncertainty in Artificial Intelligence (UAI-1999).* 1999.

Hong, Yancheng and Steven Skiena. *The Wisdom of Bookies? Sentiment Analysis vs. the NFL Point Spread*. In *Proceedings of the International Conference on Weblogs and Social Media (ICWSM-2010)*. 2010.

Hu, Minqing and Bing Liu. *Mining and summarizing customer reviews*. In *Proceedings of ACM SIGKDD International Conference on Knowledge Discovery and Data Mining (KDD-2004)*. 2004. doi:10.1145/1014052.1014073

Hu, Nan, Paul A Pavlou, and Jennifer Zhang. *Can online reviews reveal a product's true quality?: empirical findings and analytical modeling of Online word-of-mouth communication*. In *Proceedings of Electronic Commerce (EC-2006)*. 2006.

Huang, Xuanjing and W. Bruce Croft. *A unified relevance model for opinion retrieval*. In *Proceedings of ACM Confernece on Information and Knowledge Management (CIKM-2009)*. 2009. doi:10.1145/1645953.1646075

Ikeda, Daisuke, Hiroya Takamura, Lev-Arie Ratinov, and Manabu Okumura. *Learning to shift the polarity of words for sentiment classification*. In *Proceedings of the 3rd International Joint Conference on Natural Language Processing (IJCNLP-2008)*. 2008.

Indurkhya, Nitin and Fred J. Damerau. *Handbook of Natural Language Processing*, 2010: Second Edition, Chapman & Hall.

Jakob, Niklas and Iryna Gurevych. *Extracting Opinion Targets in a Single-and Cross-Domain Setting with Conditional Random Fields*. In *Proceedings of Conference on Empirical Methods in Natural Language Processing (EMNLP-2010)*. 2010.

Jia, Lifeng, Clement Yu, and Weiyi Meng. *The effect of negation on sentiment analysis and retrieval effectiveness*. In *Proceeding of the 18th ACM Conference on Information and Knowledge Management (CIKM-2009)*. 2009. doi:10.1145/1645953.1646241

Jiang, Jay J. and David W. Conrath. *Semantic similarity based on corpus statistics and lexical taxonomy*. In *Proceedings of Research in Computational Linguistics*. 1997.

Jiang, Long, Mo Yu, Ming Zhou, Xiaohua Liu, and Tiejun Zhao. *Target-dependent twitter sentiment classification*. In *Proceedings of the 49th Annual Meeting of the Association for Computational Linguistics (ACL-2011)*. 2011.

Jijkoun, Valentin , Maarten de Rijke, and Wouter Weerkamp. *Generating Focused Topic-Specific Sentiment Lexicons*. In *Proceedings of Annual Meeting of the Association for Computational Linguistics (ACL-2010)*. 2010.

Jin, Wei and Hung Hay Ho. *A novel lexicalized HMM-based learning framework for web opinion mining*. In *Proceedings of International Conference on Machine Learning (ICML-2009)*. 2009. doi:10.1145/1553374.1553435

Jindal, Nitin and Bing Liu. *Identifying comparative sentences in text documents*. In *Proceedings of ACM SIGIR Conf. on Research and Development in Information Retrieval (SIGIR-2006)*. 2006a. doi: 10.1145/1148170.1148215

Jindal, Nitin and Bing Liu. *Mining comparative sentences and relations.* In *Proceedings of National Conf. on Artificial Intelligence (AAAI-2006).* 2006b.

Jindal, Nitin and Bing Liu. *Opinion spam and analysis.* In *Proceedings of the Conference on Web Search and Web Data Mining (WSDM-2008).* 2008. doi:10.1145/1341531.1341560

Jindal, Nitin and Bing Liu. *Review spam detection.* In *Proceedings of WWW (Poster paper).* 2007. doi:10.1145/1242572.1242759

Jindal, Nitin, Bing Liu, and Ee-Peng Lim. *Finding Unusual Review Patterns Using Unexpected Rules.* In *Proceedings of ACM International Conference on Information and Knowledge Management (CIKM-2010).* 2010. doi:10.1145/1871437.1871669

Jo, Yohan and Alice Oh. *Aspect and sentiment unification model for online review analysis.* In *Proceedings of ACM Conference on Web Search and Data Mining (WSDM-2011).* 2011. doi:10.1145/1935826.1935932

Joachims, Thorsten. *Making large-Scale SVM Learning Practical,* in *Advances in Kernel Methods - Support Vector Learning,* B. Schölkopf, C. Burges, and A. Smola, Eds. 1999, MIT press.

Johansson, Richard and Alessandro Moschitti. *Reranking models in fine-grained opinion analysis.* In *Proceedings of the International Conference on Computational Linguistics (COLING-2010).* 2010.

Joshi, Mahesh, Dipanjan Das, Kevin Gimpel, and Noah A. Smith. *Movie reviews and revenues: An experiment in text regression.* In *Proceedings of the North American Chapter of the Association for Computational Linguistics Human Language Technologies Conference (NAACL 2010).* 2010.

Kaji, Nobuhiro and Masaru Kitsuregawa. *Automatic construction of polarity-tagged corpus from HTML documents.* In *Proceedings of COLING/ACL 2006 Main Conference Poster Sessions (COLING-ACL-2006).* 2006. doi:10.3115/1273073.1273132

Kaji, Nobuhiro and Masaru Kitsuregawa. *Building lexicon for sentiment analysis from massive collection of HTML documents.* In *Proceedings of the Joint Conference on Empirical Methods in Natural Language Processing and Computational Natural Language Learning (EMNLP-2007).* 2007.

Kamps, Jaap, Maarten Marx, Robert J. Mokken, and Maarten De Rijke. *Using WordNet to measure semantic orientation of adjectives.* In *Proceedings of LREC-2004.* 2004.

Kanayama, Hiroshi and Tetsuya Nasukawa. *Fully automatic lexicon expansion for domain-oriented sentiment analysis.* In *Proceedings of Conference on Empirical Methods in Natural Language Processing (EMNLP-2006).* 2006. doi:10.3115/1610075.1610125

Kennedy, Alistair and Diana Inkpen. *Sentiment classification of movie reviews using contextual valence shifters. Computational Intelligence,* 2006. **22**(2): pp. 110–125. doi:10.1111/j.1467-8640.2006.00277.x

Kennedy, Christopher. *Comparatives, Semantics of,* in *Encyclopedia of Language and Linguistics,* Second Edition, 2005, Elsevier.

Kessler, Jason S. and Nicolas Nicolov. *Targeting sentiment expressions through supervised ranking of linguistic configurations.* In *Proceedings of the Third International AAAI Conference on Weblogs and Social Media (ICWSM-2009).* 2009.

Kim, Hyun Duk and ChengXiang Zhai. *Generating comparative summaries of contradictory opinions in text.* In *Proceedings of ACM Conference on Information and Knowledge Management (CIKM-2009).* 2009. doi:10.1145/1645953.1646004

Kim, Jungi Kim, Jin-Ji Li, and Jong-Hyeok Lee. *Evaluating multilanguage-comparability of subjectivity analysis systems.* In *Proceedings of the 48th Annual Meeting of the Association for Computational Linguistics (ACL-2010).* 2010.

Kim, Jungi, Jin-Ji Li, and Jong-Hyeok Lee. *Discovering the discriminative views: Measuring term weights for sentiment analysis.* In *Proceedings of the 47th Annual Meeting of the ACL and the 4th IJCNLP of the AFNLP (ACL-2009).* 2009.

Kim, Soo-Min and Eduard Hovy. *Automatic identification of pro and con reasons in online reviews.* In *Proceedings of COLING/ACL 2006 Main Conference Poster Sessions (ACL-2006).* 2006. doi:10.3115/1273073.1273136

Kim, Soo-Min and Eduard Hovy. *Crystal: Analyzing predictive opinions on the web.* In *Proceedings of the Joint Conference on Empirical Methods in Natural Language Processing and Computational Natural Language Learning (EMNLP/CoNLL-2007).* 2007.

Kim, Soo-Min and Eduard Hovy. *Determining the sentiment of opinions.* In *Proceedings of Interntional Conference on Computational Linguistics (COLING-2004).* 2004. doi:10.3115/1220355.1220555

Kim, Soo-Min and Eduard Hovy. *Extracting opinions, opinion holders, and topics expressed in online news media text.* In *Proceedings of the Conference on Empirical Methods in Natural Language Processing (EMNLP-2006).* 2006.

Kim, Soo-Min and Eduard Hovy. *Identifying and analyzing judgment opinions.* In *Proceedings of Human Language Technology Conference of the North American Chapter of the ACL.* 2006. doi:10.3115/1220835.1220861

Kim, Soo-Min, Patrick Pantel, Tim Chklovski, and Marco Pennacchiotti. *Automatically assessing review helpfulness.* In *Proceedings of the Conference on Empirical Methods in Natural Language Processing (EMNLP-2006).* 2006. doi:10.3115/1610075.1610135

Kleinberg, Jon M. *Authoritative sources in a hyperlinked environment. Journal of the ACM (JACM),* 1999. **46**(5): pp. 604–632. doi:10.1145/324133.324140

Kobayashi, Nozomi, Ryu Iida, Kentaro Inui, and Yuji Matsumoto. *Opinion mining on the Web by extracting subject-attribute-value relations.* In *Proceedings of AAAI-CAAW'06.* 2006.

Kobayashi, Nozomi, Kentaro Inui, and Yuji Matsumoto. *Extracting aspect-evaluation and aspect-of relations in opinion mining.* In *Proceedings of the 2007 Joint Conference on Empirical Methods in Natural Language Processing and Computational Natural Language Learning.* 2007.

Kouloumpis, Efthymios, Theresa Wilson, and Johanna Moore. *Twitter Sentiment Analysis: The Good the Bad and the OMG!* in *Proceedings of the Fifth International AAAI Conference on Weblogs and Social Media (ICWSM-2011).* 2011.

Kovelamudi, Sudheer, Sethu Ramalingam, Arpit Sood, and Vasudeva Varma. *Domain Independent Model for Product Attribute Extraction from User Reviews using Wikipedia.* In *Proceedings of the 5th International Joint Conference on Natural Language Processing (IJCNLP-2010).* 2011.

Kreuz, Roger J. and Gina M. Caucci. *Lexical influences on the perception of sarcasm.* In *Proceedings of the Workshop on Computational Approaches to Figurative Language.* 2007. doi:10.3115/1611528.1611529

Kreuz, Roger J. and Sam Glucksberg. *How to be sarcastic: The echoic reminder theory of verbal irony.* Journal of Experimental Psychology: General, 1989. **118**(4): p. 374. doi:10.1037//0096-3445.118.4.374

Ku, Lun-Wei, Yu-Ting Liang, and Hsin-Hsi Chen. *Opinion extraction, summarization and tracking in news and blog corpora.* In *Proceedings of AAAI-CAAW'06.* 2006.

Lafferty, John, Andrew McCallum, and Fernando Pereira. *Conditional random fields: Probabilistic models for segmenting and labeling sequence data.* In *Proceedings of International Conference on Machine Learning (ICML-2001).* 2001.

Lakkaraju, Himabindu, Chiranjib Bhattacharyya, Indrajit Bhattacharya, and Srujana Merugu. *Exploiting Coherence for the Simultaneous Discovery of Latent Facets and associated Sentiments.* In *Proceedings of SIAM Conference on Data Mining (SDM-2011).* 2011.

Lappas, Theodoros and Dimitrios Gunopulos. *Efficient confident search in large review corpora.* In *Proceedings of ECML-PKDD 2010.* 2010. doi:10.1007/978-3-642-15883-4_13

Lee, Lillian. *Measures of distributional similarity.* In *Proceedings of Annual Meeting of the Association for Computational Linguistics (ACL-1999).* 1999. doi:10.3115/1034678.1034693

Lerman, Kevin, Sasha Blair-Goldensohn, and Ryan McDonald. *Sentiment summarization: Evaluating and learning user preferences.* In *Proceedings of the 12th Conference of the European Chapter of the Association for Computational Linguistics (EACL-2009).* 2009.

Lerman, Kevin and Ryan McDonald. *Contrastive summarization: an experiment with consumer reviews.* In *Proceedings of NAACL HLT 2009: Short Papers.* 2009.

Li, Binyang, Lanjun Zhou, Shi Feng, and Kam-Fai Wong. *A Unified Graph Model for Sentence-Based Opinion Retrieval.* In *Proceedings of Annual Meeting of the Association for Computational Linguistics (ACL-2010).* 2010.

Li, Fangtao, Chao Han, Minlie Huang, Xiaoyan Zhu, Ying-Ju Xia, Shu Zhang, and Hao Yu. *Structure-aware review mining and summarization.* In *Proceedings of the 23rd International Conference on Computational Linguistics (COLING-2010).* 2010.

Li, Fangtao, Minlie Huang, Yi Yang, and Xiaoyan Zhu. *Learning to Identify Review Spam.* In *Proceedings of the International Joint Conference on Artificial Intelligence (IJCAI-2011).* 2011.

Li, Fangtao, Minlie Huang, and Xiaoyan Zhu. *Sentiment analysis with global topics and local dependency.* In *Proceedings of the Twenty-Fourth AAAI Conference on Artificial Intelligence (AAAI-2010)*. 2010.

Li, Junhui, Guodong Zhou, Hongling Wang, and Qiaoming Zhu. *Learning the scope of negation via shallow semantic parsing.* In *Proceedings of the 23rd International Conference on Computational Linguistics (COLING-2010)*. 2010.

Li, Shasha, Chin-Yew Lin, Young-In Song, and Zhoujun Li. *Comparable entity mining from comparative questions.* In *Proceedings of Annual Meeting of the Association for Computational Linguistics (ACL-2010)*. 2010.

Li, Shoushan, Chu-Ren Huang, Guodong Zhou, and Sophia Yat Mei Lee. *Employing Personal/Impersonal Views in Supervised and Semi-Supervised Sentiment Classification.* In *Proceedings of Annual Meeting of the Association for Computational Linguistics (ACL-2010)*. 2010.

Li, Shoushan, Sophia Yat Mei Lee, Ying Chen, Chu-Ren Huang, and Guodong Zhou. *Sentiment classification and polarity shifting.* In *Proceedings of the 23rd International Conference on Computational Linguistics (COLING-2010)*. 2010.

Li, Shoushan, Zhongqing Wang, Guodong Zhou, and Sophia Yat Mei Lee. *Semi-Supervised Learning for Imbalanced Sentiment Classification.* In *Proceedings of International Joint Conference on Artificial Intelligence (IJCAI-2011)*. 2011.

Li, Tao, Yi Zhang, and Vikas Sindhwani. *A non-negative matrix tri-factorization approach to sentiment classification with lexical prior knowledge.* In *Proceedings of the Annual Meeting of the Association for Computational Linguistics (ACL-2009)*. 2009. doi:10.3115/1687878.1687914

Li, Xiao-Li, Lei Zhang, Bing Liu, and See-Kiong Ng. *Distributional similarity vs. PU learning for entity set expansion.* In *Proceedings of Annual Meeting of the Association for Computational Linguistics (ACL-2010)*. 2010.

Lim, Ee-Peng, Viet-An Nguyen, Nitin Jindal, Bing Liu, and Hady W. Lauw. *Detecting Product Review Spammers using Rating Behaviors.* In *Proceedings of ACM International Conference on Information and Knowledge Management (CIKM-2010)*. 2010. doi:10.1145/1871437.1871557

Lin, Chenghua and Yulan He. *Joint sentiment/topic model for sentiment analysis.* In *Proceedings of ACM International Conference on Information and Knowledge Management (CIKM-2009)*. 2009. doi:10.1145/1645953.1646003

Lin, Dekang. *Automatic retrieval and clustering of similar words.* In *Proccedings of 36th Annual Meeting of the Association for Computational Linguistics and 17th International Conference on Computational Linguistics (COLING-ACL-1998)*. 1998. doi:10.3115/980691.980696

Lin, Dekang. *Minipar.* http://webdocs.cs.ualberta.ca/lindek/minipar.htm. 2007.

Lin, Wei-Hao, Theresa Wilson, Janyce Wiebe, and Alexander Hauptmann. *Which side are you on?:*

Identifying perspectives at the document and sentence levels. In *Proceedings of the Conference on Natural Language Learning (CoNLL-2006).* 2006.

Liu, Bing. *Sentiment Analysis and Subjectivity,* in *Handbook of Natural Language Processing, Second Edition,* N. Indurkhya and F.J. Damerau, Eds. 2010.

Liu, Bing. *Web Data Mining: Exploring Hyperlinks, Contents, and Usage Data,* 2006 and 2011: Springer. doi:10.1007/978-3-642-19460-3_12

Liu, Bing, Wynne Hsu, and Yiming Ma. *Integrating classification and association rule mining.* In *Proceedings of International Conference on Knowledge Discovery and Data Mining (KDD-1998).* 1998.

Liu, Bing, Minqing Hu, and Junsheng Cheng. *Opinion observer: Analyzing and comparing opinions on the web.* In *Proceedings of International Conference on World Wide Web (WWW-2005).* 2005.

Liu, Bing, Wee Sun Lee, Philip S. Yu, and Xiao-Li Li. *Partially supervised classification of text documents.* In *Proceedings of International Conference on Machine Learning (ICML-2002).* 2002.

Liu, Feifan, Bin Li, and Yang Liu. *Finding Opinionated Blogs Using Statistical Classifiers and Lexical Features.* In *Proceedings of the Third International AAAI Conference on Weblogs and Social Media (ICWSM-2009).* 2009.

Liu, Feifan, Dong Wang, Bin Li, and Yang Liu. *Improving blog polarity classification via topic analysis and adaptive methods.* In *Proceedings of Human Language Technologies: The 2010 Annual Conference of the North American Chapter of the ACL (HLT-NAACL-2010).* 2010.

Liu, Jingjing, Yunbo Cao, Chin-Yew Lin, Yalou Huang, and Ming Zhou. *Low-quality product review detection in opinion summarization.* In *Proceedings of the Joint Conference on Empirical Methods in Natural Language Processing and Computational Natural Language Learning (EMNLP-CoNLL-2007).* 2007.

Liu, Jingjing and Stephanie Seneff. *Review sentiment scoring via a parse-and-paraphrase paradigm.* In *Proceedings of the 2009 Conference on Empirical Methods in Natural Language Processing (EMNLP-2009).* 2009. doi:10.3115/1699510.1699532

Liu, Yang, Xiangji Huang, Aijun An, and Xiaohui Yu. *ARSA: a sentiment-aware model for predicting sales performance using blogs.* In *Proceedings of ACM SIGIR Conf. on Research and Development in Information Retrieval (SIGIR-2007).* 2007.

Liu, Yang, Xiangji Huang, Aijun An, and Xiaohui Yu. *Modeling and predicting the helpfulness of online reviews.* In *Proceedings of ICDM-2008.* 2008. doi:10.1109/ICDM.2008.94

Long, Chong, Jie Zhang, and Xiaoyan Zhu. *A review selection approach for accurate feature rating estimation.* In *Proceedings of Coling 2010: Poster Volume.* 2010.

Lu, Bin. *Identifying opinion holders and targets with dependency parser in Chinese news texts.* In *Proceedings of Human Language Technologies: The 2010 Annual Conference of the North American Chapter of the ACL (HLT-NAACL-2010).* 2010.

Lu, Bin, Chenhao Tan, Claire Cardie, and Benjamin K. Tsou. *Joint bilingual sentiment classification with unlabeled parallel corpora.* In *Proceedings of the 49th Annual Meeting of the Association for Computational Linguistics (ACL-2011).* 2011.

Lu, Yue, Malu Castellanos, Umeshwar Dayal, and ChengXiang Zhai. *Automatic construction of a context-aware sentiment lexicon: an optimization approach.* In *Proceedings of the 20th International Conference on World wide Web (WWW-2011).* 2011.

Lu, Yue, Huizhong Duan, Hongning Wang, and ChengXiang Zhai. *Exploiting Structured Ontology to Organize Scattered Online Opinions.* In *Proceedings of Interntional Conference on Computational Linguistics (COLING-2010).* 2010.

Lu, Yue, Panayiotis Tsaparas, Alexandros Ntoulas, and Livia Polanyi. *Exploiting social context for review quality prediction.* In *Proceedings of International World Wide Web Confernece (WWW-2010).* 2010. doi:10.1145/1772690.1772761

Lu, Yue and ChengXiang Zhai. *Opinion integration through semi-supervised topic modeling.* In *Proceedings of International Conference on World Wide Web (WWW-2008).* 2008. doi:10.1145/136 7497.1367514

Lu, Yue, ChengXiang Zhai, and Neel Sundaresan. *Rated aspect summarization of short comments.* In *Proceedings of International Conference on World Wide Web (WWW-2009).* 2009. doi:10.1145/ 1526709.1526728

Ma, Tengfei and Xiaojun Wan. *Opinion target extraction in Chinese news comments.* In *Proceedings of Coling 2010 Poster Volume (COLING-2010).* 2010.

Maas, Andrew L., Raymond E. Daly, Peter T. Pham, Dan Huang, Andrew Y. Ng, and Christopher Potts. *Learning word vectors for sentiment analysis.* In *Proceedings of the 49th Annual Meeting of the Association for Computational Linguistics (ACL-2011).* 2011.

Macdonald, Craig, Iadh Ounis, and Ian Soboroff. *Overview of the TREC 2007 blog track.* 2007.

Manevitz, Larry M. and Malik Yousef. *One-class SVMs for document classification. The Journal of Machine Learning Research,* 2002. **2**: pp. 139–154.

Manning, Christopher D., Prabhakar Raghavan, and Hinrich Schutze. *Introduction to information retrieval.* Vol. 1. 2008: Cambridge University Press.

Manning, Christopher D. and Hinrich Schutze. *Foundations of statistical natural language processing.* Vol. 999. 1999: MIT Press.

Martineau, Justin and Tim Finin. *Delta tfidf: An improved feature space for sentiment analysis.* In *Proceedings of the Third International AAAI Conference on Weblogs and Social Media (ICWSM-2009).* 2009.

McDonald, Ryan, Kerry Hannan, Tyler Neylon, Mike Wells, and Jeff Reynar. *Structured models for fine-to-coarse sentiment analysis.* In *Proceedings of Annual Meeting of the Association for Computational Linguistics (ACL-2007).* 2007.

McGlohon, Mary, Natalie Glance, and Zach Reiter. *Star quality: Aggregating reviews to rank products and merchants*. In *Proceedings of the International Conference on Weblogs and Social Media (ICWSM-2010)*. 2010.

Medlock, Ben and Ted Briscoe. *Weakly supervised learning for hedge classification in scientific literature*. In *Proceedings of the 45th Annual Meeting of the Association of Computational Linguistics*. 2007.

Mei, Qiaozhu, Xu Ling, Matthew Wondra, Hang Su, and ChengXiang Zhai. *Topic sentiment mixture: modeling facets and opinions in weblogs*. In *Proceedings of International Conference on World Wide Web (WWW-2007)*. 2007.

Mejova, Yelena and Padmini Srinivasan. *Exploring Feature Definition and Selection for Sentiment Classifiers*. In *Proceedings of the Fifth International AAAI Conference on Weblogs and Social Media (ICWSM-2011)*. 2011.

Meng, Xinfan and Houfeng Wang. *Mining user reviews: from specification to summarization*. In *Proceedings of the ACL-IJCNLP 2009 Conference Short Papers*. 2009.

Mihalcea, Rada, Carmen Banea, and Janyce Wiebe. *Learning multilingual subjective language via cross-lingual projections*. In *Proceedings of the Annual Meeting of the Association for Computational Linguistics (ACL-2007)*. 2007.

Mihalcea, Rada and Carlo Strapparava. *The lie detector: Explorations in the automatic recognition of deceptive language*. In *Proceedings of the ACL-IJCNLP 2009 Conference Short Papers*. 2009.

Miller, George A., Richard Beckwith, Christiane Fellbaum, Derek Gross, and Katherine Miller. *WordNet: An on-line lexical database*. 1990: Oxford University Press. doi:10.1093/ijl/3.4.235

Miller, Mahalia, Conal Sathi, Daniel Wiesenthal, Jure Leskovec, and Christopher Potts. *Sentiment Flow Through Hyperlink Networks*. In *Proceedings of the Fifth International AAAI Conference on Weblogs and Social Media (ICWSM-2011)*. 2011.

Min, Hye-Jin and Jong C. Park. *Detecting and Blocking False Sentiment Propagation*. In *Proceedings of the 5th International Joint Conference on Natural Language Processing (IJCNLP-2010)*. 2011.

Mitchell, Tom. *Machine learning*. 1997: McGraw Hill.

Moghaddam, Samaneh and Martin Ester. *ILDA: interdependent LDA model for learning latent aspects and their ratings from online product reviews*. In *Proceedings of the Annual ACM SIGIR International conference on Research and Development in Information Retrieval (SIGIR-2011)*. 2011.

Moghaddam, Samaneh and Martin Ester. *Opinion digger: an unsupervised opinion miner from unstructured product reviews*. In *Proceeding of the ACM Conference on Information and Knowledge Management (CIKM-2010)*. 2010.

Moghaddam, Samaneh, Mohsen Jamali, and Martin Ester. *ETF: extended tensor factorization model for personalizing prediction of review helpfulness*. In *Proceedings of ACM International Conference on Web Search and Data Mining (WSDM-2012)*. 2012.

Mohammad, Saif. *From Once Upon a Time to Happily Ever After: Tracking Emotions in Novels and Fairy Tales*. In *Proceedings of the ACL 2011 Workshop on Language Technology for Cultural Heritage, Social Sciences, and Humanities (LaTeCH)*. 2011.

Mohammad, Saif and Tony Yang. *Tracking Sentiment in Mail: How Genders Differ on Emotional Axes*. In *Proceedings of the ACL Workshop on ACL 2011 Workshop on Computational Approaches to Subjectivity and Sentiment Analysis (WASSA-2011)*. 2011.

Mohammad, Saif, Cody Dunne, and Bonnie Dorr. *Generating high-coverage semantic orientation lexicons from overtly marked words and a thesaurus*. In *Proceedings of the 2009 Conference on Empirical Methods in Natural Language Processing (EMNLP-2009)*. 2009. doi:10.3115/1699571.1699591

Mohammad, Saif and Graeme Hirst. *Distributional measures of concept-distance: A task-oriented evaluation*. In *Proceedings of the Conference on Empirical Methods in Natural Language Processing (EMNLP-2006)*. 2006.

Mohammad, Saif M. and Peter D. Turney. *Emotions evoked by common words and phrases: Using mechanical turk to create an emotion lexicon*. In *Proceedings of the NAACL HLT 2010 Workshop on Computational Approaches to Analysis and Generation of Emotion in Text*. 2010.

Moilanen, Karo and Stephen Pulman. *Sentiment composition*. In *Proceedings of Recent Advances in Natural Language Processing (RANLP 2007)*. 2007.

Montague, Richard. *Formal philosophy; selected papers of Richard Montague,* 1974: Yale University Press.

Mooney, Raymond J. and Razvan Bunescu. *Mining knowledge from text using information extraction. ACM SIGKDD Explorations Newsletter,* 2005. **7**(1): pp. 3–10. doi:10.1145/1089815.1089817

Morante, Roser, Sarah Schrauwen, and Walter Daelemans. *Corpus-based approaches to processing the scope of negation cues: an evaluation of the state of the art.* In *Proceedings of the Ninth International Conference on Computational Semantics (IWCS-2011)*. 2011.

Morinaga, Satoshi, Kenji Yamanishi, Kenji Tateishi, and Toshikazu Fukushima. *Mining product reputations on the web*. In *Proceedings of ACM SIGKDD International Conference on Knowledge Discovery and Data Mining (KDD-2002)*. 2002. doi:10.1145/775094.775098

Mukherjee, Arjun and Bing Liu. *Aspect Extraction through Semi-Supervised Modeling*. In *Proceedings of 50th Anunal Meeting of Association for Computational Linguistics (ACL-2012) (Accepted for publication)*. 2012.

Mukherjee, Arjun and Bing Liu. *Modeling Review Comments*. In *Proceedings of 50th Anunal Meeting of Association for Computational Linguistics (ACL-2012) (Accepted for publication)*. 2012.

Mukherjee, Arjun, Bing Liu, and Natalie Glance. *Spotting Fake Reviewer Groups in Consumer Reviews*. In *Proceedings of International World Web Conference (WWW-2012)*. 2012. doi:10.1145/2187836.2187863

Mukherjee, Arjun, Bing Liu, Junhui Wang, Natalie Glance, and Nitin Jindal. *Detecting Group Review Spam*. In *Proceedings of International Conference on World Wide Web (WWW-2011, poster paper)*. 2011. doi:10.1145/1963192.1963240

Mukund, Smruthi and Rohini K. Srihari. *A vector space model for subjectivity classification in Urdu aided by co-training*. In *Proceedings of Coling 2010: Poster Volume*. 2010.

Mullen, Tony and Nigel Collier. *Sentiment analysis using support vector machines with diverse information sources*. In *Proceedings of EMNLP-2004*. 2004.

Murakami, Akiko and Rudy Raymond. *Support or oppose?: classifying positions in online debates from reply activities and opinion expressions*. In *Proceedings of Coling 2010: Poster Volume*. 2010.

Na, Seung-Hoon, Yeha Lee, Sang-Hyob Nam, and Jong-Hyeok Lee. *Improving opinion retrieval based on query-specific sentiment lexicon*. *Advances in Information Retrieval*, 2009: pp. 734–738. doi:10.1007/978-3-642-00958-7_76

Nakagawa, Tetsuji, Kentaro Inui, and Sadao Kurohashi. *Dependency tree-based sentiment classification using CRFs with hidden variables*. In *Proceedings of Human Language Technologies: The 2010 Annual Conference of the North American Chapter of the ACL (HAACL-2010)*. 2010.

Narayanan, Ramanathan, Bing Liu, and Alok Choudhary. *Sentiment analysis of conditional sentences*. In *Proceedings of Conference on Empirical Methods in Natural Language Processing (EMNLP-2009)*. 2009. doi:10.3115/1699510.1699534

Nasukawa, Tetsuya and Jeonghee Yi. *Sentiment analysis: Capturing favorability using natural language processing*. In *Proceedings of the K-CAP-03, 2nd International Conference on Knowledge Capture*. 2003.

Neviarouskaya, Alena, Helmut Prendinger, and Mitsuru Ishizuka. *Compositionality principle in recognition of fine-grained emotions from text*. In *Proceedings of Third International Conference on Weblogs and Social Media (ICWSM-2009)*. 2009.

Neviarouskaya, Alena, Helmut Prendinger, and Mitsuru Ishizuka. *Recognition of affect, judgment, and appreciation in text*. In *Proceedings of the 23rd International Conference on Computational Linguistics (COLING-2010)*. 2010.

Newman, Matthew L., James W. Pennebaker, Diane S. Berry, and Jane M. Richards. *Lying words: Predicting deception from linguistic styles*. *Personality and Social Psychology Bulletin*, 2003. **29**(5): p. 665. doi:10.1177/0146167203029005010

Ng, Vincent and Claire Cardie. *Improving machine learning approaches to coreference resolution*. In *Proceedings of the Annual Meeting of the Association for Computational Linguistics (ACL-2002)*. 2002. doi:10.3115/1073083.1073102

Ng, Vincent, Sajib Dasgupta, and S. M. Niaz Arifin. *Examining the role of linguistic knowledge sources in the automatic identification and classification of reviews*. In *Proceedings of COLING/ACL 2006 Main Conference Poster Sessions (COLING/ACL-2006)*. 2006. doi:10.3115/1273073.1273152

Nigam, Kamal and Matthew Hurst. *Towards a robust metric of opinion.* In *Proceedings of AAAI Spring Symp. on Exploring Attitude and Affect in Text.* 2004.

Nigam, Kamal, Andrew K. McCallum, Sebastian Thrun, and Tom Mitchell. *Text classification from labeled and unlabeled documents using EM. Machine Learning*, 2000. **39**(2): pp. 103–134. doi:10.1023/A:1007692713085

Nishikawa, Hitoshi, Takaaki Hasegawa, Yoshihiro Matsuo, and Genichiro Kikui. *Opinion summarization with integer linear programming formulation for sentence extraction and ordering.* In *Proceedings of Coling 2010: Poster Volume.* 2010a.

Nishikawa, Hitoshi, Takaaki Hasegawa, Yoshihiro Matsuo, and Genichiro Kikui. *Optimizing informativeness and readability for sentiment summarization.* In *Proceedings of Annual Meeting of the Association for Computational Linguistics (ACL-2010).* 2010b.

O'Connor, Brendan, Ramnath Balasubramanyan, Bryan R. Routledge, and Noah A. Smith. *From Tweets to Polls: Linking Text Sentiment to Public Opinion Time Series.* In *Proceedings of the International AAAI Conference on Weblogs and Social Media (ICWSM 2010).* 2010.

O'Mahony, Michael P. and Barry Smyth. *Learning to recommend helpful hotel reviews.* In *Proceedings of the third ACM Conference on Recommender Systems.* 2009.

Ott, Myle, Yejin Choi, Claire Cardie, and Jeffrey T. Hancock. *Finding deceptive opinion spam by any stretch of the imagination.* In *Proceedings of the 49th Annual Meeting of the Association for Computational Linguistics (ACL-2011).* 2011.

Ounis, Iadh, Craig Macdonald, Maarten de Rijke, Gilad Mishne, and Ian Soboroff. *Overview of the TREC-2006 blog track.* In *Proceedings of the Fifteenth Text REtrieval Conference (TREC-2006).* 2006.

Ounis, Iadh, Craig Macdonald, and Ian Soboroff. *Overview of the TREC-2008 blog track.* In *In Proceedings of the 16th Text Retrieval Conference (TREC-2008).* 2008.

Page, Lawrence, Sergey Brin, Rajeev Motwani, and Terry Winograd. *The PageRank citation ranking: Bringing order to the web.* 1999.

Paltoglou, Georgios and Mike Thelwall. *A study of information retrieval weighting schemes for sentiment analysis.* In *Proceedings of the 48th Annual Meeting of the Association for Computational Linguistics (ACL-2010).* 2010.

Pan, Sinno Jialin, Xiaochuan Ni, Jian-Tao Sun, Qiang Yang, and Zheng Chen. *Cross-domain sentiment classification via spectral feature alignment.* In *Proceedings of International Conference on World Wide Web (WWW-2010).* 2010. doi:10.1145/1772690.1772767

Pang, Bo and Lillian Lee. *Opinion mining and sentiment analysis. Foundations and Trends in Information Retrieval*, 2008. **2**(1–2): pp. 1–135. doi:10.1561/1500000011

Pang, Bo and Lillian Lee. *Seeing stars: Exploiting class relationships for sentiment categorization with respect to rating scales.* In *Proceedings of Meeting of the Association for Computational Linguistics (ACL-2005).* 2005.

Pang, Bo and Lillian Lee. *A sentimental education: Sentiment analysis using subjectivity summarization based on minimum cuts.* In *Proceedings of Meeting of the Association for Computational Linguistics (ACL-2004).* 2004.

Pang, Bo and Lillian Lee. *Using Very Simple Statistics for Review Search: An Exploration.* In *Proceedings of International Conference on Computational Linguistics, poster paper (COLING-2008).* 2008.

Pang, Bo, Lillian Lee, and Shivakumar Vaithyanathan. *Thumbs up?: sentiment classification using machine learning techniques.* In *Proceedings of Conference on Empirical Methods in Natural Language Processing (EMNLP-2002).* 2002.

Pantel, Patrick, Eric Crestan, Arkady Borkovsky, Ana-Maria Popescu, and Vishnu Vyas. *Web-scale distributional similarity and entity set expansion.* In *Proceedings of Conference on Empirical Methods in Natural Language Processing (EMNLP-2009).* 2009. doi:10.3115/1699571.1699635

Park, Do-Hyung, Jumin Lee, and Ingoo Han. *The effect of on-line consumer reviews on consumer purchasing intention: The moderating role of involvement. International Journal of Electronic Commerce,* 2007. **11**(4): pp. 125–148. doi:10.2753/JEC1086-4415110405

Park, Souneil, KyungSoon Lee, and Junehwa Song. *Contrasting opposing views of news articles on contentious issues.* In *Proceedings of the 49th Annual Meeting of the Association for Computational Linguistics (ACL-2011).* 2011.

Parrott, W. Gerrod. *Emotions in social psychology: Essential readings.* 2001: Psychology Press.

Paul, Michael J., ChengXiang Zhai, and Roxana Girju. *Summarizing Contrastive Viewpoints in Opinionated Text.* In *Proceedings of Conference on Empirical Methods in Natural Language Processing (EMNLP-2010).* 2010.

Peng, Wei and Dae Hoon Park. *Generate Adjective Sentiment Dictionary for Social Media Sentiment Analysis Using Constrained Nonnegative Matrix Factorization.* In *Proceedings of the Fifth International AAAI Conference on Weblogs and Social Media (ICWSM-2011).* 2011.

Pennebaker, James W., Cindy K. Chung, Molly Ireland, Amy Gonzales, and Roger J. Booth. *The development and psychometric properties of LIWC2007.* www.LIWC.Net, 2007.

Polanyi, Livia and Annie Zaenen. *Contextual valence shifters.* In *Proceedings of the AAAI Spring Symposium on Exploring Attitude and Affect in Text.* 2004.

Popescu, Ana-Maria and Oren Etzioni. *Extracting product features and opinions from reviews.* In *Proceedings of Conference on Empirical Methods in Natural Language Processing (EMNLP-2005).* 2005. doi:10.3115/1220575.1220618

Qiu, Guang, Bing Liu, Jiajun Bu, and Chun Chen. *Expanding domain sentiment lexicon through double propagation.* In *Proceedings of International Joint Conference on Artificial Intelligence (IJCAI-2009).* 2009.

Qiu, Guang, Bing Liu, Jiajun Bu, and Chun Chen. *Opinion Word Expansion and Target Extraction through Double Propagation. Computational Linguistics,* Vol. 37, No. 1: 9.27, 2011. doi:10.1162/coli_a_00034

Qiu, Likun, Weish Zhang, Changjian Hu, and Kai Zhao. *Selc: a self-supervised model for sentiment classification.* In *Proceeding of the 18th ACM conference on Information and knowledge management (CIKM-2009).* 2009.

Qu, Lizhen, Georgiana Ifrim, and Gerhard Weikum. *The Bag-of-Opinions Method for Review Rating Prediction from Sparse Text Patterns.* In *Proceedings of the International Conference on Computational Linguistics (COLING-2010).* 2010.

Quirk, Randolph, Sidney Greenbaum, Geoffrey Leech, and Jan Svartvik. *A comprehensive grammar of the English language.* Vol. 397. 1985: Cambridge University Press.

Raaijmakers, Stephan and Wessel Kraaij. *A shallow approach to subjectivity classification,* In *Proceedings of ICWSM-2008,* 2008. pp. 216–217.

Raaijmakers, Stephan, Khiet Truong, and Theresa Wilson. *Multimodal subjectivity analysis of multiparty conversation.* In *Proceedings of Conference on Empirical Methods in Natural Language Processing (EMNLP-2008).* 2008. doi:10.3115/1613715.1613774

Rabiner, Lawrence R. *A tutorial on hidden Markov models and selected applications in speech recognition.* Proceedings of the IEEE, 1989. **77**(2): pp. 257–286. doi:10.1109/5.18626

Radev, Dragomir R., Simone Teufel, Horacio Saggion, Wai Lam, John Blitzer, Hong Qi, Arda Celebi, Danyu Liu, and Elliott Drabek. *Evaluation challenges in large-scale document summarization.* In *Proceedings of the Annual Meeting of the Association for Computational Linguistics (ACL-2003).* 2003. doi:10.3115/1075096.1075144

Rao, Delip and Deepak Ravichandran. *Semi-supervised polarity lexicon induction.* In *Proceedings of the 12th Conference of the European Chapter of the ACL (EACL-2009).* 2009. doi:10.3115/1609067.1609142

Ravichandran, Deepak and Eduard Hovy. *Learning surface text patterns for a question answering system.* In *Proceedings of the Annual Meeting of the Association for Computational Linguistics (ACL-2002).* 2002.

Riloff, Ellen. *Automatically constructing a dictionary for information extraction tasks.* In *Processing of AAAI-2003.* 1993.

Riloff, Ellen. *Automatically generating extraction patterns from untagged text.* In *Proceedings of AAAI-1996.* 1996. doi:10.3115/1610075.1610137

Riloff, Ellen, Siddharth Patwardhan, and Janyce Wiebe. *Feature subsumption for opinion analysis.* In *Proceedings of the Conference on Empirical Methods in Natural Language Processing (EMNLP-2006).* 2006. doi:10.3115/1119355.1119369

Riloff, Ellen and Janyce Wiebe. *Learning extraction patterns for subjective expressions.* In *Proceedings of Conference on Empirical Methods in Natural Language Processing (EMNLP-2003).* 2003.

Ruppenhofer, Josef, Swapna Somasundaran, and Janyce Wiebe. *Finding the sources and targets of subjective expressions.* In *Proceedings of LREC.* 2008.

Sadikov, Eldar, Aditya Parameswaran, and Petros Venetis. *Blogs as predictors of movie success.* In *Proceedings of the Third International Conference on Weblogs and Social Media (ICWSM-2009).* 2009.

Sakunkoo, Patty and Nathan Sakunkoo. *Analysis of Social Influence in Online Book Reviews.* In *Proceedings of third International AAAI Conference on Weblogs and Social Media (ICWSM-2009).* 2009.

Santorini, Beatrice. *Part-of-speech tagging guidelines for the Penn Treebank Project,* 1990: University of Pennsylvania, School of Engineering and Applied Science, Dept. of Computer and Information Science.

Sarawagi, Sunita. *Information extraction.* Foundations and Trends in Databases, 2008. **1**(3): pp. 261–377.

Sauper, Christina, Aria Haghighi, and Regina Barzilay. *Content models with attitude.* In *Proceedings of the 49th Annual Meeting of the Association for Computational Linguistics (ACL-2011).* 2011.

Scaffidi, Christopher, Kevin Bierhoff, Eric Chang, Mikhael Felker, Herman Ng, and Chun Jin. *Red Opal: product-feature scoring from reviews.* In *Proceedings of Twelfth ACM Conference on Electronic Commerce (EC-2007).* 2007.

Schapire, Robert E. and Yoram Singer. *BoosTexter: A boosting-based system for text categorization.* Machine Learning, 2000. **39**(2): pp. 135–168. doi:10.1023/A:1007649029923

Seki, Yohei, Koji Eguchi, Noriko Kando, and Masaki Aono. *Opinion-focused summarization and its analysis at DUC 2006.* In *Proceedings of the Document Understanding Conference (DUC).* 2006.

Shanahan, James G., Yan Qu, and Janyce Wiebe. *Computing attitude and affect in text: theory and applications.* Vol. 20. 2006: Springer-Verlag, New York. doi:10.1007/1-4020-4102-0

Shawe-Taylor, John and Nello Cristianini. *Support Vector Machines,* 2000, Cambridge University Press.

Snyder, Benjamin and Regina Barzilay. *Multiple aspect ranking using the good grief algorithm.* In *Proceedings of the Conference of the North American Chapter of the Association for Computational Linguistics: Human Language Technologies (NAACL/HLT-2007).* 2007.

Socher, R., J. Pennington, E. H. Huang, A.Y. Ng, and C.D. Manning. *Semi-Supervised Recursive Autoencoders for Predicting Sentiment Distributions.* In *Proceedings of the Conference on Empirical Methods in Natural Language Processing (EMNLP-2011).* 2011.

Somasundaran, S., J. Ruppenhofer, and J. Wiebe. *Discourse level opinion relations: An annotation study.* In *Proceedings of the 9th SIGdial Workshop on Discourse and Dialogue.* 2008.

Somasundaran, Swapna, Galileo Namata, Lise Getoor, and Janyce Wiebe. *Opinion graphs for polarity and discourse classification.* In *Proceedings of the 2009 Workshop on Graph-based Methods for Natural Language Processing.* 2009. doi:10.3115/1708124.1708138

Somasundaran, Swapna and Janyce Wiebe. *Recognizing stances in online debates.* In *Proceedings of the 47th Annual Meeting of the ACL and the 4th IJCNLP of the AFNLP (ACL-IJCNLP-2009).* 2009.

Steyvers, Mark and Thomas L. Griffiths. *Probabilistic topic models. Handbook of latent semantic analysis*, 2007. **427**(7): pp. 424–440.

Stone, Philip. *The general inquirer: A computer approach to content analysis. Journal of Regional Science*, 1968. **8**(1).

Stoyanov, Veselin and Claire Cardie. *Partially supervised coreference resolution for opinion summarization through structured rule learning.* In *Proceedings of Conference on Empirical Methods in Natural Language Processing (EMNLP-2006)*. 2006.

Stoyanov, Veselin and Claire Cardie. *Topic identification for fine-grained opinion analysis.* In *Proceedings of the International Conference on Computational Linguistics (COLING-2008)*. 2008. doi:10.3115/1599081.1599184

Strapparava, Carlo and Alessandro Valitutti. *WordNet-Affect: an affective extension of WordNet.* In *Proceedings of the International Conference on Language Resources and Evaluation*. 2004.

Su, Fangzhong and Katja Markert. *From words to senses: a case study of subjectivity recognition.* In *Proceedings of the 22nd International Conference on Computational Linguistics (COLING-2008)*. 2008.

Su, Fangzhong and Katja Markert. *Word sense subjectivity for cross-lingual lexical substitution.* In *Proceedings of Human Language Technologies: The 2010 Annual Conference of the North American Chapter of the ACL (HLT-NAACL-2010)*. 2010.

Su, Qi, Xinying Xu, Honglei Guo, Zhili Guo, Xian Wu, Xiaoxun Zhang, Bin Swen, and Zhong Su. *Hidden sentiment association in chinese web opinion mining.* In *Proceedings of International Conference on World Wide Web (WWW-2008)*. 2008. doi:10.1145/1367497.1367627

Taboada, Maite, Julian Brooke, Milan Tofiloski, Kimberly Voll, and Manfred Stede. *Lexicon-based methods for sentiment analysis. Computational Linguistics*, 2011. **37**(2): pp. 267–307. doi:10.1162/COLI_a_00049

Täckström, Oscar and Ryan McDonald. *Discovering fine-grained sentiment with latent variable structured prediction models.* Advances in Information Retrieval, 2011: pp. 368–374. doi:10.1007/978-3-642-20161-5_37

Täckström, Oscar and Ryan McDonald. *Semi-supervised latent variable models for sentence-level sentiment analysis.* In *Proceedings of the 49th Annual Meeting of the Association for Computational Linguistics:shortpapers (ACL-2011)*. 2011.

Takamura, Hiroya, Takashi Inui, and Manabu Okumura. *Extracting semantic orientations of phrases from dictionary.* In *Proceedings of the Joint Human Language Technology/North American Chapter of the ACL Conference (HLT-NAACL-2007)*. 2007.

Takamura, Hiroya, Takashi Inui, and Manabu Okumura. *Extracting semantic orientations of words using spin model.* In *Proceedings of the Annual Meeting of the Association for Computational Linguistics (ACL-2005)*. 2005. doi:10.3115/1219840.1219857

Takamura, Hiroya, Takashi Inui, and Manabu Okumura. *Latent variable models for semantic orientations of phrases.* In *Proceedings of the Conference of the European Chapter of the Association for Computational Linguistics (EACL-2006).* 2006.

Tan, Songbo, Gaowei Wu, Huifeng Tang, and Xueqi Cheng. *A novel scheme for domain-transfer problem in the context of sentiment analysis.* In *Proceeding of the ACM conference on Information and knowledge management (CIKM-2007).* 2007. doi:10.1145/1321440.1321590

Tata, Swati and Barbara Di Eugenio. *Generating fine-grained reviews of songs from album reviews.* In *Proceedings of Annual Meeting of the Association for Computational Linguistics (ACL-2010).* 2010.

Tesniere, L. *Éléments de syntaxe structurale: Préf. de Jean Fourquet.* 1959: C. Klincksieck.

Titov, Ivan and Ryan McDonald. *A joint model of text and aspect ratings for sentiment summarization.* In *Proceedings of Annual Meeting of the Association for Computational Linguistics (ACL-2008).* 2008.

Titov, Ivan and Ryan McDonald. *Modeling online reviews with multi-grain topic models.* In *Proceedings of International Conference on World Wide Web (WWW-2008).* 2008. doi:10.1145/1367497.1367513

Tokuhisa, Ryoko, Kentaro Inui, and Yuji Matsumoto. *Emotion classification using massive examples extracted from the web.* In *Proceedings of the 22nd International Conference on Computational Linguistics (COLING-2008).* 2008. doi:10.3115/1599081.1599192

Tong, Richard M. *An operational system for detecting and tracking opinions in on-line discussion.* In *Proceedings of SIGIR Workshop on Operational Text Classification.* 2001.

Toprak, Cigdem, Niklas Jakob, and Iryna Gurevych. *Sentence and expression level annotation of opinions in user-generated discourse.* In *Proceedings of the 48th Annual Meeting of the Association for Computational Linguistics (ACL-2010).* 2010.

Tsaparas, Panayiotis, Alexandros Ntoulas, and Evimaria Terzi. *Selecting a Comprehensive Set of Reviews.* In *Proceedings of the ACM SIGKDD Conference on Knowledge Discovery and Data Mining (KDD-2011).* 2011. doi:10.1145/2020408.2020440

Tsur, Oren, Dmitry Davidov, and Ari Rappoport. *A Great Catchy Name: Semi-Supervised Recognition of Sarcastic Sentences in Online Product Reviews.* In *Proceedings of the Fourth International AAAI Conference on Weblogs and Social Media (ICWSM-2010).* 2010.

Tsur, Oren and Ari Rappoport. *Revrank: A fully unsupervised algorithm for selecting the most helpful book reviews.* In *Proceedings of the International AAAI Conference on Weblogs and Social Media (ICWSM-2009).* 2009.

Tumasjan, Andranik, Timm O. Sprenger, Philipp G. Sandner, and Isabell M. Welpe. *Predicting elections with twitter: What 140 characters reveal about political sentiment.* In *roceedings of the International Conference on Weblogs and Social Media (ICWSM-2010).* 2010.

Turney, Peter D. *Thumbs up or thumbs down?: semantic orientation applied to unsupervised classification of reviews*. In *Proceedings of Annual Meeting of the Association for Computational Linguistics (ACL-2002)*. 2002.

Turney, Peter D. and Micharel L. Littman. *Measuring praise and criticism: Inference of semantic orientation from association. ACM Transactions on Information Systems*, 2003. doi:10.1145/944012.944013

Utsumi, Akira. *Verbal irony as implicit display of ironic environment: Distinguishing ironic utterances from nonirony.* Journal of Pragmatics, 2000. **32**(12): pp. 1777–1806. doi:10.1016/S0378-2166(99)00116-2

Valitutti, Alessandro, Carlo Strapparava, and Oliviero Stock. *Developing affective lexical resources.* PsychNology Journal, 2004. **2**(1): pp. 61–83.

Velikovich, Leonid, Sasha Blair-Goldensohn, Kerry Hannan, and Ryan McDonald. *The viability of web-derived polarity lexicons.* In *Proceedings of Annual Conference of the North American Chapter of the Association for Computational Linguistics (HAACL-2010)*. 2010.

Vrij, Aldert. *Detecting lies and deceit: Pitfalls and opportunities*, 2008: Wiley-Interscience.

Wan, Xiaojun. *Co-training for cross-lingual sentiment classification.* In *Proceedings of the 47th Annual Meeting of the ACL and the 4th IJCNLP of the AFNLP (ACL-IJCNLP-2009)*. 2009. doi:10.3115/1687878.1687913

Wan, Xiaojun. *Using bilingual knowledge and ensemble techniques for unsupervised Chinese sentiment analysis.* In *Proceedings of Conference on Empirical Methods in Natural Language Processing (EMNLP-2008)*. 2008. doi:10.3115/1613715.1613783

Wang, Dong and Yang Liu. *A pilot study of opinion summarization in conversations.* In *Proceedings of the 49th Annual Meeting of the Association for Computational Linguistics (ACL-2011)*. 2011.

Wang, Guan, Sihong Xie, Bing Liu, and Philip S. Yu. *Identify Online Store Review Spammers via Social Review Graph. ACM Transactions on Intelligent Systems and Technology*, Accepted for publication, 2011.

Wang, Hongning, Yue Lu, and Chengxiang Zhai. *Latent aspect rating analysis on review text data: a rating regression approach.* In *Proceedings of ACM SIGKDD International Conference on Knowledge Discovery and Data Mining (KDD-2010)*. 2010.

Wang, Tong and Graeme Hirst. *Refining the Notions of Depth and Density in WordNet-based Semantic Similarity Measures.* In *Proceedings of the Conference on Empirical Methods in Natural Language Processing (EMNLP-2011)*. 2011.

Wang, Xiaolong, Furu Wei, Xiaohua Liu, Ming Zhou, and Ming Zhang. *Topic sentiment analysis in twitter: a graph-based hashtag sentiment classification approach.* In *Proceeding of the ACM conference on Information and knowledge management (CIKM-2011)*. 2011.

Wei, Bin and Christopher Pal. *Cross lingual adaptation: an experiment on sentiment classifications.* In *Proceedings of the ACL 2010 Conference Short Papers (ACL-2010).* 2010.

Wei, Wei and Jon Atle Gulla. *Sentiment learning on product reviews via sentiment ontology tree.* In *Proceedings of Annual Meeting of the Association for Computational Linguistics (ACL-2010).* 2010.

Wen, Miaomiao and Yunfang Wu. *Mining the Sentiment Expectation of Nouns Using Bootstrapping Method.* In *Proceedings of the 5th International Joint Conference on Natural Language Processing (IJCNLP-2010).* 2011.

Wiebe, Janyce. *Identifying subjective characters in narrative.* In *Proceedings of the International Conference on Computational Linguistics (COLING-1990).* 1990. doi:10.3115/997939.998008

Wiebe, Janyce. *Learning subjective adjectives from corpora.* In *Proceedings of National Conf. on Artificial Intelligence (AAAI-2000).* 2000. doi:10.1145/337897.338001

Wiebe, Janyce. *Tracking point of view in narrative.* Computational Linguistics, 1994. **20**: pp. 233–287.

Wiebe, Janyce and Rada Mihalcea. *Word sense and subjectivity.* In *Proceedings of Intl. Conf. on Computational Linguistics and 44th Annual Meeting of the ACL (COLING/ACL-2006).* 2006. doi: 10.3115/1220175.1220309

Wiebe, Janyce, Rebecca F. Bruce, and Thomas P. O'Hara. *Development and use of a gold-standard data set for subjectivity classifications.* In *Proceedings of the Association for Computational Linguistics (ACL-1999).* 1999.

Wiebe, Janyce and Ellen Riloff. *Creating subjective and objective sentence classifiers from unannotated texts.* Computational Linguistics and Intelligent Text Processing, 2005: pp. 486–497. doi:10.1007/978-3-540-30586-6_53

Wiebe, Janyce, Theresa Wilson, Rebecca F. Bruce, Matthew Bell, and Melanie Martin. *Learning subjective language.* Computational Linguistics, 2004. **30**(3): pp. 277–308. doi:10.1162/089120 1041850885

Wiebe, Janyce, Theresa Wilson, and Claire Cardie. *Annotating expressions of opinions and emotions in language.* Language Resources and Evaluation, 2005. **39**(2): pp. 165–210. doi:10.1007/ s10579-005-7880-9

Wiegand, M. and D. Klakow. *Convolution kernels for opinion holder extraction.* In *Proceedings of Human Language Technologies: The 2010 Annual Conference of the North American Chapter of the ACL (HAACL-2010).* 2010.

Williams, Gbolahan K. and Sarabjot Singh Anand. *Predicting the polarity strength of adjectives using wordnet.* In *Proceedings of the Third International AAAI Conference on Weblogs and Social Media (ICWSM-2009).* 2009.

Wilson, Theresa and Stephan Raaijmakers. *Comparing word, character, and phoneme n-grams for subjective utterance recognition.* In *Proceedings of Interspeech.* 2008.

Wilson, Theresa, Janyce Wiebe, and Paul Hoffmann. *Recognizing contextual polarity in phrase-level sentiment analysis.* In *Proceedings of the Human Language Technology Conference and the Conference on Empirical Methods in Natural Language Processing (HLT/EMNLP-2005).* 2005. doi:10 .3115/1220575.1220619

Wilson, Theresa, Janyce Wiebe, and Rebecca Hwa. *Just how mad are you? Finding strong and weak opinion clauses.* In *Proceedings of National Conference on Artificial Intelligence (AAAI-2004).* 2004.

Wilson, Theresa, Janyce Wiebe, and Rebecca Hwa. *Recognizing strong and weak opinion clauses.* Computational Intelligence, 2006. **22**(2): pp. 73–99. doi:10.1111/j.1467-8640.2006.00275.x

Wu, Guangyu, Derek Greene, Barry Smyth, and Pádraig Cunningham. *Distortion as a validation criterion in the identification of suspicious reviews.* In *Proceedings of Social Media Analytics.* 2010.

Wu, Qion, Songbo Tan, and Xueqi Cheng. *Graph ranking for sentiment transfer.* In *Proceedings of the ACL-IJCNLP 2009 Conference Short Papers (ACL-IJCNLP-2009).* 2009. doi:10.3115/16675 83.1667681

Wu, Yuanbin, Qi Zhang, Xuanjing Huang, and Lide Wu. *Phrase dependency parsing for opinion mining.* In *Proceedings of Conference on Empirical Methods in Natural Language Processing (EMNLP-2009).* 2009. doi:10.3115/1699648.1699700

Wu, Yuanbin, Qi Zhang, Xuanjing Huang, and Lide Wu. *Structural opinion mining for graph-based sentiment representation.* In *Proceedings of the 2011 Conference on Empirical Methods in Natural Language Processing (EMNLP-2011).* 2011.

Wu, Yunfang and Miaomiao Wen. *Disambiguating dynamic sentiment ambiguous adjectives.* In *Proceedings of the 23rd International Conference on Computational Linguistics (Coling 2010).* 2010.

Xia, Rui and Chengqing Zong. *Exploring the use of word relation features for sentiment classification.* In *Proceedings of Coling 2010: Poster Volume.* 2010.

Xia, Rui and Chengqing Zong. *A POS-based ensemble model for cross-domain sentiment classification.* In *Proceedings of the 5th International Joint Conference on Natural Language Processing (IJCNLP-2010).* 2011.

Xu, G., X. Meng, and H. Wang. *Build Chinese emotion lexicons using a graph-based algorithm and multiple resources.* In *Proceedings of the 23rd International Conference on Computational Linguistics (Coling 2010).* 2010.

Yang, Hui, Luo Si, and Jamie Callan. *Knowledge transfer and opinion detection in the TREC2006 blog track.* In *Proceedings of TREC.* 2006.

Yang, Seon and Youngjoong Ko. *Extracting comparative entities and predicates from texts using comparative type classification.* In *Proceedings of the 49th Annual Meeting of the Association for Computational Linguistics (ACL-2011).* 2011.

Yano, Tae and Noah A. Smith. *What's Worthy of Comment? Content and Comment Volume in Political Blogs.* In *Proceedings of the International AAAI Conference on Weblogs and Social Media (ICWSM 2010).* 2010.

Yatani, Koji, Michael Novati, Andrew Trusty, and Khai N. Truong. *Analysis of Adjective-Noun Word Pair Extraction Methods for Online Review Summarization.* In *Proceedings of International Joint Conference on Artificial Intelligence (IJCAI-2011).* 2011.

Yessenalina, Ainur and Claire Cardie. *Compositional Matrix-Space Models for Sentiment Analysis.* In *Proceedings of the Conference on Empirical Methods in Natural Language Processing (EMNLP-2011).* 2011.

Yessenalina, Ainur, Yejin Choi, and Claire Cardie. *Automatically generating annotator rationales to improve sentiment classification.* In *Proceedings of the ACL 2010 Conference Short Papers.* 2010.

Yessenalina, Ainur, Yison Yue, and Claire Cardie. *Multi-level Structured Models for Document-level Sentiment Classification.* In *Proceedings of Conference on Empirical Methods in Natural Language Processing (EMNLP-2010).* 2010.

Yi, Jeonghee, Tetsuya Nasukawa, Razvan Bunescu, and Wayne Niblack. *Sentiment analyzer: Extracting sentiments about a given topic using natural language processing techniques.* In *Proceedings of IEEE International Conference on Data Mining (ICDM-2003).* 2003. doi:10.1109/ICDM.2003.1250949

Yoshida, Yasuhisa, Tsutomu Hirao, Tomoharu Iwata, Masaaki Nagata, and Yuji Matsumoto. *Transfer Learning for Multiple-Domain Sentiment Analysis—Identifying Domain Dependent/Independent Word Polarity.* In *Proceedings of the Twenty-Fifth AAAI Conference on Artificial Intelligence (AAAI-2011).* 2011.

Yu, Hong and Vasileios Hatzivassiloglou. *Towards answering opinion questions: Separating facts from opinions and identifying the polarity of opinion sentences.* In *Proceedings of Conference on Empirical Methods in Natural Language Processing (EMNLP-2003).* 2003.

Yu, Jianxing, Zheng-Jun Zha, Meng Wang, and Tat-Seng Chua. *Aspect ranking: identifying important product aspects from online consumer reviews.* In *Proceedings of the 49th Annual Meeting of the Association for Computational Linguistics.* 2011.

Yu, Jianxing, Zheng-Jun Zha, Meng Wang, Kai Wang, and Tat-Seng Chua. *Domain-Assisted Product Aspect Hierarchy Generation: Towards Hierarchical Organization of Unstructured Consumer Reviews.* In *Proceedings of the Conference on Empirical Methods in Natural Language Processing (EMNLP-2011).* 2011.

Zhai, Zhongwu, Bing Liu, Hua Xu, and Peifa Jia. *Clustering Product Features for Opinion Mining.* In *Proceedings of ACM International Conference on Web Search and Data Mining (WSDM-2011).* 2011. doi:10.1145/1935826.1935884

Zhai, Zhongwu, Bing Liu, Hua Xu, and Peifa Jia. *Constrained LDA for Grouping Product Features in Opinion Mining.* In *Proceedings of PAKDD-2011.* 2011. doi:10.1109/MIS.2011.38

Zhai, Zhongwu, Bing Liu, Hua Xu, and Peifa Jia. *Grouping Product Features Using Semi-Supervised Learning with Soft-Constraints.* In *Proceedings of International Conference on Computational Linguistics (COLING-2010).* 2010. doi:10.1007/978-3-642-19460-3_11

Zhai, Zhongwu, Bing Liu, Lei Zhang, Hua Xu, and Peifa Jia. *Identifying evaluative opinions in online discussions.* In *Proceedings of AAAI.* 2011.

Zhang, Lei and Bing Liu. *Extracting Resource Terms for Sentiment Analysis.* In *Proceedings of IJCNLP-2011.* 2011a.

Zhang, Lei and Bing Liu. *Identifying noun product features that imply opinions.* In *Proceedings of the Annual Meeting of the Association for Computational Linguistics (short paper) (ACL-2011).* 2011b.

Zhang, Lei, Bing Liu, Suk Hwan Lim, and Eamonn O'Brien-Strain. *Extracting and Ranking Product Features in Opinion Documents.* In *Proceedings of International Conference on Computational Linguistics (COLING-2010).* 2010.

Zhang, Min and Xingyao Ye. *A generation model to unify topic relevance and lexicon-based sentiment for opinion retrieval.* In *Proceedings of the Annual ACM SIGIR International conference on Research and Development in Information Retrieval (SIGIR-2008).* 2008. doi:10.1145/1390334 .1390405

Zhang, Wei, Lifeng Jia, Clement Yu, and Weiyi Meng. *Improve the effectiveness of the opinion retrieval and opinion polarity classification.* In *Proceedings of ACM International Conference on Information and Knowledge Management (CIKM-2008).* 2008. doi:10.1145/1458082.1458309

Zhang, Wei and Clement Yu. *UIC at TREC 2007 Blog Report,* 2007.

Zhang, Wenbin and Steven Skiena. *Trading strategies to exploit blog and news sentiment.* In *Proceedings of the International Conference on Weblogs and Social Media (ICWSM 2020).* 2010.

Zhang, Zhu and Balaji Varadarajan. *Utility scoring of product reviews.* In *Proceedings of ACM International Conference on Information and Knowledge Management (CIKM-2006).* 2006. doi:10 .1145/1183614.1183626

Zhao, Wayne Xin, Jing Jiang, Hongfei Yan, and Xiaoming Li. *Jointly modeling aspects and opinions with a MaxEnt-LDA hybrid.* In *Proceedings of Conference on Empirical Methods in Natural Language Processing (EMNLP-2010).* 2010.

Zhou, Lanjun, Binyang Li, Wei Gao, Zhongyu Wei, and Kam-Fai Wong. *Unsupervised discovery of discourse relations for eliminating intra-sentence polarity ambiguities.* In *Proceedings of the Conference on Empirical Methods in Natural Language Processing (EMNLP-2011).* 2011.

Zhou, Lina, Yongmei Shi, and Dongsong Zhang. *A Statistical Language Modeling Approach to Online Deception Detection. IEEE Transactions on Knowledge and Data Engineering*, 2008: pp. 1077–1081.

Zhou, Shusen, Qingcai Chen, and Xiaolong Wang. *Active deep networks for semi-supervised sentiment classification*. In *Proceedings of Coling 2010: Poster Volume*. 2010.

Zhu, Jingbo, Huizhen Wang, Benjamin K. Tsou, and Muhua Zhu. *Multi-aspect opinion polling from textual reviews*. In *Proceedings of ACM International Conference on Information and Knowledge Management (CIKM-2009)*. 2009. doi:10.1145/1645953.1646233

Zhu, Xiaojin and Zoubin Ghahramani. *Learning from labeled and unlabeled data with label propagation*. School of Computer Science, Carnegie Mellon University, Pittsburgh, PA, Tech. Rep. CMU-CALD-02-107, 2002.

Zhuang, Li, Feng Jing, and Xiaoyan Zhu. *Movie review mining and summarization*. In *Proceedings of ACM International Conference on Information and Knowledge Management (CIKM-2006)*. 2006. doi:10.1145/1183614.1183625

Zirn, Cäcilia, Mathias Niepert, Heiner Stuckenschmidt, and Michael Strube. *Fine-Grained Sentiment Analysis with Structural Features*. In *Proceedings of the 5th International Joint Conference on Natural Language Processing (IJCNLP-2011)*. 2011.

Author Biography

Bing Liu is a professor of Computer Science at the University of Illinois at Chicago (UIC). He received his PhD in Artificial Intelligence from the University of Edinburgh. Before joining UIC, he was with the National University of Singapore. His current research interests are sentiment analysis and opinion mining, opinion spam detection, and social media modeling. He has published extensively in leading conferences and journals on these topics, e.g., ACL, EMNLP, COLING, KDD, WWW, AAAI, IJCAI, SIGIR, Computational Linguistics and ACM Transactions on Intelligent Systems and Technology. He has also given more than thirty invited and keynote speeches. Due to his work on opinion spam detection, he was featured in a front page article of The New York Times on Jan 27, 2012. Prof. Liu's earlier research was in the fields of data mining, Web mining and machine learning, where he also published numerous papers in prestigious conferences and journals, e.g., KDD, WWW, ICML, AAAI, IJCAI, ICDM, WSDM, and IEEE Transactions on Knowledge and Data Engineering. He has written a textbook titled "Web Data Mining: Exploring Hyperlinks, Contents and Usage Data" published by Springer (first edition in 2006, and second edition in 2011). Due to his research achievements, he has served as program chairs of ACM SIGKDD International Conference on Knowledge Discovery and Data Mining (KDD), IEEE International Conference on Data Mining (ICDM), ACM Conference on Web Search and Data Mining (WSDM), SIAM Conference on Data Mining (SDM), ACM Conference on Information and Knowledge Management (CIKM), and Pacific Asia Conference on Data Mining (PAKDD). He has also served extensively as areas chairs, track chairs, and senior program committee members for natural language processing, data mining, Web technology, and Artificial Intelligence conferences. Additionally, he has been on the editorial boards of many leading journals including Data Mining and Knowledge Discovery (DMKD), ACM Transactions on the Web (TWEB), and IEEE Transactions on Knowledge and Data Engineering (TKDE).

Printed in the United States
by Baker & Taylor Publisher Services